Question&Answer

CONTRACT LAW

Develop your legal skills

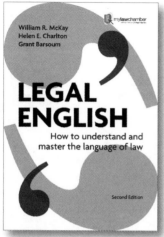

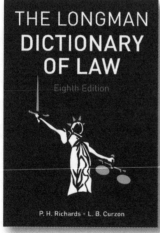
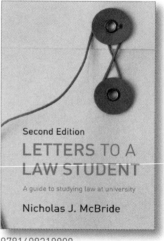

Question&Answer

CONTRACT LAW

2nd edition

Marina Hamilton
University of Hertfordshire

Harlow, England • London • New York • Boston • San Francisco • Toronto • Sydney • Auckland • Singapore • Hong Kong
Tokyo • Seoul • Taipei • New Delhi • Cape Town • São Paulo • Mexico City • Madrid • Amsterdam • Munich • Paris • Milan

Pearson Education Limited
Edinburgh Gate
Harlow CM20 2JE
United Kingdom
Tel: +44 (0)1279 623623
Web: **www.pearson.com/uk**

First published 2012 (print)
Second edition published 2014 (print and electronic)

ISBN: 978-0-273-78367-1 (print)
 978-0-273-78370-1 (PDF)
 978-0-273-78368-8 (eText)

British Library Cataloguing-in-Publication Data
A catalogue record for the print edition is available from the British Library

Library of Congress Cataloging-in-Publication Data
A catalog record for the print edition is available from the Library of Congress

10 9 8 7 6 5 4 3 2 1
17 16 15 14 13

Print edition typeset in 10/13pt Helvetica Neue LT Pro by 35
Print edition printed in Malaysia (CTP - KHL)

NOTE THAT ANY PAGE CROSS REFERENCES REFER TO THE PRINT EDITION

Contents

Supporting resources

Visit the series companion website at **www.pearsoned.co.uk/lawexpressqa** to find valuable learning material including:

- **Additional essay and problem questions** arranged by topic for each chapter give you more opportunity to practise and hone your exam skills.
- **Diagram plans** for all additional questions assist you in structuring and writing your answers.
- **You be the marker** questions allow you to see through the eyes of the examiner by marking essay and problem questions on every topic covered in the book.
- Download and print all **Attack the question** diagrams and **Diagram plans** from the book.

Also: The companion website provides the following features:

- Search tool to help locate specific items of content.
- Online help and support to assist with website usage and troubleshooting.

For more information please contact your local Pearson sales representative or visit **www.pearsoned.co.uk/lawexpressqa**

Acknowledgements

To Peter, Jessica, Christopher, and the spare room for giving me the peace and solitude in which to work.

Publisher's acknowledgements

Our thanks go to all reviewers who contributed to the development of this text, including students who participated in research and focus groups that helped to shape the series format.

What you need to do for every question in Contract Law

Contract law is predominantly taught and assessed through problem scenarios. These scenarios can be long and the facts complicated; for instance, a question on offer and acceptance can have a series of communications between the parties involved. It is essential that you identify the legal issues raised by the question; so ask yourself what the status of each communication is, and what is the authority for such an assertion. Having a plan before you write will assist with this. Ensure that you do not retell the facts of the problem: focus on the issues raised by those facts. Once you have identified, discussed and supported your legal argument, apply that analysis back to the facts of the question. There will be multiple issues in contract problems: deal with them logically and ensure that the answer has a natural flow. Equally with essays; answer the question set. Do not write everything you know on that topic area. For instance, if an essay concerns silence and misrepresentation, you will not gain marks for discussing statements of opinion.

A strong introduction can often focus your structure and attention on the question set. A conclusion draws together all the lines of argument and analysis into a succinct answer to the issues raised by that question.

The best way to cope with large amounts of case law is to learn your authorities as you learn the principle concerned. One of the commonest criticisms of contract law papers is a lack of supporting authority for the point made.

Guided tour

What you need to do for every question in Contract Law

HOW TO USE THIS BOOK

Books in the *Question and Answer* series focus on the *why* of a good answer alongside the *what*, thereby helping you to build your question answering skills and technique.

This guide should not be used as a substitute for learning the material thoroughly. It will help you to make the most out of what you have already learned from lecture notes, materials and textbooks when answering an exam or coursework question.

Focus on the question set. Examiners are interested in how you use your knowledge. Do not try to memorise the answers given here; instead, use the answers and the other features to understand what goes into a good answer and why.

A well-structured answer will allow you to explore each issue you raise in depth, before developing your argument into the next point. Always plan before you write.

Contract law is predominantly taught and assessed through problem scenarios. These scenarios can be long and the facts complicated; for instance, a question on offer and acceptance can have a series of communications between the parties involved. It is essential that you identify the legal issues raised by the question; so ask yourself what the status of each communication is, and what is the authority for such an assertion. Having a plan before you write will assist with this. Ensure that you do not retell the facts of the problem: focus on the issues raised by those facts. Once you have identified, discussed and supported your legal argument, apply that analysis back to the facts of the question.

What to do for every question – Identify the key things you should look for in any question and answer on the subject ensuring you give every one of your answers a great chance from the start.

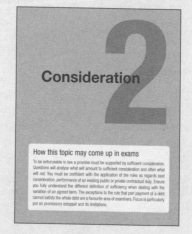

Consideration

2

How this topic may come up in exams

To be enforceable in law a promise must be supported by sufficient consideration. Questions will analyse what will amount to sufficient consideration and often what will not. You must be confident with the application of the rules as regards past consideration, performance of an existing public or private contractual duty. Ensure you fully understand the different definition of sufficiency when dealing with the variation of an agreed term. The exceptions to the rule that part payment of a debt cannot satisfy the whole debt are a favourite area of examiners. Focus is particularly put on promissory estoppel and its limitations.

How this topic may come up in exams – Understand how to tackle any question on this topic by using the handy tips and advice relevant to both essay and problem questions. In-text symbols clearly identify each question type as they occur.

 Essay question

 Problem question

Attack the question – Use these diagrams as a step-by-step guide to help you confidently identify the main points covered in any question asked.

Answer plans and Diagram plans – Clear and concise answer plans and diagram plans support the planning and structuring of your answers whatever your preferred learning style.

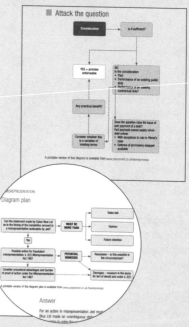

■ Attack the question

A printable version of this diagram is available from www.pearsoned.co.uk/lawexpressqa

Answer plan

→ Define economic duress and its effect on a contract.

→ Determine whether the action of the Administrative Dock Workers' Union is unlawful, as commercial pressure exerted is illegitimate where a tort or criminal offence has been committed.

→ Consider the test in *DSDN Subsea Ltd* v *Petroleum Geo-Services* as to the situation with DSTR threatening to breach the contract with LN Ltd.

→ Evaluate whether it is possible to have lawful act duress in the context of Gloop plc refusing credit.

MISREPRESENTATION
Diagram plan

A printable version of this diagram is available from www.pearsoned.co.uk/lawexpressqa

Answer

For an action in misrepresentation Jed must [...]
Blue Ltd made an unambiguous stat[...]

Answer with accompanying guidance – Make the most out of every question by using the guidance to recognise what makes a good answer and why. Answers are the length you could realistically hope to produce in an exam to show you how to gain marks quickly when under pressure.

Case names clearly highlighted – Easy to spot bold text makes those all important case names stand out from the rest of the answer, ensuring they are much easier to remember in revision and in an exam.

Make your answer stand out – Really impress your examiners by going the extra mile and including these additional points and further reading to illustrate your deeper knowledge of the subject, fully maximising your marks.

Don't be tempted to – Points out common mistakes ensuring you avoid losing easy marks by understanding where students most often trip up in exams.

Bibliography – Use this list of further reading to really delve into and explore areas in more depth, enabling you to excel in exams.

Answer

An award of contractual damages attempts, as far as a monetary award can do so, to put the innocent party to a breach in the position they would have been in had the contract been performed, satisfying expectation interest. Contractual damages are, however, not punitive and therefore as Sally has not actually suffered any economic loss as a result of any of the breaches of contract, the measure of damages will be quantified on a potentially less generous measure.[1]

The expectation measure of damages seeks to put the innocent party to a breach of contract in the financial position they would have been in had the enforceable promise made to them been performed. This measure of damages therefore goes beyond just putting the parties back in the position they were in before the contract was made: it will aim to recompense for potential loss of profit.[2]

In the problem, there is an available market in meercats and therefore the losses are easily calculable as being the difference in the

[1] The introduction recognises that an understanding of the principles is involved in determining in a *quantum meruit* of damages where no actual pecuniary loss has been sustained.

Stating the general rule here [...] you to articulate the [...]

Skinner [2001] All ER 801. It can be argued that **Ruxley Electronics and Construction Ltd v Forsyth** recognises the economic value of exact performance and made an award only for this element of disappointment. The courts in **McLaren Murdoch & Hamilton Ltd v The Abercromby Motor Group Ltd** (2003) SCLR 323 held that the decision not to award cost of cure damages means that the cost must be manifestly disproportionate to the benefit to be received.[5] No real benefit would be gained by the very expensive work required to render exact and precise performance with regard to the waterfall features. A claimant cannot be forced to spend an award in a particular way and the decision in **Ruxley Electronics and Construction Ltd v Forsyth** prevents a claimant being overcom-

[5] Reinforcing the principle with a more recent authority demonstrates currency of knowledge.

✓ Make your answer stand out

- Consider if the UK courts might follow the lead of the Canadian case of *Whiten v Pilot Insurance Co.* 2002 SCC 18, where it was held that where there is an independent actionable wrong arising out of the same facts as a breach of contract then a punitive award would be possible.
- Support your analysis with the use of some academic authority, such as B. Coote's (1997) article Contract damages, *Ruxley* and the performance interest, *CLJ* 537, or perhaps A. Loke (1996) Cost of cure or difference in market value? Towards a sound choice in the basis for quantifying expectation damages, 10 *JCL* 189.
- Add depth to your answer by reading and possible reference to D. Pearce and R. Halson's (2008) article Damages for breach of contract: compensation, restitution, and vindication, 28 *OJLS* 73, which picks up on the themes of what the law is actually trying to compensate for.

! Don't be tempted to . . .

- Miss out the limitation on the recovery of losses which the claimant could have mitigated. The question openly directs you to the other losses. Higher marks will be gained by recognising this issue. Only the better answers would do this.
- Lose the opportunity to give depth to your analysis: in this question you really have the chance to have a good look at the decision in *Hadley v Baxendale*.
- Forget to do your application as you progress through your answer. It is tempting to cover all the complex issues surrounding remoteness and apply the test to both potential amounts claimed at the end. If you do this as you go along, it does also help illustrate the legal point you are making and so is doubly effective.

Bibliography

Andrews, N. (2001) Strangers to justice no longer – the reversal of the privity rule under the Contracts (Rights of Third Parties) Act 1999, *Cambridge Law Journal* 353.

Atiyah, P.S. (1986) Consideration: a re-statement, in *Essays on Contract*, Oxford: Oxford University Press, p. 179.

Guided tour of the companion website

Book resources are available to download. Print your own **Attack the question** and **Diagram plans** to pin to your wall or add to your own revision notes.

Additional Essay and Problem questions with **Diagram plans** arranged by topic for each chapter give you more opportunity to practise and hone your exam skills. Print and email your answers.

You be the marker gives you a chance to evaluate sample exam answers for different question types for each topic and understand how and why an examiner awards marks. Use the accompanying guidance to get the most out of every question and recognise what makes a good answer.

All of this and more can be found when you visit
www.pearsoned.co.uk/lawexpressqa

Table of cases and statutes

■ Cases

TABLE OF CASES AND STATUTES

Formation of a contract

How this topic may come up in exams

The rules with regards to offer and acceptance are the same whatever the apparent complexity of the scenario or essay question. To allow stronger candidates to demonstrate their knowledge examiners may throw in more complex issues such as the specific rules relating to auctions or unilateral offers. Remember the same very basic principles apply: you need an offer and an acceptance to have an enforceable contract.

■ Attack the question

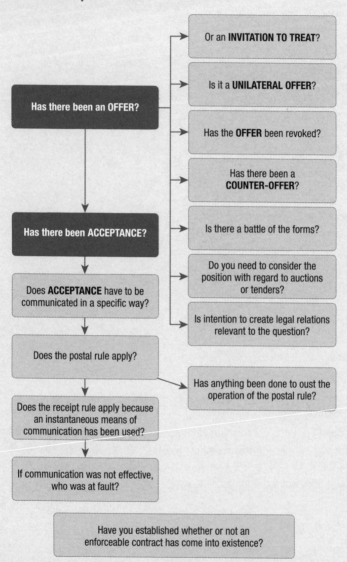

Has there been an OFFER?
→ Or an **INVITATION TO TREAT**?
→ Is it a **UNILATERAL OFFER**?
→ Has the **OFFER** been revoked?
→ Has there been a **COUNTER-OFFER**?

Has there been ACCEPTANCE?
→ Is there a battle of the forms?
→ Do you need to consider the position with regard to auctions or tenders?
→ Is intention to create legal relations relevant to the question?

Does **ACCEPTANCE** have to be communicated in a specific way?

Does the postal rule apply?
→ Has anything been done to oust the operation of the postal rule?

Does the receipt rule apply because an instantaneous means of communication has been used?

If communication was not effective, who was at fault?

Have you established whether or not an enforceable contract has come into existence?

A printable version of this diagram is available from www.pearsoned.co.uk/lawexpressqa

? Question 1

Logoplat Ltd design plates. Ten thousand dining plates with a 'Le Chat Noir' design on the side have been produced. On 1 May at 9.00 a.m. Logoplat Ltd post a note on their website indicating that 'Le Chat Noir' plates are for sale at a price of £1.00 per plate.

Sebastian, owner of Le Chat Noir restaurant, sees the advertisement. He emails Logoplat Ltd at 10.00 a.m. on 1 May asking to have 500 of the plates at £1.00 per plate or 2000 at 50p per plate. Logoplat Ltd reply at 10.05 a.m. saying that they will sell 2000 at 70p per plate. Sebastian drafts an email at 11.30 a.m. confirming the order for 2000 plates at 70p. When he presses 'send' he is not connected to the internet. As a result his email is stored in his outbox and sent the following morning, 2 May, at 10.30.

The Black Swan Brewery Ltd wants the whole consignment of plates for the launch of their new 'Le Chat Noir' beer. They send a van to the premises of Logoplat Ltd with enough cash to pay at £1 per plate. The van arrives at 4.00 p.m. on 1 May and the plates are loaded and sent on their way by 4.30 p.m. At 4.54 p.m. Logoplat Ltd email Sebastian withdrawing their offer. Sebastian reads the email at 10.30 a.m. on 2 May when he logs back onto the internet.

Advise Logoplat Ltd as Sebastian is claiming that the rules on offer and acceptance mean that an enforceable contract was formed with him prior to the plates being sold to the Black Swan Brewery Ltd.

Answer plan

→ Identify the website advertisement as an invitation to treat.

→ Sebastian's reply could be considered as an invitation to treat, as it is uncertain as to terms, or potentially two offers.

→ Logoplat Ltd's response is either an offer or a counter-offer, either of which is capable of acceptance.

→ Applying the decision in *Entores*, does the acceptance of Logoplat Ltd's offer take effect before or after the offer is withdrawn?

→ An enforceable contract is formed with the Black Swan Brewery Ltd.

Diagram plan

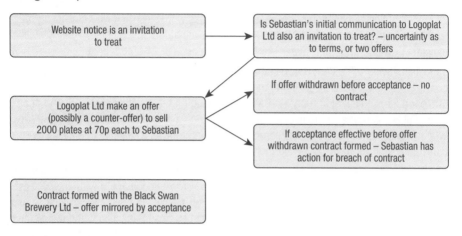

A printable version of this diagram plan is available from www.pearsoned.co.uk/lawexpressqa

Answer

[1] A strong opening identifies the core issues raised by the question.

In order to have an enforceable contract there must be an offer which is accepted prior to any revocation of that offer.[1] Whether Sebastian had formed a contract with Logoplat Ltd before they purported to withdraw their offer, having sold the goods elsewhere, will involve an analysis of the traditional rules of offer and acceptance. These principles continue to be applied to technologies which did not exist at the time the authorities themselves were decided.

[2] Simply stated but this point is then developed through clear, precise application and use of authority.

As a general rule, advertisements are invitations to treat, not offers.[2] An offer is an expression of willingness to be bound on acceptance of that offer on certain terms. An invitation to treat by comparison is inviting offers to be made. The website states the availability of plates for sale and gives a price but gives no indication as to how many are in stock. It is, therefore, unlikely to be capable of being an offer as it is looking to generate interest rather than finalise a deal. The website notice is analogous to a notice in a catalogue (***Grainger v Gough*** [1896] AC 325) or even a display in a shop window (***Fisher v Bell*** [1961] 1 QB 394).

Sebastian's first communication to Logoplat Ltd could again be interpreted as invitation to treat as it is uncertain as to terms, ***Loftus v Roberts*** (1902) 18 TLR 532. However, as Treitel (Peel, 2011)

points out, determining whether an offer or invitation has been made is a question of intention[3] (**Harvey v Facey** [1893] AC 552). From this viewpoint, Sebastian's email could be deemed to contain two offers, either of which he would intend to be bound by on acceptance by Logoplat Ltd.[4]

Logoplat Ltd's response is an offer which is capable of being accepted, if Sebastian's first email is found to be an invitation to treat. The terms are certain and there is an expression of willingness to be bound. If it were determined that Sebastian's first email was an offer, then Logoplat Ltd's response is a counter-offer as it proposes different terms, which has the effect of rejecting the original offer (**Hyde v Wrench** (1840) 3 Beav 334). Sebastian is free to accept or reject this offer.[5]

Sebastian's second email is intended to be an acceptance of Logoplat Ltd's offer to sell the plates at 70p each. The acceptance must mirror the terms offered and must be effectively communicated to the offeror[6] (**Entores Ltd v Miles Far East Corporation** [1955] 2 QB 327). The method of communication of acceptance has not been prescribed and email is appropriate in the circumstances, as it the same mode used for the offer[7] (**Quenerduaine v Cole** (1883) 32 WR 185). However, any offer can be revoked at any time prior to acceptance (**Byrne v Van Tienhoven** (1880) 5 CPD 344). Both a revocation of an offer and an acceptance by an instantaneous[8] means of communication take effect on receipt. Therefore it has to be determined which was received first: the revocation or the acceptance?

Issues surrounding effective communication of acceptance are discussed in Denning's judgment in **Entores**.[9] Denning identified two types of communication of acceptance: instantaneous and non-instantaneous.[10] Non-instantaneous applies to the post only and acceptance takes effect on posting (**Adams v Lindsell** (1818) 1 B & Ald 681). Instantaneous means of communication apply to everything else, even new technologies developed after this decision that are capable of message storage (**Brinkibon Ltd v Stahag Stahl und Stahlwarenhandel GmbH** [1982] 2 WLR 264). **Brinkibon** does not give a precise ruling as to when acceptance will take place in such circumstances. Potentially it could be when the message is sent, on receipt in the storage device, or when it is actually heard/read.[11] **Brinkibon** suggests that in the absence of a precise intention[12] expressed by the parties determining when acceptance takes place depends on the business practice concerned or a judgement as to where the risks of acceptance/non-acceptance should lie. The basic principles in **Entores** apply as to the risk of non-effective communication of acceptance. In not connecting to the internet it would appear that Sebastian has not communicated his acceptance effectively and therefore the revocation of the offer would take effect before the message purporting to accept the offer was sent. If the fault for the non-connection to the internet was not his, but equally not Logoplat Ltd's, then the risk according to Denning's judgment will still lie with Sebastian.[13] The time of receipt does not have to be the time the message is actually read (**Tenax Steamship Co. v Owners of the Motor Vessel Brimnes** The Brimnes [1975] QB 851).

[13] Effective link back to the point made in *Brinkibon* through the application of Denning's key judgment.

Logoplat Ltd made an offer capable of acceptance to Sebastian. Sebastian did not effectively communicate his acceptance of this offer until after the offer was withdrawn.[14] An enforceable contract was made with the Black Swan Brewery Ltd. The offer and acceptance have been communicated by conduct (**Brogden v Metropolitan Railway Company** [1877] 2 App Cas 666). However, had the email sent by Sebastian gone through successfully at 11.30 a.m. on 1 May, then acceptance would have been effective before the offer was withdrawn and Logoplat Ltd would have been in breach of contract with Sebastian, damages being available as of right.[15]

[14] Good clear application to the problem.

[15] Interesting finish, demonstrating a depth of knowledge and sound understanding of the topic area.

✓ Make your answer stand out

- Consider expanding the point you raise in reference to Treitel's determination of whether an invitation to treat or an offer has been made by doing a comparison of *Gibson* v *Manchester County Council* [1978] 1 WLR 520 and *Storer* v *Manchester County Council* [1974] 1 WLR 1403.
- Build depth into your answer: explore the rationale for not expanding the postal rule.
- Note that the rule was introduced to encourage the expansion of the use of the newly formed postal service but the rule was criticised from its inception, *Byrne* v *Van Tienhoven*.
- Draw on the above and include some academic opinion critical of the postal rule and that despite its evident similarities with email it is unlikely to be expanded: S. Hill, 'Flogging a dead horse: the postal acceptance rule and email' (2001) 17 *JCL* 151.

! Don't be tempted to . . .

- Stop before you have followed a complete analysis of the issues raised. This question demands an understanding of the postal rule, but also its avoidance.
- Panic if there are two potential arguments: identify both and choose the most logical application. If your marker disagrees with your application you will have at least demonstrated that you understand both sides of the legal issue.

Question 2

Discuss the continued application of the postal rule in today's commercial environment, with particular reference as to why new technologies such as email should be considered an instantaneous means of communication when determining whether acceptance has been effectively communicated.

Answer plan

→ Consider the difference between instantaneous and non-instantaneous means of communication and the postal rather than the receipt rule.
→ Investigate the potential difficulties raised by the postal rule and how to avoid its application.
→ Evaluate the similarities between post and email.
→ The receipt rule raises problems with email and particularly the timing of acceptance.

Diagram plan

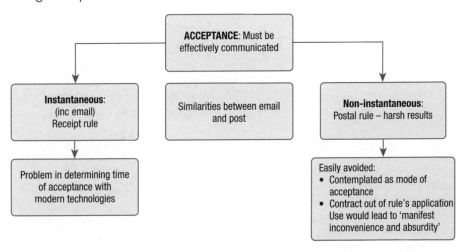

A printable version of this diagram plan is available from www.pearsoned.co.uk/lawexpressqa

Answer

Acceptance is a final and unqualified assent to the terms of an offer. Once an offer has been accepted, there is an enforceable contract. Acceptance must be effectively communicated to the offeror unless the need for communication has been waived, as in *Carlill v Carbolic Smoke Ball Co.* [1893] 1 QB 256, or the postal rule operates.[1]

[1] This covers all the exceptions to the receipt rule.

The postal rule provides that acceptance takes place on posting (*Adams v Lindsell* (1818) 1 B & Ald 681). At the time of this decision the post could take a considerable time to arrive and therefore, in having acceptance on posting, it provided certainty as to the time at which a contract was concluded, it being easier to prove posting than receipt.[2]

[2] In giving the historical context for the rationale of the rule, you are directly focusing on the question set and will gain marks for demonstrating a depth of understanding of the issues involved.

Provided that the letter has been properly stamped and addressed, then a binding contract will be formed when a letter is dropped in the post box, even if that letter is never received (*Household Fire Insurance v Grant* (1879) 4 Ex D 216). As such, an offeror may not actually know that they are subject to an enforceable agreement. This can appear to be a rather harsh repercussion of the rule.

The postal rule is also at odds with the law on revocation of offers which will only be effective on receipt. In *Henthorn v Fraser* [1892] 2 Ch 27 an acceptance taking effect on posting took precedence over a withdrawal of the same offer which was posted first but did not reach the offeree until after the acceptance was posted. *Byrne & Co. v Van Tienhoven & Co.* (1880) 5 CPD 344 expressed similar discomfort with the application of the postal rule in the situation where it would take precedence over the withdrawal of an offer which is subject to the receipt rule, binding the offeror to a bargain they no longer wished to be a party to.

[3] This draws together analysis from the previous two paragraphs and flows naturally into a discussion of the ability to lessen the impact of the postal rule.

The risk of the potential adverse effects of the postal rule appear to rest heavily on the offeror.[3] They can, however, contract out of the postal rule by determining in their offer the method and timing of the communicating acceptance (*Tinn v Hoffman & Co.* (1873) 29 LT 271). The mode of communication may be inferred from the circumstances, so if an offer is made by email suggesting a reply by the close of business that day, it is likely to be interpreted by the courts as the offeror expecting a reply by email or an equally expeditious means of communication. The courts have been willing to interpret contracts as ousting the postal rule where it would lead to 'manifest inconvenience or absurdity' (**Holwell Securities Ltd v Hughes** [1974] 1 WLR 155). This case demonstrates that it is unlikely that the postal rule will be abandoned; however, its application is likely to remain limited and only the exceptions to it developed in a modern commercial context.[4]

[4] This exemplifies good essay skill: remembering to relate analysis back to the question.

Email has a lot of the characteristics of the post. The communication is delivered by a third party; it may not be read immediately on delivery; it can get lost/damaged and arrive in an incomprehensible form; and it has to be opened.[5]

[5] This is a good link from previous points that it is unlikely that there will be expansion of the postal rule in spite of similarities in name and shared characteristics with email (even the now iconic symbol of the envelope).

Lord Denning in **Entores Ltd v Miles Far East Corporation** [1955] 2 QB 327 draws only a distinction between instantaneous and non-instantaneous forms of communication with regard to acceptance. Instantaneous forms of communication were subject to the receipt rule, that is to say acceptance would only take place when the acceptance had been effectively communicated to the offeror. In 1955 the only form of non-instantaneous messaging would be the post and telegrams. Technology has moved on and it is possible to store messages electronically to be read or heard at a later date, including email; however, as discussed above, it is unlikely that the postal rule will be expanded: only the exceptions to it will be developed.

There is no UK legislation as to when acceptance takes place when using email, or any decided UK cases on that point. To be consistent, for instance, with the Vienna Convention on Contracts for the International Sale of Goods, the Unidroit Principles of International and Commercial Contracts, and the Principles of European Contract Law, the UK would have to operate the receipt rule with regard to email communication of acceptance. Even in 1955 in **Entores** Lord Denning stated that 'it is very important that the countries of the world should have the same rule'.[6]

[6] The analysis reflects an appreciation of and reflection on Denning's judgment for certainty and pragmatism in the law which is just as relevant in the context of twenty-first century technologies.

By 1983 and the decision in **Brinkibon Ltd v Stahag Stahl und Stahlwarenhandel GmbH** [1982] 2 WLR 264, the ability to store communications electronically was becoming commonplace and therefore questions had to be asked as to when acceptance actually took place. It was clear from the **Brinkibon** decision that there would be no expansion of the postal rule. The actual time that acceptance took place would depend on the intention of the parties, in other words that they could stipulate that an email acceptance would only take place once read. Alternatively, timing of acceptance might be determined by sound business practice or a judgement as to where the risks should lie. This is rather analogous to the postal rule which leaves the risk with the offeror, with the option to decide how acceptance will be communicated and how it will take effect.[7]

[7] Drawing previous lines of analysis together gives depth to your analysis.

The postal rule will be confined to the use of the post. It is unlikely to have application to private couriers where, if delivery is not made, there will be a potential action for breach of contract between sender and carrier. Almost since its inception the postal rule has been viewed with cynicism and it is no surprise to find its application curtailed rather than encouraged. With regard to email, it is unlikely that the courts would seek to deal with the complexities of distinguishing between web transactions which have the characteristics of being instantaneous modes of communications and internet emails which share more characteristics with a state mail service.[8]

[8] Recognising this distinction demonstrates your rounded understanding of the topic area.

[9] A strong conclusion to a well-reasoned argument will impress any marker.

The timing of acceptance of email transactions, as with other means of electronic communication, remains uncertain; however, what is clear is that it will not be on sending.[9]

✓ Make your answer stand out

- Put in academic opinion to support the proposition that the postal rule belongs in its time (S. Gardner (1992) Thrashing with Trollope: a deconstruction of the postal rule in contract, 12 *OJLS* 170).

- Considering that the justification for the postal rule is weak, make an argument that the receipt rule should apply to email, treating it as an instantaneous means of communication.

- Provide support for the above line of argument by evaluating S. Hill (2001) Flogging a dead horse: the postal acceptance rule and email, 17 *JCL* 151.

- Consider including the recent Privy Council decision in *Chwee Kin Keong* v *Digilandmall.com Pte Ltd* [2004] SGHC 71, which suggests that if you are to expand the use of the postal rule, then web transactions have the characteristics of instantaneous transactions and internet communications share some characteristics of the post. Following the line of argument formulated in the answer, such a distinction would be an unnecessary and unjustifiable complication hampering certainty in the commercial markets of today.

> **!** **Don't be tempted to . . .**
>
> ■ Run scared of this question as at heart it is only asking why the postal rule will not be expanded.

❓ Question 3

Film Buff Stores has put the following notice in its shop window:

> Free to the first 10 individual purchasers of the new *Monsters from Mars* DVD, autographed filmset photographs of its star Jimmy De Roi. Available from Monday morning at 9.00 a.m.

On Sunday night, Victor, the owner of Film Buff Stores hears of Jimmy De Roi's death. Realising the photos may be now quite valuable, he calls Karl and Maya, two dealers in film memorabilia to ascertain whether they would be interested in purchasing five signed photos each for £1,000. Maya says she wants to think about it and will call him in the morning. Karl is not in so Victor leaves a voicemail message saying that if he doesn't hear from him he will presume that Karl has accepted his offer.

Maya calls Victor in the morning at 6.30 a.m. saying that she accepts Victor's offer. Victor inadvertently deletes the message without ascertaining who it was from. At 9.10 a.m. Victor remembers to take the notice down concerning the photographs.

Simon has been waiting outside the store since 5.00 a.m. to ensure he is one of the first to purchase the DVD. At 9.01 a.m. the shop assistant sells Simon the DVD but refuses to give him the free photo as she has been told, by Victor, that the offer has been withdrawn.

Karl arrives at Film Buff Stores at 10.15 a.m. to collect his five signed photographs.

Discuss with whom, if anyone, Victor has formed a contract as regards the Jimmy De Roi photographs.

Answer plan

→ Determine if the advertisement in the shop window is an invitation to treat or a unilateral offer.

→ If the advertisement is a unilateral offer, had Simon accepted this offer before it was revoked by Victor?

→ Whether a contract has been made with Maya will depend on whether she communicated her acceptance of Victor's offer effectively.

→ Silence cannot constitute acceptance and bind Karl to the offer made by Victor, but Victor can waive the need to communicate acceptance.

→ Has Karl accepted Victor's offer by conduct?

Diagram plan

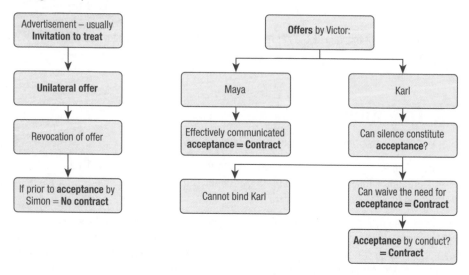

A printable version of this diagram plan is available from www.pearsoned.co.uk/lawexpressqa

Answer

The common rules of offer and acceptance need to be considered in determining if Victor has formed a contract with Maya, Karl or Simon. A binding contract is formed when an offer on certain terms is accepted on those terms by the offeree, and that acceptance has been effectively communicated to the offeror. An offer may be revoked at any time prior to acceptance.[1]

[1] A good identification in the introduction of the legal issues raised by the question puts an examiner in a positive frame of mind that the following piece of work is going to be focused and on task.

An offer is a declaration of a willingness to be legally bound on acceptance of the terms and conditions put forward. Prices and goods on display in a shop window are usually to be considered invitations to treat (*Fisher v Bell* [1961] 1 QB 394). Advertisements are also usually invitations to treat inviting offers. In *Partridge v Crittenden* [1968] 2 All ER 421 the vendor had a finite supply of birds and could not have intended to supply all those that responded to the advertisement, but was instead inviting negotiations with individual potential buyers. By contrast, the sign in the window of Film Buff Stores promising the first 10 purchasers the signed photographs indicated the supply is clearly limited.[2] The case of

[2] Immediately distinguishing the instant case as to why this is an offer not an invitation to treat.

Carlill v *Carbolic Smoke Ball Co.* [1893] 1 QB 256 provides authority that unilateral offers can be made to the whole world or specified groups of people where the offer can be accepted without any further negotiation between the parties and there is an intention to be bound on those terms. In *Lefkowicz* v *Great Minneapolis Stores* (1957) 86 NW 2d 689 an advertisement stating that three mink coats were available at a special price on a first come first served basis. This amounted to a unilateral offer, which was accepted by the customer performing the condition of being the first served. Although this judgment is of persuasive value as it is from the United States, it does follow the line of reasoning put forward in *Carlill* and subsequently in *Bowerman* v *Association of British Travel Agents Ltd* [1996] CLC 451, whereby a sign stating ABTA's obligations in a travel agent's window to reimburse monies paid out in respect of a holiday was a unilateral offer accepted by the customer in contracting with the ABTA member.[3] The purchase of the *Monsters from Mars* DVD will communicate Simon's acceptance of the unilateral offer made by Film Buff Stores as to the signed photographs. A customer makes an offer to buy goods displayed in a shop when they put them in a basket or carry them around the shop. It is the 'shopkeeper' that is free to accept or reject this offer when the goods are brought to the checkout for payment (*Pharmaceutical Society of Great Britain* v *Boots Cash Chemist (Southern) Ltd* [1952] 2 QB 795). Simon will accept the unilateral offer of the photographs by concluding the contract for the purchase of the *Monsters from Mars* DVD.[4]

An offer can be revoked at any time prior to acceptance provided that it is effectively communicated to the offeree (*Byrne* v *Van Tienhoven* (1880) 5 CPD 344). A unilateral offer can be revoked prior to acceptance. As it may be impractical to notify everyone who may have had notice of the offer individually, it will suffice to communicate by the same method as the original offer (*Shuey* v *United States* (1875) 92 US 73). Victor does this, but arguably after there has been acceptance by Simon at the checkout.[5] Revocation can be effective if it is communicated by someone other than the offeree as long as the source of information is reliable (*Dickinson* v *Dodds* (1876) 2 Ch D 463). The shop assistant is a reliable source of information. Therefore provided she informed Simon before the contract was concluded at the checkout, the revocation will be effective.[6]

[3] Explaining the facts of the cited cases here does illustrate your application.

[4] Things look promising for Simon at this point.

[5] This builds threads of an argument and links to previous points of analysis.

[6] The final application on this point has drawn together the last two paragraphs of analysis clearly. Having a well-structured flow to an argument will achieve this.

[7] In one sentence the receipt rule is articulated as opposed to the postal rule.

Victor has made an offer to Maya. Acceptance must mirror the terms of the offer and must be effectively communicated to the other party. All forms of communication with the exception of the post are deemed to be instantaneous means of communication and acceptance takes place on receipt[7] (*Entores Ltd* v *Miles Far East Corporation* [1955] 2 QB 327). The question arising with regard to Maya's acceptance is whether or not she communicated her acceptance effectively. Lord Denning in *Entores* articulated that predominantly the onus lies on the offeree to ensure that their communication is received. If a telephone line goes dead or the voicemail system is faulty there will be no contract until the offeree has repeated their acceptance to the offeror.[8] The only exception to this is if the offeree believes that acceptance has been made but by some fault on the offeror's part it has not. Maya has left a voicemail message and the non-receipt of the message is Victor's fault. As such, Victor would be estopped from claiming he did not receive the message and will be bound by Maya's acceptance.

[8] Stating the usual presumption against the offeree emphasises your application to the problem.

Offerors are free to stipulate how acceptance is to be made; they cannot, however, bind an offeree to a contractual obligation by stating that their silence will be acceptance (*Felthouse* v *Bindley* (1862) 6 LT 157). It can, however, remain open to an offeror to waive the need to communicate acceptance, and this is most common with unilateral contracts but can apply to bilateral contracts if the offeror wishes to assume that risk[9] (*Carlill* v *Carbolic Smoke Ball Co.*). In arriving at the shop Karl has also communicated his acceptance by conduct (*Brogden* v *Metropolitan Railway Co.* (1877) LR 2 App Cas 666).

[9] In dealing with the more complex argument rather than going for the simpler solution straight away, a greater understanding of the topic area is shown.

Victor is contractually bound to sell the photographs to Maya and Karl. In spite of Simon's early arrival the revocation of the offer was communicated to him before his acceptance, albeit by a third party.

✓ Make your answer stand out

- Perhaps in your discussion on the potential revocation of the unilateral offer you might consider including the possible alternative argument in *Daulia Ltd* v *Four Millbank Nominees Ltd* [1978] Ch 231 where the proposition was put forward, obiter, that once performance has been embarked upon it is not possible to revoke a unilateral offer.
- Remember, however, a distinction must be drawn between commencement of performance and merely preparing to perform (*Errington* v *Errington* [1952] 1 KB 290).
- In the light of the two points above ensure you apply your analysis to the facts of the question: Simon, in arriving early, was securing his place in any potential queue to be one of the first purchasers, rather than embarking on performance of the contract and as such the revocation by the shop assistant of the unilateral offer will have been communicated prior to acceptance.

! Don't be tempted to . . .

- Fail to consider all the facts: remember you are told the notice of revocation is late, but why would you be told about the shop assistant having knowledge of the situation if it wasn't relevant?
- Ignore potential exceptions to hard-and-fast general rules such as silence cannot constitute acceptance.

Question 4

Discuss the problems inherent in the common law rules on offer and acceptance in determining exactly if and when a bilateral contract was formed particularly where commercial parties use their own standard terms.

Answer plan

→ Distinguishing between an offer and an invitation to treat can be difficult in lengthy and complex negotiations.

→ Acceptance must mirror terms; issue as to whose terms have been accepted in 'battle of the form' scenarios.

→ If there is material agreement, it's more likely a contract is in existence.

→ Rules on communication of acceptance and time at which acceptance takes place can be crucial and not certain.

Diagram plan

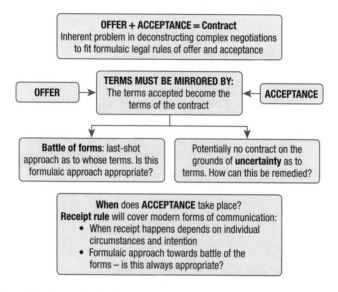

OFFER + ACCEPTANCE = Contract
Inherent problem in deconstructing complex negotiations to fit formulaic legal rules of offer and acceptance

OFFER →

TERMS MUST BE MIRRORED BY:
The terms accepted become the terms of the contract

← **ACCEPTANCE**

Battle of forms: last-shot approach as to whose terms. Is this formulaic approach appropriate?

Potentially no contract on the grounds of **uncertainty** as to terms. How can this be remedied?

When does **ACCEPTANCE** take place?
Receipt rule will cover modern forms of communication:
• When receipt happens depends on individual circumstances and intention
• Formulaic approach towards battle of the forms – is this always appropriate?

A printable version of this diagram plan is available from www.pearsoned.co.uk/lawexpressqa

Answer

To have an enforceable contract there must be offer and acceptance. Acceptance will be a mirror of the terms of the offer. Those terms will be the terms of the contract. Parties to a contract are focused predominantly on 'the deal' rather than the approach a court may take to dissecting their negotiations and rearticulating them in terms of offer and acceptance.[1] Many of the common law rules applied to modern contracts predate the technology now available and in everyday use. This can add a level of complexity in their application.[2]

Distinctions between invitations to treat and an offer can be difficult to draw. If the statement made by one party is a final proposition which the maker intends to be bound to on acceptance, it will be an offer. If it is merely a statement as to their current position at that stage of the negotiations, it will be an invitation to treat. The distinction is clear in law but can be harder to determine from the facts of a particular case.[3] This can be illustrated by the cases of ***Gibson v Manchester City Council*** [1978] 1 WLR 520. As the correspondence

[1] This identification of a tension between commercial reality and potential legal dogma is key to answering the question set.

[2] This point immediately focuses on the 'inherent' problem – old rules/new technologies.

[3] Make sure you include clear definitions with illustration.

between the council and Mr Gibson only amounted to an invitation to treat, there could be no acceptance as there had been no offer. The Court of Appeal questioned whether or not it was always necessary to use a formulaic approach to the rules on offer and acceptance; the House of Lords saw no reason to deviate from the conventional approach in this situation. A mechanical approach to the rules on offer and acceptance can make the law appear detached from commercial reality.[4]

[4] This leads neatly into the next line of argument.

Acceptance must be an unqualified assent to the terms of the offer. If it does not mirror the terms of the offer, then there has been a counter-offer which if accepted will lead to an enforceable agreement on those terms. If the counter-offer is not accepted, it operates as a rejection of the original offer which cannot then later be accepted (*Hyde v Wrench* (1840) 3 Beav 334).[5] Many commercial contracts use standard forms. As such, an offeror may make an offer on their standard terms and in response the offeree sends their standard terms, which do not exactly mirror the original offer. Following *Hyde v Wrench* the second set of terms constitute a counter-offer which the original offeror is free to accept or reject (*Butler Machine Tool v Ex-Cell-O Corp* [1979] 1 WLR 401). This fits with the offer/acceptance analysis, but where terms vary in the detail the decision can turn on chance events as to who made the last communication and the response to it. In using the last-shot approach, it is possible that a party is bound by terms that they did not intend to be bound by.[6]

[5] This is a good lead into how general principles apply to the battle of the forms.

[6] You should reflect back to the question asked here that this is the 'inherent' problem.

There is also a danger that if terms are too inconsistent or uncertain on a material term that no contract will be found to exist.[7] In *Nicolene v Simmonds* [1953] 1 QB 543 the courts were willing to ignore uncertainty where it concerned a subsidiary matter, but this will not be the case if the fundamental terms remained uncertain even though substantial performance had been made (*British Steel Corporation v Cleveland Bridge and Engineering Co. Ltd* [1984] 1 All ER 504). The courts can also resolve an issue of uncertainty by implying a term using custom and practice, previous course of dealings, a statutory implied term, or the officious bystander test. A court will not usually allow a party to escape from an obligation on a technicality where there has been partial or substantial performance. In *Hillas & Co. Ltd v Arcos* (1932) 43 LT Rep 359 the courts were very clear in their assertion that they were not 'the

[7] The following paragraph identifies the means by which the courts have been able to find a contract to be in existence in spite of rules of offer and acceptance.

destroyer of bargains' and were willing to imply a standard of reasonableness to make an otherwise vague statement certain.

The time at which a contract is formed will depend on the method of acceptance used.[8] An offeror can prescribe how and when acceptance will take place (***Tinn v Hoffman*** (1873) 29 LT 271). Where no such requirements are articulated in the offer, the common law provides two general rules for the time at which acceptance takes place. If the post is used, then acceptance takes place on posting (***Adams v Lindsell*** (1918) 1 B & Ald 681). Providing the letter was properly stamped and addressed, this could mean that the offeror is bound even if they never actually receive the acceptance. The rule is contrary to all other means of communication of acceptance which are subject to the receipt rule (***Entores Ltd v Miles Far East Corporation*** [1955] 2 QB 327). As such, acceptance takes effect when it has been effectively communicated to the other party. ***Entores*** was decided in 1955 and distinguished between instantaneous and non-instantaneous means of communication. Instantaneous means of communication would be subject to the receipt rule and non-instantaneous the postal rule. The advent of new technologies has enabled instantaneous means of communication such as the telephone or email to be stored and retrieved at a different time to the time of communication. Even though the retrieval of the acceptance is later, it is unlikely that the postal rule will be expanded beyond the use of the Royal Mail. This then leaves open the question of when acceptance takes place. Is it when a message of this type is sent, or perhaps when it is received in the recipient's storage device, or when it is actually read by the recipient?[9] No decision has actually been made on this point as regards the timing of acceptance. In ***Brinkibon Ltd v Stahag Stahl und Stahlwarenhandel GmbH*** [1982] 2 WLR 264 Lord Wilberforce suggested that no universal rule could cover such cases, and the timing of acceptance would depend on the intention of the parties, by sound business practice, or in some cases where a court feels the risk should lie.

The potential clash of standard form terms is still being decided on nineteenth-century principles of offer and counter-offer and the last-shot approach is still the most favoured. The problem inherent in this approach is that in determining whose terms have been

[8] Having dealt with 'if', now consider the 'when' demanded by the question.

[9] The analysis recognises what is still an unresolved issue in B2B transactions.

agreed upon, a formulaic approach may be reflective of the chance chronology of events rather than the party's intentions. Ironically, in determining the time at which a contract came into being where modern technologies allow the storing of communications is left very much to be dependent on individual circumstances and modes of trading rather than a hard-and-fast rule.[10]

[10] A strong finish pulls together all the arguments and focuses conclusions directly on the question set.

✓ Make your answer stand out

- An examiner will be impressed if you can include an appreciation of a wider global context in the age of e-contracts. Consider discussing the following issues:

  (i) The UK courts use the traditional formulaic approach of offer and acceptance wherever possible in dealing with the battle of the forms. However, UK law is consistent with other jurisdictions and conventions, such as the American Uniform Commercial Code, the Vienna Convention on Contracts for the International Sale of Goods 1980 and Principles of European Contract Law, in not allowing trivial inconsistencies to defeat the existence of a contract. What will be considered sufficiently material to preclude the existence of a contract does still vary.

  (ii) Some electronic means of communication are now governed by specific legislation. The Electronic Commerce (EC Directive) Regulations 2002 for instance now covers the timing of acceptance as being the time at which the receiving party is able to access the requisite communications, but does not define what constitutes acceptance. This would apply to internet transactions but not email which would still be governed by the rules in *Entores* and *Brinkibon*.

- *Clark* v *Dunraven* [1897] AC 59 could be worth including as an example of where the rules on offer and acceptance provide no assistance and yet a contract was found to exist between individual members of a yacht club to comply with the rules of the club.

! Don't be tempted to . . .

- Be superficial in your analysis: inherent problems suggest you need to be looking for a critique of the application of the traditional approach to the requirement of offer and acceptance.
- Miss the clues: 'if and when' give direction as to the 'inherent' problems involved.

❓ Question 5

Jack and Imogen have booked a table at the 'Blue Parrot' restaurant. They are greeted by Wilf the head waiter. Imogen leaves the group. While she is gone Wilf tells Jack that the restaurant is named after the owner's pet bird which escaped that afternoon. He tells Jack that the owners are offering a £1,000 reward for information leading to its recovery. Posters have been put up to that effect on lamp posts and trees in the area.

Once seated Imogen tells Jack about a parrot she found locked in her greenhouse. She says she was late for her date with Jack and has not reported her find to anyone. Jack tells her not to worry and that he will report it for her.

Jack leaves the table, gives Wilf Imogen's address, his name for the reward cheque, and a time at which to collect the parrot. Jack informs Imogen that he has arranged for the bird's collection. On the way home Imogen sees one of the posters offering the reward. Imogen is furious with Jack as he had not mentioned the reward and she says that at least half if not all the reward money should be hers.

Later that evening the parrot's owners turn up at Imogen's house. The owners refuse to pay Jack as they feel he did nothing towards the recovery of the bird. They thank Imogen for her help, but say that as she did not know of the reward she cannot be entitled to it.

Advise Imogen and Jack if they have any legal claim to the reward money offered.

Answer plan

→ Discuss how offers of a reward can be unilateral offers.

→ Explain how acceptance by conduct has taken place in giving the information to Wilf.

→ Discuss how Jack's knowledge of the offer will create a binding contract, but Imogen's ignorance of the reward will defeat her claim.

→ Consider if Jack has any legal obligation to share any of the reward money with Imogen.

Diagram plan

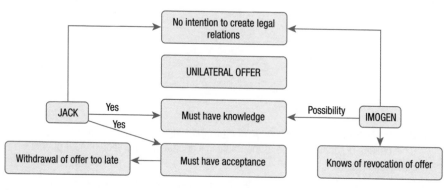

A printable version of this diagram plan is available from www.pearsoned.co.uk/lawexpressqa

Answer

The placing of an advertisement, poster or circular providing for a reward in return for a given act can amount to a unilateral offer capable of acceptance and creating an enforceable agreement. The owners of the parrot have made a unilateral offer capable of acceptance in the provision of information leading to the recovery of the parrot. Knowledge of the offer is a prerequisite to acceptance and this may be especially problematic for Imogen. As with all offers, unilateral offers can be withdrawn at any time prior to acceptance.[1]

The posters put on the lamp posts and trees by the owners of the parrot are unilateral offers, capable of acceptance by providing information that led to the recovery of the parrot. The poster is a unilateral offer rather than an invitation to treat as it demonstrates an intention to be bound and invites no further negotiation (**Carlill v Carbolic Smoke Ball Co.** [1893] 1 QB 256).[2] Furthermore, in such circumstances the need to communicate acceptance is waived and acceptance is provided by conduct in completing performance (**Daulia v Four Millbank Nominees Ltd** [1978] Ch 231).[3]

[2] This is good use of case law as it paraphrases the key elements from the relevant decision.

[3] Note complete not partial performance here, which leads to more complex issues.

In the above scenario, providing information that leads to the recovery of the parrot rather than actually locating the parrot is required. Jack has complied with that condition and the owners of the parrot cannot then prevaricate on the quality of performance of their condition, unless some element of their offer had not been complied with.[4] On giving the information that led to the recovery of the missing parrot, Jack has accepted the unilateral offer by conduct. An offer can be revoked at any time prior to acceptance. Any attempt to withdraw an offer after acceptance has taken place is a breach of contract (**Payne v Cave** (1789) 3 Term Rep 148). Acceptance of the unilateral offer took place in the restaurant at which point a binding contract between the owners and Jack came into being. The refusal to pay the reward when the terms of the offer have been complied with is a breach of contract by the parrot's owners.

[4] This is a pertinent point to make; nothing in the problem would suggest so.

Knowledge of the offer of a reward is necessary in order for there to be acceptance and a legally binding contract even if that is not the primary motivation for performance (**Williams v Carwardine** (1833) 4 B & Ad 621). Jack has knowledge of the offer, even though it was not directly from the source. He also knew of the actual source of the unilateral offer and the reward money was potentially a motivation for giving Wilf the information so as to claim the reward. **Gibbons v Proctor** (1891) 64 LT 594, the only UK case on this point, suggests that motive is irrelevant and that only the intention to be bound need be demonstrated;[5] again Jack satisfies this requirement. By contrast Imogen did not know of the reward until she was walking home with Jack. It can be argued that she had already completed performance in finding the parrot; however, the offer referred to information leading to the recovery of the parrot and this she did by telling Jack of her find. This, however, was done in total ignorance of the offer of a reward.

[5] Using the case law in this way dispenses with any counter-arguments to Jack's claim.

In the Australian case of **R v Clarke** (1927) 40 CLR 227 the claimant could not recover a promised reward, as at the time he gave the information he had forgotten (and therefore had no knowledge of the reward at the time the information was given) about the reward offered. This would appear to defeat any claim that Imogen might have to the reward money. The only English case in this area, **Gibbons v Proctor**, however, allowed recovery of a reward in ignorance of the offer when the principal became aware of the offer before his agent's effective communication of the information to the offeror, even though at the time that he delivered the information to the agent he had no knowledge of the offer. Imogen has no knowledge of the offer at the time she finds the parrot; she still does not know of the offer when it is communicated through Jack to Wilf, who are both mere conduits of information. If Imogen sees the poster before the message is delivered to the owners of the parrot by Wilf, she may be able to claim the reward relying on the UK authority of **Gibbons v Proctor**. If she only has knowledge of the offer after the owners of the parrot have received the information, her claim would also appear to be defeated.

Following the decision in **Dickinson v Dodds** (1876) 2 Ch D 463, it can be argued that Imogen knows that the information has already been given to the owners of the parrot and that the offer is no longer open when she sees the poster.[6]

[6] Astute application of legal principles needs to be shown in spite of where any sympathies may lie.

Imogen gave the information to Jack to see the parrot returned to its owners. There is no obligation in UK law to act in good faith (**Smith v Hughes** (1871) LR 6 QB 597) and therefore Jack was under no obligation to inform Imogen of the offer of a reward. Imogen believed Jack to be acting on her behalf in reporting her find and may argue that there was an intention to create legal relations as to the outcome of this joint venture. With regard to domestic and social arrangements there has been a presumption by the courts that no intention to create legal relations exists unless there is evidence to rebut this presumption (**Wilson v Burnett** [2007] EWCA Civ 1170).[7]

[7] It is perfectly acceptable to use better known cases such as *Balfour* v *Balfour* [1919] 2 KB 571 or *Simpkins* v *Pays* [1955] 1 WLR 975.

Jack completed performance as required by the parrot owners and therefore an enforceable contract exists between them. Jack is entitled to the reward of £1,000. It is too late at this point for the parrot's owners to withdraw their offer. Imogen has no knowledge of the offer at the time she gives the information to Jack, and, even if she acquired that knowledge before the information reached the parrot's owners, in gaining that knowledge she also knew simultaneously that the offer had already been accepted and performance rendered by Jack and was no longer open. A court would be unlikely to find that Jack and Imogen intended to create legal relations between themselves and, as such, Jack would have no legal obligation to share the reward with Imogen.[8]

[8] A conclusion which draws all threads of analysis and application together gives a polished finish to the answer.

✓ Make your answer stand out

- Consider supplementing an answer with some academic opinion: for example, P. Mitchell and J. Phillips (2002) argue that UK law requires knowledge of an offer, that that knowledge demonstrates the intention to accept a unilateral offer and that motivation is irrelevant – The contractual nexus: is reliance essential?, 22 *OJLS* 115.

! Don't be tempted to . . .

- Avoid applying the legal rules as you do not like the 'unfairness' of the outcome. Imogen does not have a claim legally, her choice of friends is another matter.
- Miss the detail in considering the attempted withdrawal of the offer to Jack and the termination of the offer as regards Imogen.

 Question 6

Examine how the legal distinction between an invitation to treat and an offer has been applied to auction sales and sales by tender, having particular regard to the creation of enforceable collateral contracts.

Answer plan

→ Explain why a distinction between an invitation to treat and an offer is important.

→ Explain how advertisement of an auction or invitation to submit tenders are subject to the general definitions above.

→ Investigate the role collateral contracts have in these areas, citing cases specifically relevant to these particular situations.

→ Evaluate the potential consequences of breach of these collateral contracts.

Diagram plan

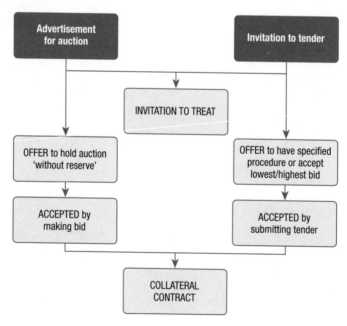

A printable version of this diagram plan is available from www.pearsoned.co.uk/lawexpressqa

Answer

The legal definitions of invitation to treat and offer apply to auction sales and sales by tender just as they would to any other contractual relationship. There is a presumption that an advertisement of an auction or an invitation to tender will be treated as invitations to treat. This presumption can be rebutted where evidence of a contrary intention is demonstrated. Therefore, there is the possibility of the creation of a collateral contract which is enforceable where there has been a promise made that an auction sale or tender process will be operated in a specified way.[1]

An offer is an expression of a definite willingness to be bound on certain terms which becomes an enforceable agreement on being accepted by the offeree. By contrast an invitation to treat is inviting further negotiation or offers. Advertisements usually fall into this category as the aim of an advertisement is to interest prospective customers into making an offer for the goods or service (**Partridge v Crittenden** [1968] 2 All ER 421). In **Harris v Nickerson** (1873) LR 8 QB 286, this point was decided with particular reference to auctions when the plaintiff was unable to recover his travelling expenses in attending an advertised but cancelled auction. To have found otherwise would have made anyone who advertises an event liable in damages to all who attempted to attend before they were made aware of the cancellation.[2] Furthermore, the auctioneers request for bids is also an invitation to treat; an offer is made by the bidder which the auctioneer is free to accept or reject (**Payne v Cave** (1789) 3 Term Rep 148): this position has found statutory recognition in section 57(2) of the Sale of Goods Act 1979. At any time before acceptance the bidder may withdraw their offer (the bid), and the auctioneer is not free to return to accept an earlier bid as that will have been rejected in favour of the new bid/offer. Equally a request for tenders is also regarded as an invitation to treat with the submission of the tender being an offer which the party asking for the submission of tenders is free to accept or reject (**Spencer v Harding** (1870) LR 5 CP 561).[3]

Although the general rule is that an advertisement or an invitation to tender will be no more than an invitation to treat, it is possible that

[1] Your introduction should be concise, outlining the main points for discussion and focus on the question set.

[2] This pragmatic analysis hints at your knowledge of revocation.

[3] You can mirror analysis of an auction case while building on general application of legal principles which are applied to both types of situation.

it may amount to a unilateral offer if it is specific enough on the performance of a specified condition to become binding (*Carlill* **v** *Carbolic Smoke Ball Co.* [1893] 1 QB 256). In *Warlow* **v** *Harrison* (1895) 1 E&E 309 it was said, obiter, that if an auction was advertised as being held 'without reserve', there was a contractual obligation to sell to the highest bidder. A unilateral offer had been made by the auctioneer in the advertisement to sell to the highest bidder and that offer was accepted by the prospective purchasers placing a bid. The contract formed is between the auctioneer and the highest bidder, not the owner of the property being auctioned. This line of reasoning was followed in *Barry* **v** *Heathcote Ball & Co. Ltd* [2000] 1 WLR 1962, in which the court found that in advertising that the auction would be held without reserve a collateral contract had been formed with the highest bidder. It is interesting to note that if the auction was not held at all, there would have been no breach of contract and no cause of action.[4] It would also appear that a collateral contract is formed with every bidder, but only the highest bidder whose offer is rejected would be able to show loss and therefore would be the only one to gain from a possible action for breach of contract. In *Harvela Investments Ltd* **v** *Royal Trust Co. of Canada (CI) Ltd* [1986] AC 207, the court used similar reasoning with regard to the promise to accept the highest offer on the purchase of shares being accepted by making an offer. As such, a collateral contract was formed with the party submitting the highest offer. Some sympathy lies with the offeror in this situation, however, as the bid that was accepted was a referential bid in that it offered a fixed amount or C$2,100,000 above any other offer received. To have decided otherwise would, however, have meant that others submitting tenders would never have a real opportunity to have their offers accepted.[5] *Blackpool and Fylde Aero Club Ltd* **v** *Blackpool Borough Council* [1990] 3 All ER 25 provides authority for the proposition that while there is no obligation to accept tenders at all if a process by which tenders will be considered is promised, that promise can form a collateral contract. In this case the local council believed the plaintiffs' tender to have been submitted late which it had not been. The invitation to tender amounted to a unilateral offer to consider any tender that was submitted in accordance with their rules;[6] this offer was accepted by anyone correctly making a tender. In not considering Blackpool and Fylde Aero Club Ltd's tender the council were in breach of contract.

[4] A good student will make the point to define the extent of potential obligations.

[5] It is important to show the examiner you have understood the rationale behind the decision by providing a good explanation.

[6] This point shows you have recognised the creation of wider obligation where a particular process is promised.

The advertisement of auction sales, the inviting of bids and invitations to tender will prima facie be considered to be mere invitations to treat and not binding agreements. Through the use of the rules on offer and acceptance, and particularly the distinction between an invitation to treat and an offer, a collateral contract will be found to exist where there is an intention to adhere to a given process or promise to accept the highest bid. Without such a protection the holder of the auction would be able to entice interest without running any risk of loss, and with regard to tender the offeror could fail to abide by an agreed process and potentially have an unfair selection process.[7] Breach of these collateral contracts may prove expensive as contractual damages where possible reflect expectation interest, which with regard to auctions would be the difference between market value and the amount bid; with a tender, if expectation loss is too speculative, then a measure of damages could be quantified on the loss of chance and/or reliance damages for costs incurred in preparing the tender.

[7] The analysis of the traditional rules of offer and acceptance enable you to articulate why such an exercise is necessary.

✓ Make your answer stand out

- Consider impressing an examiner by demonstrating a depth of understanding of the measure and rationale for damages awarded: in *Barry* v *Heathcote Ball & Co. Ltd* damages were awarded for the difference between the amount bid and the market value, rather than the ultimate sum realised for the sale of the machinery.

- In contrast, consider the rationale behind the measure of damages awarded in *Blackpool and Fylde Aero Club Ltd* v *Blackpool Borough Council*: as there was no guarantee that they would have secured the tender, an amount was awarded to reflect the loss of chance as in *Chaplin* v *Hicks* [1911] 2 KB 786.

- Add some incisive comment to your analysis, evaluating the possibility that the common law has moved towards an almost public law style of protection when looking at the protection afforded tenders and a promised procedure. This is an increasingly regulated area of law, particularly in the public sector.

! Don't be tempted to . . .

- Miss out on higher marks by describing the rules as defined by case law without attempting some rationale as to why the law has developed in this way.

❓ Question 7

George's Perfect Pizzas Ltd has been in lengthy negotiations with Fiorentina Foods Ltd for the supply of buffalo mozzarella.

Following a demonstration of the products by the representatives of Fiorentina Foods Ltd, the buyers at George's Perfect Pizzas Ltd complete an order form for a monthly supply of 5,000 kg at £1.00 per kg. The order form has their standard terms and conditions on the reverse of the document, which provide that termination of the agreement will require three months' notice and all payments for goods will be made quarterly.

Fiorentina Foods Ltd respond by thanking George's Perfect Pizzas Ltd for their order and attach a form entitled 'Delivery Request' which has their own terms and conditions on the back of the form, which stipulate that deliveries will be made weekly on a regular day of the customer's choice and that payment will be due within fourteen days of each delivery. The document is silent as to termination of the agreement.

The buyers at George's Perfect Pizzas Ltd do not fill in the request form but ring Fiorentina Foods Ltd to suggest Monday as being the regular day for delivery. Fiorentina Foods Ltd has made deliveries for two months but no payments as yet have been received. Furthermore, George's Perfect Pizzas Ltd has said that with immediate effect they wish to cancel their order as they have found an alternative supplier.

Advise Fiorentina Foods Ltd as they believe they are entitled to three months' notice of termination, but George's Perfect Pizzas Ltd assert that no contract ever existed between them as they never formally agreed specified terms.

Diagram plan

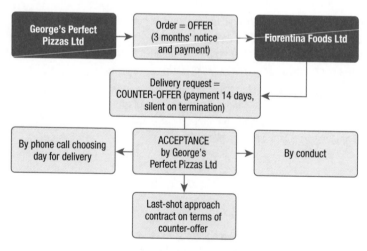

A printable version of this diagram plan is available from www.pearsoned.co.uk/lawexpressqa

Answer plan

→ Outline the traditional doctrine of offer and acceptance as prerequisites for an enforceable agreement in a battle of the forms scenario.

→ Discuss the courts' likely response to the argument that no contract was ever formed.

→ Using the last-shot approach it is unlikely that Fiorentina will be able to rely on the three-month notice provision in the original order form as it is their own terms which operated as a counter-offer which was accepted.

Answer

The traditional doctrine of offer and acceptance requires both elements to be present. George's Perfect Pizzas Ltd and Fiorentina Foods Ltd each purport to have contracted on their own differing standard terms. If a strict adherence to the rules on offer and acceptance is adopted, it is necessary to determine whether or not a contract was formed and if so on whose terms.

The courts have demonstrated a reluctance to find there to be no contract in existence where there has been substantial performance and there is material agreement (**Nicolene v Simmonds** [1953] 1 QB 543).[1] However, the courts will find that no contract had come into existence in spite of substantial performance where fundamental terms remain uncertain (**British Steel Corporation v Cleveland Bridge and Engineering Co. Ltd** [1984] 1 All ER 504). The fundamental terms as to price, quantity and delivery have been agreed between George's Perfect Pizzas Ltd and Fiorentina Foods Ltd; what remains uncertain is the notice period required for termination of the contract and the time of payment. To find that no contract came into existence would be to allow George's Perfect Pizzas Ltd to escape from their contractual obligations on a technicality, having found a more lucrative deal elsewhere.[2]

An offer is an expression of willingness to be bound to those certain terms on acceptance by the offeree. In completing the order form, George's Perfect Pizzas Ltd demonstrated their willingness to be bound on their standard terms, including a provision requiring three months' notice to terminate the contract and quarterly payments. On acceptance by Fiorentina Foods Ltd, the contract would have been concluded and those terms binding on the parties. Treitel (Peel,

[1] Succinct, to the point and clearly addresses the first issue – is there a contract?

[2] The application here demonstrates a commercial awareness of the practical repercussions of an overly formulaic approach to the rules on offer and acceptance.

[3] Use of academic authority demonstrates breadth of knowledge and research.

2007) defines acceptance as being 'a final and unqualified assent to all the terms of an offer'.[3] This reinforces the decision in **Taylor v Laird** (1856) 1 H & N 266 that requires that the acceptance must mirror the terms of the offer exactly. Fiorentina Foods Ltd's response did not operate as a 'final unqualified acceptance of the offer': it introduced a new term as to time of payment and as such also did not mirror the terms of the offer.

A mere acknowledgement of receipt of an offer will not be an acceptance unless in that context it is a clear indication of agreement to particular terms. The inclusion of alternative terms and conditions here by Fiorentina Foods Ltd would suggest that the thanking for the order is just that and not an acceptance. The inclusion of alternative terms as to payment times is not an unqualified acceptance of the offer and as such may be construed as being a counter-offer (**Hyde v Wrench** (1840) 3 Beav 334),[4] which in order to form an enforceable contract must be accepted.

[4] While still focusing on application to the problem, you have introduced the idea of counter-offers in these situations.

The traditional offer, counter-offer and acceptance rules have been used to ensure a finding of the existence of a contract in the battle of the form scenarios, as in the given problem, where both parties believe they are contracting on their own standard terms and conditions (**Butler Machine Tool Co. Ltd v Ex-Cell-O Corporation (England) Ltd** [1979] 1 WLR 401). Where standard terms and conditions are exchanged in this way, the last-shot approach is taken to determine whose terms will prevail and be enforceable.

In the above scenario the phone call by George's Perfect Pizzas Ltd can be construed as acceptance of the counter-offer and therefore the terms contained in the counter-offer will take precedence. The irony of this would be that George's Perfect Pizzas Ltd would not be bound by the three-month notice period which was in their own terms and conditions, and using the last-shot approach would not apply.[5]

[5] The irony of the situation is acknowledged and is important, as in this area of law the true intention of the parties can be lost in a strict adherence to the last-shot approach.

It could be argued that the telephone call is merely a response to an enquiry as to a delivery date and is not in itself an acceptance. Even if this were to be the case, it is unlikely that there would be a finding that no contract had ever been formed for want of acceptance. As in **Butler Machine Tool Co. Ltd v Ex-Cell-O Corporation (England) Ltd**, the Court of Appeal suggested, obiter, that there would have been acceptance once the goods had been delivered and accepted by the buyer. George's Perfect Pizzas Ltd and Fiorentina Foods Ltd have been making and accepting deliveries over the last two months. Therefore it can argued that Fiorentina Foods Ltd's counter-offer has been accepted by conduct (*Brogden* v *Metropolitan Rail Co.* (1877) LR 2 App Cas 666).[6] Again, the last-shot approach would come into play and the counter-offer would be the prevailing terms, with no three-month notice period, but George's Perfect Pizzas Ltd being overdue with their payment.

[6] Two potential viewpoints, but same outcome.

In using the last-shot approach, it is possible that a party is bound by terms they did not intend to be bound by (*Tekdata Interconnections Ltd* v *Amphenol Ltd* [2009] EWCA Civ 1209),[7] and it can be argued that effect is not being given to the parties' intentions. George's Perfect Pizzas Ltd will be able to escape from their obligation to give three months' notice unless some evidence can be brought to show a contrary intention to be bound by alternative terms.

[7] This use of case law demonstrates to the examiner a currency of knowledge and an understanding of the application of the principles you are discussing.

An element of chance is introduced by the interpretation of the parties' negotiations in terms of offer, counter-offer and acceptance. Lord Denning in *Butler Machine Tool Co. Ltd* v *Ex-Cell-O Corp (England) Ltd* questioned whether or not the formulaic approach to offer and acceptance was only appropriate to the extent of determining that a contract had come in existence and that the terms should be determined by a more sophisticated construction of the parties' true intentions. This split approach has been repeatedly refuted by the House of Lords who will, where possible, adopt the traditional approach to offer and acceptance.[8] George's Perfect Pizzas and Fiorentina do have a contractual relationship. The last-shot approach favoured by the courts will mean that the term requiring three months' notice will not be part of the contractual terms agreed to.[9] The courts will need extremely good cause to move away from the traditional approach.

[8] This demonstrates a depth of knowledge behind the main decision.

[9] Final application: this should be focused and clearly articulated in terms of the problem set.

✓ Make your answer stand out

- Consider taking the academic argument one step further. In *G Percy Trentham Ltd* v *Archital Luxfer* [1993] 1 Lloyd's Rep 25 the possibility was raised that, where an acknowledgement contained substantially the same terms as the offer, it would not interpreted as a counter-offer.

- Remember to apply the analysis above specifically to the problem; is the difference in the payment date enough to argue that the delivery request was an acceptance rather than a counter-offer? Unlikely: the answer would probably be the same, as the difference is sufficient to amount to a counter-offer.

- Higher marks are given for the ability to evaluate the law. In *Balmoral Group Ltd* v *Borealis* (UK) Ltd [2006] EWHC 1900 (Comm) the point was clearly made that parties to a contract are focused on the deal rather than a legal deconstruction of their negotiations in terms of offer and acceptance and, as such, the terms contracted on a matter of chance rather than planning.

- Consider reinforcing your point further. Even where this has been thought about and a prevailing clause term is used, you should declare that the standard terms will be those used and no others. It will not be legally enforceable if superseded by a counter-offer which is later deemed to be accepted (*Butler Machine Tool Co. Ltd* v *Ex-Cell-O Corp (England)*).

! Don't be tempted to . . .

- Miss the need to apply your analysis to the problem set in becoming involved in the deeper legal analysis of offer and acceptance as regards the battle of the form scenarios.

- Avoid the question in fear of some of the complexities involved; easy marks are achieved by your basic knowledge of offer/acceptance and counter-offer.

 Question 8

Discuss the legal definition of a unilateral offer and the potential difficulties arising from the purported revocation of such an offer.

Answer plan

→ Define unilateral offer, distinguishing it from an invitation to treat.

→ Discuss the means by which such offers are accepted and the waiving of the need to communicate that acceptance.

→ Consider that revocation of a unilateral offer can be made at any time prior to acceptance as with any other offer; difficulties arise with communication of the revocation and where performance has been commenced but not yet completed.

Diagram plan

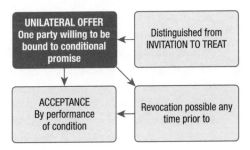

A printable version of this diagram plan is available from www.pearsoned.co.uk/lawexpressqa

Answer

A unilateral offer occurs where one party offers to be bound to a conditional promise: for example, the offer of £100 for the return of a lost wallet. It is unilateral as only one party is making a promise. Acceptance is effective when the condition is acted upon. As with all offers revocation can take place at any time before acceptance; however, it is unclear as to whether or not revocation can be effective if performance has been embarked upon.[1]

[1] This is a good start. The answer is well focused on the question; it gives a definition, an illustrative example, and raises the issue surrounding revocation.

Advertisements, circulars and notices addressed to the whole world usually amount to invitations to treat (***Partridge v Crittenden*** [1968] 2 All ER 421). An invitation to treat does not express a willingness to be bound on acceptance but is an invitation to negotiate or to make an offer which can then be accepted or rejected.

The courts, aware that advertisers, in particular, are hoping to increase interest in their products or activities, will not find a unilateral offer to exist if the statement in question is a 'mere puff' (**Carlill v Carbolic Smoke Ball Co.** [1893] 1 QB 256). It must be understood to be an offer which could be acted upon.[2]

[2] It is important to try to draw the line between hype and obligation.

An offer is defined as being an expression of willingness to be bound on certain terms on acceptance of that offer.[3] A unilateral offer is also an expression of willingness to be bound without further negotiation on performance of the condition. As with any other offer an enforceable agreement is formed on acceptance. In **Carlill v Carbolic Smoke Ball Co.** the defendants had offered £100 to any person contracting influenza after the proper use of their product. Mrs Carlill purchased the smoke ball, used it, and caught influenza.[4] The company argued that no contract existed as it is impossible to make an offer to the whole world. This argument was rejected, as an offer could be made to the whole world which would become a contract with a limited number of persons who performed the condition in accordance with the advertisement. Furthermore, there was evidence of the intention of the company to be bound to the promise, as the advertisement asserted that £1,000 had been deposited in the bank to satisfy such claims. In **Bowerman v ABTA** [1996] CLC 451 a notice displayed on a tour operator's premises promising reimbursement in the event of the operator's insolvency created a direct contractual relationship between ABTA and the customer.[5] The offer was a unilateral one which customers accepted in purchasing the holiday from the ABTA member. Customers seeing the notice would expect the promise to be one that would create a legal obligation: otherwise what would be the purpose of such a statement?

[3] Do not spurn the easy marks by not giving the basic key definition.

[4] Good use of facts to illustrate the promise (£100) in return for the performance of the condition (using the product – or perhaps arguably catching influenza!).

[5] This is an excellent use of a modern case to reinforce the point on intention.

The defendants in **Carlill v Carbolic Smoke Ball Co.** also argued that there had been no acceptance of the offer. The court held that the offer is accepted by the performance of the condition and that it could be implied from the circumstances that the need to communicate acceptance had been waived. However, the person claiming the benefit of the promise must have known of the offer in order to be able to accept it[6] (**R v Clarke** (1927) 40 CLR 227), even if that was not the primary motivation for fulfilling the condition (**Williams v Carwardine** (1833) 4 B & Ad 621). Neither **R v Clarke** nor **Williams v Cawardine** are UK decisions and are therefore persuasive authorities only. In the UK case of **Gibbons v Proctor** (1891) 64 LT 594, it was sufficient that the claimant did not know of an offer of a reward for information concerning a crime at the time he passed

[6] Fully expanding on the issues will gain higher marks.

the information on to an intermediary, but did know of it before the information was received by the offeror.

An offer can be revoked at any time before acceptance, and this principle applies equally to unilateral offers.[7] In a bilateral contract revocation of an offer can only be effective if it has been communicated (***Dickinson v Dodds*** (1876) 2 Ch D 463). Unilateral offers have a practicable problem in that an offer is made to the world at large: a revocation communicated in the same way may not be seen by all of the people who knew of the offer. There is no UK decision on this point but the US case of ***Shuey v United States*** (1875) 92 US 73 would suggest that, if the revocation is communicated in the same manner as the offer was made, then that will be sufficient to operate as a withdrawal of the offer and any subsequent acceptance would be too late. Reasonable steps must have been taken to bring the withdrawal to the notice of potentially affected persons even if in reality not all of them will hear of it.

Perhaps more problematic is the revocation of a unilateral offer after performance has been started. In ***Daulia Ltd v Four Millbank Nominees Ltd*** [1978] Ch 231 the court held that once performance had commenced it was too late to revoke the offer; however, the offeror is entitled to complete performance of their condition before they have to make any payment. This prevents an unscrupulous offeror withdrawing their offer almost at the point of completion of the condition, but equally ensures that the offeree will receive no payment or reward unless they give complete performance of that condition.[8]

Carlill v Carbolic Smoke Ball Co. provided a legal definition of unilateral offers and contracts which is still relevant today in protecting the performer of a condition from an empty promise (***O'Brien v MGN Ltd*** [2001] EWCA Civ 1279). The need to communicate acceptance is waived and the performance of the condition is acceptance. The offeror is also prevented from a last-minute revocation once performance has been started upon, while still being entitled to complete performance of their condition.

[7] This demonstrates a clear understanding of the legal point as regards revocation and the difficulties raised by unilateral offers.

[8] The analysis has depth in explaining the balance that has to be struck.

✓ Make your answer stand out

- Picking up on the more subtle points of analysis will enhance marks. Consider including the following academic debate as it will demonstrate a deeper understanding of the topic area and broader reading.

- In *Luxor (Eastborne) Ltd* v *Cooper* [1941] AC 108, it was held that the owner of a house could revoke his promise as regards paying commission to an estate agent at any point up to a buyer being found, even though the estate agent had been making great efforts to secure a buyer. The offer was unilateral as the vendor of the property is promising payment on fulfilment of a condition – the finding of a buyer.

- Following the reasoning in *Daulia*, the offeror would not be able to withdraw from the arrangement once the estate agent began looking for a buyer.

- The solution to this is debatable: Lord Denning favoured relying on the concept of promissory estoppel (*Errington* v *Errington* [1952] 1 KB 290), whereas some academics, such as Cheshire, Fifoot and Furmston, appear to prefer the recognition of a collateral contract being implied that the offer will not be revoked once performance has begun (M.P. Furmston (2010) *Cheshire, Fifoot and Furmston's Law of Contract*, 16th edn, Oxford: OUP).

! Don't be tempted to . . .

- Miss potential depth to your analysis; it would be easy to miss these points:
  (i) Although there is no need to communicate acceptance you must know of the offer made.
  (ii) Revocation is possible prior to acceptance but limited if performance has been embarked upon.

www.pearsoned.co.uk/lawexpressqa

 Go online to access more revision support including additional essay and problem questions with diagram plans, You be the marker questions, and download all diagrams from the book.

Consideration

2

How this topic may come up in exams

To be enforceable in law a promise must be supported by sufficient consideration. Questions will analyse what will amount to sufficient consideration and often what will not. You must be confident with the application of the rules as regards past consideration, performance of an existing public or private contractual duty. Ensure you fully understand the different definition of sufficiency when dealing with the variation of an agreed term. The exceptions to the rule that part payment of a debt cannot satisfy the whole debt are a favourite area of examiners. Focus is particularly put on promissory estoppel and its limitations.

Attack the question

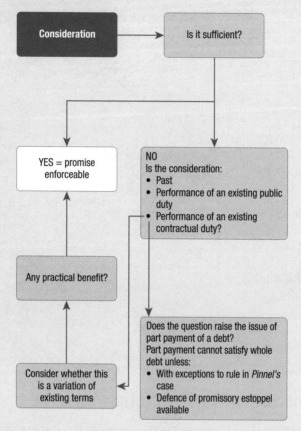

A printable version of this diagram is available from www.pearsoned.co.uk/lawexpressqa

 Question 1

'Consideration must be something "which is of value in the eye of the law"', Lord Thomas, *Chappell & Co.* v *Nestlé Co. Ltd* [1960] AC 87. Evaluate what will and will not amount to value to satisfy the legal requirement that a bargain to be enforceable must be supported by sufficient consideration.

Answer plan

→ Evaluate the requirement that consideration must be present in order that a contract be enforceable and identify that it is a low threshold.

→ Explain that consideration must be recognised as existing in law to be sufficient, but the law is not concerned with a value judgement as to the adequacy of the bargain itself.

→ Consider the following limitations to the sufficiency of consideration: if performance is past, or is of an existing contractual or a public duty.

Diagram plan

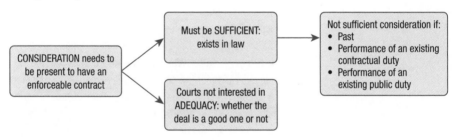

A printable version of this diagram plan is available from www.pearsoned.co.uk/lawexpressqa

Answer

To have an enforceable contract consideration must be provided. The courts are not concerned with determining the value of the bargain. Consideration must be sufficient and have some value recognised by the law. The economic value of the consideration can be negligible, but it cannot be in recognition of past performance, nor can it be the performance of an existing contractual or public duty.[1]

By not evaluating the value of the bargain, the courts give effect to the principle of the freedom of contract. In the view of Treitel (Peel,

[1] A good introduction will focus on the question set and introduce the issues raised by that question.

[2] Good use of academic
authority focused on the
evaluation required by the
question.

2011) the provision of consideration demonstrates a clear intention to be bound. This provides the rationale for the continued existence of a technically complicated and functionally obscure doctrine.[2] Regardless of academic argument in this context the courts are pragmatic in their approach to the doctrine. In ***Johnson* v *Gore Woods & Co. (A Firm)*** [2001] 1 All ER 481 Lord Goff pointed out that the doctrine of consideration is a part of our law and as such must be applied by the courts.

In ***Chappell & Co. Ltd* v *Nestlé Co. Ltd*** [1960] AC 87 Nestlé, in order to promote chocolate sales, were discounting the price of a record: selling it for a cash sum and three chocolate wrappers. Nestlé argued that the wrappers were of no value to them, being discarded on receipt, and therefore did not form part of the consideration. The House of Lords held that the value of the wrappers was irrelevant and that they did form part of the consideration,[3] and as such the royalties payable on the sale of the record were a percentage of the cash price and chocolate bar sales.

[3] The facts of the case, from which the quotation in the question is taken, highlight the legal issues raised by the question.

It would appear that 'sufficient consideration' does not have to have a 'great deal' of economic value but the question arises, can the value be other than economic? The answer would appear to be yes. In ***Ward* v *Byam*** [1959] 1 WLR 496, making a child 'happy' was sufficient consideration for the promise of maintenance payments as in doing so the promise had gone beyond the statutory duty of caring for the child. However, in ***White* v *Bluett*** (1853) 23 LJ Ex 36 a father's promise, to release his son from his liability under a promissory note if the son ceased to complain about his intentions as to the distribution of his estate after his death, was unenforceable for lack of consideration. The son had no right to complain and, as such, refraining from doing something he had no right to do could not amount to sufficient consideration. The US case of ***Hamer* v *Sidway*** (1881) 124 NY 538 provides persuasive authority that refraining from doing a lawful act, such as in this case not drinking, swearing, gambling or smoking before the promisee's twenty-first birthday, can amount to consideration even though both the benefit and the detriment appear to lie with the promisee.

Consideration must be given in return for the specific promise made; as such, a promise for an act already performed is not enforceable as the consideration is past. In ***Re McArdle*** [1951] Ch 669 the

Lampleigh v Braithwait

promise to reimburse the costs of home improvements done to a property could not be recovered because the promise to pay was made after the works had been done. An exception to this rule exists where the past consideration was provided at the promisor's request. In **Lampleigh v Braithwait** (1615) Hob 105 the plaintiff secured a pardon for the defendant. Braithwait promised the sum of £100. Ostensibly this would appear to be past consideration but the court held that there was an implied promise that payment would be made, and this was good consideration even though the precise amount was only decided on later.[4]

[4] Providing the exception to the rule demonstrates to the marker a depth of knowledge and understanding.

[5] A clear statement of the general rule allows you to develop a logical flow to your argument.

Performance of an existing contractual duty cannot provide valuable consideration for a fresh promise to the promisee.[5] In **Stilk v Myrick** (1809) 2 Camp 317 the extra work of two missing crewmen shared amongst the remaining crew was held to be merely the performance of an existing contractual duty to complete a voyage. The promise of an extra payment was unenforceable for want of consideration. By contrast, in **Hartley v Ponsonby** (1857) 7 E & B 872, a ship's crew were able to claim extra wages promised when half the crew deserted. The conditions undertaken for the return journey was so different from those originally agreed to that the old contract had been terminated and a new contract formed with new terms. In **Williams v Roffey** [1991] 1 QB 1 a 'practical benefit' received by the promisor was consideration for an additional promise. In **Williams v Roffey** the main contractors, Roffey, promised Williams an additional payment of money for the completion on time of the refurbishment of flats, which was an existing contractual obligation. It was held that, although **Stilk v Myrick** is still good law, in the absence of duress and where the increased payment is the promisor's suggestion consideration can be established by the receipt of a practical benefit.[6] Roffey's practical benefit was in not having to suffer a penalty clause by not being in breach of his own contractual arrangements, rearranging the scheme for payment, reorganising the work plans, and not having to find an alternative contractor. Providing a 'practical benefit' will not apply to part payment of a debt (**Re Selectmove Ltd** [1995] 1 WLR 474).[7]

[6] Defining the limitation of when 'practical benefit' can amount to consideration shows you understand the complexities of the issue.

[7] Excellent depth provided to your answer here in that the 'practical benefit' of some money will not be sufficient consideration to discharge the whole debt.

Similarly, consideration cannot be provided by performing an existing public duty (**Collins v Godefroy** (1831) 1 B & Ad 950). However, in **Harris v Sheffield United Football Club Ltd** [1988] QB 77, the cost of extra policing at football matches was good consideration as, although there is a public duty on the police to maintain law and order, a Saturday would encourage a larger crowd and therefore created a bigger self-induced risk, necessitating a larger police presence which is beyond the existing public duty.

Consideration does have to be sufficient; without it, a bargain is unenforceable unless the doctrine of promissory estoppel could apply.[8] Sufficiency makes no evaluation of the bargain itself but must have a 'value' recognised in law. What will be sufficient is often a reflection of the parties' intention to be bound, subject to any hint of economic duress. Consideration will not be sufficient if the promise is made after the consideration asked has already been given or it is the performance of an existing public or contractual duty.

[8] Hinting at a broader level of knowledge beyond the question asked.

 Make your answer stand out

- An excellent answer might add depth to the analysis of issues raised by this question by examining some of the academic writing challenging the very rationale for the existence of the doctrine:
  - Halson, R. (1990) Sailors, subcontractors and consideration, 106 *LQR* 183.
  - Atiyah, P.S. (1986) Consideration: a re-statement, in *Essays on Contract*, Oxford: OUP.
  - G. Treitel's (1974) contrasting view Consideration: a critical analysis of Professor Atiyah's fundamental restatement, 50 *ALJ* 439 and (2002) *Some Landmarks of Twentieth Century Contract Law*, Oxford: OUP, Chapter 1.

! **Don't be tempted to . . .**

- Forget to consider what might not be sufficient for consideration.
- Miss fully expanding your analysis to consider any expansions to the traditional limitations to the doctrine's application: for example, in *Williams* v *Roffey*.

❓ Question 2

past not good

Ramsey White is the owner of a well-known local gastro pub, the Fox and Grapes. Ramsey promises Michel, his chef, a £50 bonus for the wedding cake he specially prepared for Ramsey's daughter's wedding last week. He has also promised Michel £100 a month extra if he will stop moaning about the extra work involved in corporate bookings.

The Gastro Publicans Association publish the *Great Gastro Pub Guide* which Ramsey has been selling for £1 and three wine corks from bottles consumed on the premises. Ramsey has agreed to pay the Gastro Publicans Association 10 per cent of the money made from sales of the book in return for his inclusion in the publication. The Gastro Publicans Association are claiming that 10 per cent of the sale price is 10 per cent of the book price and three bottles of wine, representing an average of £6–10 rather than 10p per copy.

Ramsey has also received a £5,000 bill from Yorkester Metropolitan Police Force to cover the extra costs incurred, at his request, in providing protection for the leader of a local right-wing extremist party during their annual conference dinner held at the Fox and Grapes.

Advise Ramsey as to whether or not he has a legal obligation to pay any of these sums in the light of the doctrine of consideration.

Answer plan

→ Focus closely on the application that the bonus for the cake would amount to past consideration.

→ Consider if the monthly increase is for the performance of an existing contractual duty.

→ The amount due to Gastro Publicans Association will depend on whether or not the corks form part of the consideration paid for the book. Focus the discussion on the court's requirement of sufficiency rather than adequacy of consideration.

→ Evaluate whether the payment to the police is for services they provided over and above those required as part of their public duty.

Diagram plan

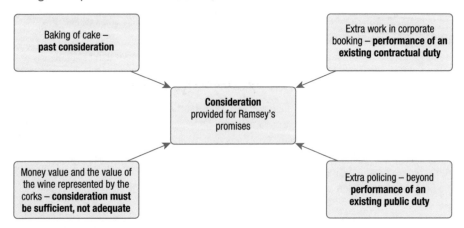

A printable version of this diagram plan is available from www.pearsoned.co.uk/lawexpressqa

Answer

Promises are only enforceable if they are supported by consideration. Consideration is that which is given in return for a promise which has sufficient value in law. Consideration cannot be past, nor can the performance of an existing contractual or public duty provide consideration for a fresh promise.[1]

[1] The marker immediately knows you have recognised the pertinent legal issues raised by the question.

Consideration must be given in return for the promise or act of the other party. If there is no consideration, then the promise is a gratuitous one which may impose a moral but not a legal obligation. A promise that is made to reward an act already completed is also unenforceable as the consideration is past. The consideration does not support the promise made as it has already been given. In *Re McArdle* [1951] Ch 669 the promise of reimbursement from other family members, who had an interest in the property, of expenses incurred in making house improvements by the residents was made after the work had been done. Therefore the promise was unenforceable as a gratuitous promise was unsupported by consideration and not made under deed.[2] The promise to pay a bonus for the baking of the wedding cake was made after the cake had been made and presented at the wedding. The offer of the bonus was made after

*Re v
McArdle*

[2] This additional point raised demonstrates that such a gratuitous promise could be enforceable but only if made under deed.

[3] Giving both sides of the legal argument provides a practical dimension to your answer, showing a strong application/understanding of legal principles.

Michel had completed performance: as such, the consideration was past. The promised bonus is not enforceable in law unless it could be established that Michel baked the cake at Ramsey's request and that it was understood that he would receive some payment in return.[3] This line of argument was successful in the case of **Lampleigh v Braithwait** (1615) Hob 105 and also later in **Pao On v Lau Yiu Long** [1980] AC 614 with the additional proviso that the promise must have been legally enforceable if promised in advance of performance.

Stilk Myn CR

— Stilk v. Myrick

Performance of an existing contractual duty cannot as a general rule provide consideration for a fresh promise (**Stilk v Myrick** (1809) 2 Camp 317). Michel would, therefore, have to show that in cooking for the corporate bookings he is doing something over and above what he was already contractually obliged to do. In **Hartley v Ponsonby** (1857) 7 E & B 872 the extra duties required of the seamen were such that the old contract had been abandoned and a new one with the new terms commenced.[4] The problem suggests that the extra money is being given in return for Michel's change in behaviour in ceasing to moan. Consideration only has to be sufficient and cases such as **Currie v Misa** (1875) LR 10 Ex 153 look, inter alia, only for some 'forbearance', which ceasing to moan would be. It is unlikely that it will be sufficient consideration for the extra £100 per month promised. In **White v Bluett** (1853) 23 LJ Ex 36 the promise by the father to forgo the repayment of a loan if the son would stop complaining about how the father's estate would be distributed on his death was not enforceable for want of consideration. In ceasing to complain the son had not provided sufficient consideration as he had no legal right to complain as to the disposition of the estate. Michel is employed as a chef and unless his duties are greater than his contractual obligation he too has no legal right to complain, and therefore it would be unlikely that ceasing to moan would amount to sufficient consideration.[5] The case of **Williams v Roffey** [1991] 1 QB 1 provides a refinement to the rule in **Stilk v Myrick** in so far as consideration for a variation in contractual terms can be provided if the promisor has received some practical benefit from the promise, and it was their idea with no hint of duress or illegitimate pressure. Potentially, Ramsey will have a practical benefit in that his chef will stop complaining and a better working relationship will ensue. It

— Hartley vs Ponsonby

[4] A modern example of this is *Compagnie Noga D'Importation et D'Exportation SA* v *Abacha (No. 2)* [2003] EWCA Civ 1100. Extra credit will be given for currency of knowledge and up-to-date application of the law, even though the traditional authority is sufficient for your needs.

White vs Bluett

[5] This clear application of the principles surrounding sufficiency will demonstrate your clear understanding of those principles to the examiner.

— Stilk v Myrick — illegitimate press

could be argued that Michel's moaning is illegitimate pressure, but it would be hard to establish that this fell within the narrow application of the doctrine of duress.[6]

[6] Providing a potential use of *Williams* v *Roffey* in this way adds depth to the analysis and highlights some of the academic debate surrounding the need perhaps to clarify the decision's limitations.

Consideration must be sufficient in order for a bargain to be enforceable. The law does not look into the adequacy of the consideration; as long as consideration is present in the eyes of the law, whether a good bargain has been made or not is irrelevant. In ***Chappell & Co. Ltd*** v ***Nestlé Co. Ltd*** [1960] AC 87 the consideration requested by the defendants was an amount in money and three chocolate wrappers for the purchase of a record. The wrappers were discarded on receipt and had no economic value to the defendants; however, it was held that this was still part of the consideration.[7] The courts stressed that they did not require the consideration to be adequate, in other words a good deal, simply that it was sufficient, that is to say recognised by the law. The situation with Ramsey and the Gastro Publicans Association is analogous and the consideration paid for the book is £1 and an amount representative of three bottles of wine. Therefore the Gastro Publicans Association is correct in their demand for the higher sum due to them.

[7] This reinforces the key point that the courts are not interested in the value of the bargain struck by the parties: just that there is a bargain.

Performance of a public duty is not usually good consideration for an additional promise (***Collins*** v ***Godefroy*** (1831) 1 B & Ad 950). A charge can be made for the performance of a public duty where the provision of the public service requested is greater than that deemed to be necessary (***Glasbrook Bros Ltd*** v ***Glamorgan County Council*** [1925] AC 270) or the provision necessary is greater than usual because of the actions of the party promising the consideration (***Harris*** v ***Sheffield United Football Club Ltd*** [1988] QB 77).[8] In ***Harris*** the large police presence was necessary because of the football club choosing to maximise attendance by the timing of the fixtures. Ramsey has chosen to allow the annual conference dinner to be held at his premises and had asked for extra police support, which was provided.

[8] These cases show the subtle distinction between the two decisions, both of which are relevant to the scenario.

Ramsey will be bound by the promises he has made to Yorkester Metropolitan Police Force and the Gastro Publicans Association as they have provided him with consideration. Michel has a contractual right to the £50 promised if he can demonstrate that it was always understood he would be paid. Michel will only be able to insist on the pay rise if he can establish that he is providing some fresh consideration beyond his existing contractual obligations: it is unlikely that ceasing to moan will be sufficient.[9]

[9] It is always a good idea to draw all your application together succinctly when you have been dealing with a complex problem. Then if perhaps you weren't clear in part of your answer, you can remove any doubt from the examiner's mind that you did know what you were talking about.

✓ Make your answer stand out

■ Consider opposing views to the moaning being sufficient consideration as in the case of *Hamer* v *Sidway* (1881) 124 NY 538, which provides persuasive authority as an American case that refraining from lawful acts such as smoking, gambling or drinking can be sufficient consideration in a domestic context. This case can be distinguished from the present problem as Michel and Ramsey are in a commercial relationship.

■ Equally consider whether the removal of 'vexatious' behaviour in *Pitt* v *PHH Asset Management Ltd* [1994] 1 WLR 327 was sufficient consideration; in that situation there was a promise to complete a conveyance within two weeks, so it is questionable whether the removal of the annoyance itself would have been sufficient.

! Don't be tempted to . . .

■ Leap to conclusions and miss giving a balanced argument: for instance, the baking of the cake looks like an obvious example of past consideration but most probably isn't if there was an implicit promise that some reward would be given.

■ Focus on one solution. Some of the issues are equivocal, so do not be afraid to put both possible solutions. Your marker will be looking at the strength of your legal argument as well as your application. This issue was particularly difficult in discussions on whether or not ceasing to moan could be sufficient consideration.

Question 3

To what extent is a creditor who accepts part payment of a debt in full and final settlement of that amount bound to that promise not to enforce their legal rights to claim the full amount?

Answer plan

→ Consider the general rule that part payment of a debt cannot satisfy the whole debt, subject to exceptions laid out in *Pinnel's Case*.

→ Discuss whether a *Williams* v *Roffey* type practical benefit can provide consideration for the variation in terms, i.e. the accepting of a lesser sum.

→ Recognise and focus on the exception to the general rule provided by the equitable doctrine of promissory estoppel.

→ Evaluate the scope and limitations of the doctrine: it must be a shield not a sword, whether there has been reliance, and whether it would be inequitable to enforce the strict legal rights.

Diagram plan

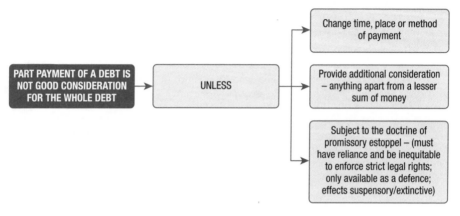

A printable version of this diagram plan is available from www.pearsoned.co.uk/lawexpressqa

Answer

Agreeing to accept a lesser sum of money than is actually due is to make a promise which is unenforceable unless supported by consideration, or the doctrine of promissory estoppel can be relied upon as a defence to stop the promisor going back on that promise.[1]

[1] From the outset the answer directly applies the main principles of law to the question set. Focus gains marks, irrelevant material loses them.

Pinnel's Case (1602) 5 Co Rep 117 lays down the general rule that part payment of a debt cannot provide good consideration for the whole debt. The decision was reinforced in **Foakes v Beer** (1884) 9 App Cas 605 where the agreement to forgo the interest due on a judgment debt was not enforceable. More recently, in **Re Selectmove** [1995] 1 WLR 474 an agreement to collect tax arrears by instalments was unenforceable for want of consideration.[2]

[2] These cases demonstrate the strict consistent and current application of the rule, which as we will see can be easily avoided.

Part payment of a debt is only part performance of an existing contractual duty already owed to the promisee. Payment at an earlier date, a different place or by using a different method of payment, however, will satisfy the requirement of providing additional consideration for the acceptance of a lesser sum and be an exception to the general rule. The additional consideration for acceptance of a lesser sum has to be sufficient, not adequate[3] (**Chappell & Co. Ltd v Nestlé Co. Ltd** [1960] AC 87). Therefore any chattel accepted with the lesser sum of money will be good consideration, even if the

[3] Remember general principles relating to the doctrine of consideration are used where anything other than a lesser sum of money is offered to satisfy a debt.

consideration has no economic value to the recipient as long as there has been no economic duress present to gain acceptance of the lesser sum. The provision of consideration by way of an additional chattel, or change in the arrangements for payment, would mean that a promise to accept a lesser sum of money 'in full and final settlement' would be enforceable.

Williams v Roffey [1991] 1 QB 1 raises the potential that in accepting a lesser sum of money a creditor has received some practical benefit. Therefore a promise to accept such a sum in full and final settlement would be supported by consideration and be enforceable. The effect of such a finding would be to undermine the rule in **Pinnel's Case**, as affirmed in **Foakes v Beer**. In **Re Selectmove** the Court of Appeal stressed that the principle in **Williams v Roffey** would not be extended to a **Foakes v Beer** situation. As such, having some money will not be sufficient consideration for the satisfaction of the promise to accept a lesser sum.[4]

The doctrine of promissory estoppel can operate to enforce a promisor's promise to accept part payment of a debt as total satisfaction of that debt, in spite of there being no consideration to support that promise.[5] The promisor is estopped from going back on their promise. The doctrine has its roots in the case of **Hughes v Metropolitan Railway Co.** (1877) 2 App Cas 439, whereby an implied promise not to enforce the legal right of forfeiture of a lease for the failure to repair premises during a period of negotiation for the sale of the property was binding on the promisor. The leaseholder had promised to suspend the legal right of forfeiture until the negotiations of the sale of the property had ended: the promisee had relied on this and it would have been inequitable to allow the promisor to go back on this promise.[6] The doctrine was later applied in **Central London Property Trust Ltd v High Trees House Ltd** [1947] KB 130, whereby the owners of a block of flats agreed to receive only half of the ground rents due from the leaseholder who would be unable to rent out the flats during the war years. The reduced rent was to last until either the end of the war or all the flats were once again occupied. As such, the owners were entitled to the full ground rents for the last two quarters of 1945. Lord Denning also added, obiter, that even though the promise to accept a lesser sum than contractually agreed to during the war years was not supported by consideration that amount could not be recovered because of the

[handwritten note: Hughes vs Metropolitan Railway]

[4] This sentence reinforces and fully develops earlier analysis that almost anything can be given to support the promise to accept a lesser sum of money except the lesser sum of money itself.

[5] It is argued by some academics that the doctrine of consideration is unnecessary, as the doctrines of economic duress and promissory estoppel can perform the same functions.

[6] These are the parameters within which the doctrine operates. Identifying them initially through the case law allows you to develop fully the analysis as to the limitations of the doctrine on a point-by-point basis later.

equitable principles laid down in **Hughes**. Furthermore, those amounts would never be recoverable as the rights to the arrears had been permanently lost rather than suspended until the leaseholders could afford to pay.

The doctrine of promissory estoppel can therefore apply to a promisor who agrees to accept part payment of a debt in full and final settlement.[7] There must be a pre-existing legal right which the promisor has made an unambiguous promise not to enforce. With regard to part payment of a debt, that will be not to seek the full amount due, although, legally, unless the part payment is supported by some form of consideration, there is a legal right to do so: this was the situation in the **High Trees** case. There must also be reliance on that promise: in **High Trees** there was a continued effort to find tenants rather than sell on their leasehold interest. The doctrine can only be used as a defence and not as a cause of action (**Combe v Combe** [1951] 2 KB 215).[8] Furthermore, as an equitable doctrine the promisor will only be estopped from reneging on their promise if it would be inequitable for them to do so. If the party attempting to rely on promissory estoppel does not come to equity with clean hands, they will be unable to rely on the doctrine. In **D & C Builders Ltd v Rees** [1966] 2 QB 617 the defendants knew of the financial difficulties of the plaintiffs and paid a lesser sum than agreed to in the contract in full and final settlement of the agreement. The plaintiffs subsequently sued for the balance. The payment of a lesser sum would of course be contrary to a straightforward application of the rule in **Pinnel's Case**, but the defence of promissory estoppel was not available to them as a result of their own behaviour in trying to take advantage of the plaintiff's predicament.[9]

A creditor is only bound by a promise to accept part payment of a debt if they have received consideration for doing so. They can accept something of negligible value to bind themselves to this. Alternatively, the court will accept the defence of promissory estoppel against their claim for the full amount of the debt where it would be inequitable to allow the creditor to go back on their promise.

[7] Higher marks are always achieved by focusing analysis on the question set.

[8] This limitation to the operation of the doctrine was not identified earlier and fits well into the flow of your answer here.

[9] *D & C Builders* v *Rees* works well here. It demonstrates the application of the issue raised by the question, as well as drawing together the rule in *Pinnel's Case* and an important limitation to the operation of the doctrine of promissory estoppel.

✓ **Make your answer stand out**

- Expand your analysis into a consideration of why 'practical benefit' is acceptable as consideration where an increased payment is offered but not for a lesser amount, making use of an academic authority such as O'Sullivan, J. (1996) In defence of *Foakes* v *Beer*, *CLJ* 219.
- Consider also the extinctive effects of promissory estoppel – will it cancel the debt forever or merely suspend it? David Capper's article investigates this issue and the importance of promisee reliance – (2008) The extinctive effect of promissory estoppel, 37(2) *CLWR* 105.

! **Don't be tempted to . . .**

- Miss identifying the possibility of the promise to accept a lesser sum being enforceable if supported by consideration.
- Stop your analysis too soon. To score highly in this question you must fully develop your answer. For example, investigating why if practical benefit can be good consideration for a promise to pay a greater sum of money it cannot be good consideration for payment of a lesser sum.

❓ Question 4

Toby has completed the refurbishment of Vera's houseboat, *The Alberta Rose*. The contract price for the work was £5,000.

Vera knows that Toby is looking to expand his business and needs cash quickly to secure additional premises next to the canal. If Toby does not secure this deal, it is unlikely that he will ever have the opportunity again as the land will be sold to a housing developer.

Vera tells Toby that she will be unemployed from the following week and cannot afford to pay him the full £5,000 in one go and asks him to either accept £4,000 now in full and final settlement of the debt or wait for her redundancy payment.

Toby reluctantly agrees to accept the £4,000 in full and final settlement of the debt in order to be able to continue with his plans. Toby later hears that Vera resigned her job voluntarily in order to go touring in her newly refurbished houseboat and there will be no redundancy payment.

Advise Toby as to whether he is bound by his promise to accept the part payment of the debt in full and final settlement of the whole debt or whether he is still entitled to recover the remaining £1,000.

Answer plan

→ Identify the key legal issue that part payment of a debt cannot satisfy the whole debt.

→ Discuss whether Vera can argue that Toby received a practical benefit which amounts to consideration for the variation in payments terms. He received a payment immediately, rather than a larger sum later, which allowed Toby to proceed with his plans.

→ Consider the likelihood of success if Vera relies on the application of the equitable doctrine of promissory estoppel as a defence to any action brought by Toby to recover the remaining £1,000.

→ Evaluate whether the effects of promissory estoppel are suspensory or extinctive.

→ Discuss if it would be inequitable for Toby to go back on his promise.

Diagram plan

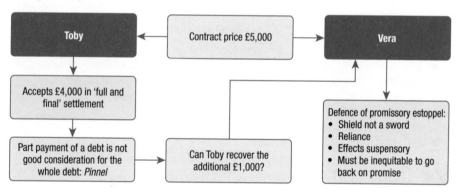

A printable version of this diagram plan is available from www.pearsoned.co.uk/lawexpressqa

Answer

Vera has a contractual obligation to pay Toby £5,000 for the work done. The rule in **Pinnel's Case** (1602) 5 Co Rep 117 provides that part payment of a debt will not satisfy the whole debt and as such the unpaid amount will remain due. This rule is subject to exceptions, including promissory estoppel, a defence available to Vera which may prevent Toby going back on his promise to accept a lesser amount of money.[1]

The amount of money owed to Toby is not in dispute; payment has not been made earlier, in a different place or by a different method;

[1] This is a clear statement of the general legal principal and the main line of argument which Toby will have to overcome if he is to be able to claim the full amount of money due to him.

payment has not been made by a third party, nor is part payment offered as part of a compromise agreement and as such will not fall under those exceptions to the rule in **Pinnel's Case**.[2] All variations in a contract are enforceable if supported by fresh consideration; however, with regard to part payment of a debt any consideration proffered will be sufficient apart from a lesser sum of money (**Foakes v Beer** (1884) 9 App Cas 605). Had Vera given Toby £4,000 and a rusty nail that would have been capable of satisfying the whole debt. The courts are not interested in the adequacy of consideration, that is to say the value, merely its presence.[3]

In receiving some money the creditor, in this case Toby, has potentially received a practical benefit, which can amount to consideration as defined in **Williams v Roffey** [1991] 1 QB 1. In **Re Selectmove** [1995] 1 WLR 474 the adjustment available to other variations of a pre-existing contractual obligation available following **Williams v Roffey** will not extend to part payment of a debt. This confirms the decision in **Foalkes v Beer** that part payment of a debt will not satisfy the whole of the debt, and furthermore **Williams v Roffey** type consideration will not extend to a **Foalkes v Beer** situation.[4] As such, Toby will remain entitled to the full £5,000, as any consideration provided would be deemed sufficient apart from the lesser sum of £4,000.

Hughes v Metropolitan Railway Co

The doctrine of promissory estoppel is an equitable doctrine that will bind a promisor to a promise not to pursue their legal rights even though that promise is not supported by consideration. The roots of this doctrine can be found in **Hughes v Metropolitan Railway Co.** (1877) 2 App Cas 439 and further developed in **Central London Property Trust Ltd v High Trees House Ltd** [1947] 1 KB 130. In **Hughes** the landlords agreed to suspend their right to forfeit a lease while negotiations for the sale of the lease continued. Here Toby is entitled to the full payment of £5,000 and is promising not to enforce his contractual right to the remaining £1,000.[5]

Combe v Combe

In **Combe v Combe** [1951] 2 KB 215 promissory estoppel was described as 'a shield not a sword'. The doctrine is available only as a defence and not a cause of action. Vera is relying on the doctrine as a defence to Toby's action for the outstanding £1,000.[6]

The effects in **Hughes** were suspensory, and once negotiations for the sale of the property had failed they could reissue the forfeiture

---

[2] Without straying too far from the question set and becoming irrelevant, this demonstrates an awareness of all the exceptions – not just those of immediate interest.

[3] A core understanding is evident from the articulation of the general rule and its relationship to part payment of the whole debt; this will impress an examiner.

[4] In this short paragraph you have dealt with the complexities of the developments in *Williams v Roffey* while clearly articulating a limitation to its application.

[5] The application here articulates the requirement in *Hughes* that, for the doctrine of promisor estoppel to apply, the promisor must have promised not to enforce their strict contractual rights.

[6] Again you are identifying the constituent parts of the doctrine and applying those directly to the facts of the problem given.

[7] This is a good lead into establishing that the doctrine can have permanent effects and some of the uncertainties surrounding the law on this point.

notice. This would suggest that the effects of promissory estoppel are not capable of permanent effect and that Toby should be able to recover the full amount on giving the appropriate notice to do so.[7] In *High Trees* the landlord had willingly agreed to accept a lower rent during the war years and then reinstated the full rents after the war was over. Lord Denning, obiter, provided that the lesser amount paid during the war years would extinguish the whole debt for that period permanently, as it would be inequitable to allow the promisor to go back on that promise. Denning is therefore suggesting that a promise to accept part payment should be capable of discharging the whole of the original debt permanently. This would be logical in agreements to accept lesser payments in full and final settlement of a debt, as, if the effects were only suspensory, the creditor would be able to come back for the full amount at any time on giving appropriate notice.

Toby therefore potentially will have to rely on the doctrine not being applied on other grounds, such as Vera being unable to demonstrate any reliance on the promise to accept part payment or that it would not be inequitable for him to go back on his promise.[8]

[8] The logical flow in your argument has led to the likelihood of the doctrine having permanent effect and the need for an alternative means of avoiding its operation.

[9] Such an understanding of the subtleties involved in reliance will gain higher marks.

The definition of reliance in the context of promissory estoppel is still uncertain. In *Tool Metal Manufacturing* v *Tungsten Electric Co. Ltd* [1955] 2 All ER 657 it was suggested that the act of reliance requires the promisee to have suffered a disadvantage; no such requirement is mentioned in either *High Trees* or *Hughes*.[9] It would appear to be sufficient that it has influenced their conduct. Vera has not suffered a disadvantage but her conduct may have been influenced by having £1,000 extra for her trip.

[10] Note any lawyers' reluctance to say 'unfair' in a judgment or a commentary – a good phrase that could be used is to say that you must come to equity 'with clean hands'.

The doctrine of promissory estoppel will only be applied where it would be inequitable for the promisor not to be held to their promise. The doctrine will not be applied if the promisee has behaved in any way which could be construed as being inappropriate for them to rely on it.[10] In *D & C Builders Ltd* v *Rees* [1966] 2 QB 617 the defendants, knowing the builders were having financial difficulties, when pressed for payment offered a part payment or nothing. Reluctantly the builders agreed and later successfully sued for the balance owed. It was held in this case that the rule in *Pinnel's Case* would apply here and no defence of promissory estoppel could be accepted, as their own behaviour would make it inequitable for the doctrine to be used. Similarly, Vera knew of Toby's immediate need for payment. Apparently her trip was already planned, as was her unemployment rather than her loss of income being an unforeseen circumstance.[11] It is unlikely in these circumstances that Vera would be allowed to use the defence of promissory estoppel against an action by Toby for the remaining £1,000.

[11] Good use of all the facts logical in application following the in-depth analysis of why it would not be inequitable for Toby to break his promise not to sue for the remaining money.

Toby will be able to recover the £1,000 still owed to him, as Vera will be unable to bring herself within any of the exceptions to *Pinnel's Case* and the courts would be unwilling to allow a defence of promissory estoppel where the defendant's behaviour has been questionable.

✓ Make your answer stand out

- Consider using the recent authority of *Collier* v *P & MJ Wright (Holdings) Ltd* [2007] EWCA Civ 1329, which illustrates the courts' continued adherence to the decisions in *Foakes* v *Beer* and the limitations imposed by *Re Selectmove* while demonstrating the courts' more sympathetic attitude to arguments surrounding promissory estoppel where there is genuine agreement between the parties.

- Read The extinctive effect of promissory estoppel by David Capper (2008) 37(2) *CLWR* 105 for an up-to-date analysis of cases and academic opinion surrounding the requirements and limitations of the application of promissory estoppel in *Foakes* v *Beer* type situations.

! Don't be tempted to . . .

- Avoid a full discussion of the legal issues surrounding part payment of a debt in an attempt to solve the 'problem'. Problem questions also gain marks for full developments of legal analysis, just as with essay questions.

- Miss out on marks by detailing the more complex areas of law surrounding promissory estoppel and then not applying that analysis to the question.

D and C Builders Ltd v Rees

Question 5

Discuss the impact of the decision in *Williams* v *Roffey Bros & Nicholls (Contractors) Ltd* [1991] 1 QB 1 on the doctrine of consideration.

Answer plan

→ Define consideration and its necessary presence in order to have an enforceable agreement.

→ Discuss the low threshold of what will be sufficient consideration but that it cannot be performance of an existing contractual duty.

→ Explain the decision in *Williams* v *Roffey* and the definition of 'practical benefit' and how the case has refined and limited the rule in *Stilk* v *Myrick* but not overruled it.

→ Explore why the *Williams* v *Roffey* 'practical benefit' will not be sufficient consideration for part payment of a debt.

Diagram plan

```
┌─────────────────────────┐     ┌─────────────────────┐     ┌─────────────────────────┐
│ Performance of an existing │     │                     │     │                         │
│ contractual duty is not good │ ──▶ │   Unless receive:   │ ──▶ │ Will operate for variations to │
│ consideration for a fresh  │     │  Practical benefit  │     │ contracts for goods and services │
│ promise                    │     │                     │     │                         │
└─────────────────────────┘     └─────────────────────┘     └─────────────────────────┘
                                          │
                                          ▼
                                ┌─────────────────────┐
                                │ Will not be good consideration │
                                │ to support part payment │
                                │      of a debt      │
                                └─────────────────────┘
```

A printable version of this diagram plan is available from www.pearsoned.co.uk/lawexpressqa

Answer

A promise is not legally binding unless supported by consideration. The law requires consideration to be present, but does not put a value on the bargain struck. This reinforces the idea of the freedom of contract, but difficulties can be encountered when there is a proposed variation in terms, as the law requires fresh consideration to be provided for the fresh promise. It is not sufficient for the performance of an existing contractual duty to provide consideration for the new promise.[1] The decision in **Williams v Roffey Bros & Nicholls (Contractors) Ltd** [1991] 1 QB 1 appears to have relaxed the strict interpretation of what can amount to good consideration in these circumstances.

[1] Outlining the legal context in *Williams* v *Roffey* immediately gives a logical structure to the analysis.

The sufficiency of consideration to support a bargain is not a high threshold. In **Chappell & Co. Ltd v Nestlé Co. Ltd** [1960] AC 87 three chocolate bar wrappers were part of the consideration paid for the purchase of a record; it was irrelevant that they had no actual economic value to the recipient. It was enough that the promisor had asked for them and was willing to accept them in payment for the goods supplied. However, where a variation of terms of an existing agreement is promised, that promise will only be enforceable if supported by fresh consideration. The performance of an existing contractual duty will not be sufficient.[2] In **Stilk v Myrick** (1809) 2 Camp 317 a ship's captain promised increased wages to his crew for sailing short-handed. On completing the journey the additional wages were not paid. The sailors sued for the extra remuneration promised. The promise of extra wages was unenforceable for lack of consideration. The crew were contractually obliged to sail to the ship's destination and back. They had done no more than this. The case of **Stilk v Myrick** was decided before the doctrine of economic duress was developed. On public policy grounds it was a concern that it would be possible to take unfair advantage of the promisor and demand higher remuneration than originally agreed to for the same contractual performance.[3] In contrast, the case of **Hartley v Ponsonby** (1857) 7 E & B 872 found that in making a return voyage with almost half the crew missing, this had fundamentally changed the contractual obligations. Therefore the old contract had been discharged and a new one entered into. This line of reasoning deals with the issue of consideration but only where the performance required is so different that a new contract is deemed to have been negotiated.[4] The question still remains as to what would amount to sufficient consideration going beyond the performance of an existing contractual duty to make a new promise on an existing contract enforceable.

Following the decision in **Stilk v Myrick** the threshold is much higher than the consideration required for the original contract. **Williams v Roffey Bros & Nicholls (Contractors) Ltd** has refined and perhaps redrawn the limitations imposed by the rule in **Stilk v Myrick**.

In **Williams v Roffey Bros & Nicholls (Contractors) Ltd** the defendants had subcontracted the joinery work required for the refurbishment of flats to the plaintiff. Williams was to receive payments in stages as sections of the work were completed. About

[2] The difference in the threshold of sufficiency is key to understanding the thinking behind the decision in *Williams* v *Roffey* and the subsequent limitations to its application.

[3] Perhaps this explains why the courts were more willing to take a more generous line with *Williams* v *Roffey*. If there had been economic duress, the defendants, Roffey, would have an alternative remedy.

[4] By emphasising the difference in the performance required in *Hartley* v *Ponsonby*, you have also drawn attention to the difference between the sufficiency required for a variation in agreed terms and the sufficiency required simply to have an enforceable contract.

80 per cent of the work had been done and paid for when it became evident that Williams was in financial difficulties. He had under-estimated the price of the job and had not managed his workforce effectively. The defendants had a liquidated damages clause in their main contract that would apply if completion was late.[5] To ensure that the refurbishment was completed on time, the defendants agreed to pay an additional £575 per flat for that promise. The plaintiff completed a further eight flats for which the defendants paid a proportion of the original price. The plaintiff stopped work and sued for the outstanding amended amount. The defendants argued that Williams had not provided sufficient consideration for the promise of an additional payment as he was already contractually obliged to complete the refurbishment. The court agreed that there was an existing contractual duty to refurbish the flats and that could not amount to good consideration, nor could the courts rewrite a bad bargain. However, in return for the promise of an extra payment, the defendants had received a 'practical benefit' which could amount to sufficient consideration.[6] The practical benefit in this case was that the defendants would not have to pay a penalty charge for late com-pletion, they reorganised the work and the payment for that work, and they did not have to find an alternative contractor. Lord Glidewell described the decision in this case to be a refinement and limitation on the rule in **Stilk v Myrick**; it does not overrule it. The decision relates only to the variation of obligations within an existing contract, not to the rules concerning consideration at the point of formation of a contract.[7] There must be no hint of duress or illegitimate pressure and it would appear that the variation must be at the instigation of the promisor.

Williams v Roffey Bros & Nicholls (Contractors) Ltd refined the rule in **Stilk v Myrick** but was subsequently subject to limitation. The rule in **Pinnel's Case** (1602) 5 Co Rep 117, as affirmed in **Foakes v Beer** (1884) 9 App Cas 605, provides that part payment of a debt cannot be good consideration for the whole debt, unless some other consideration is provided with the lesser sum of money. It soon became apparent that receiving a 'practical benefit' would arise in the context of part payment of a debt as amounting to suf-ficient consideration to satisfy the whole debt. Surely having some of the money owed will always have a practical benefit? In **Re Selectmove** [1995] 2 All ER 531 it was held that a **Williams v**

[5] Remember good use of technical language; this will illustrate your depth of understanding beyond the immediate topic.

[6] A clear articulation of how the rule in *Stilk* v *Myrick* was applied in *Williams* v *Roffey* and still remains good law. Understanding these subtleties will gain higher marks.

[7] This justification for the difference in what will be sufficient when a contract is formed and a higher requirement for a variation in terms will impress the examiner, as it demonstrates a thorough understanding of the case law discussed.

Roffey consideration in providing a 'practical benefit' could not apply to a *Foakes* v *Beer* situation, that is to say part payment of a debt. This in itself appears rational; however, in **Re Selectmove** the creditor was trying to enforce a promise to accept payments by instalments, not to pay only part of what was owed.[8]

[8] Recognition of a contradiction or potential conflict with commercial reality, where an inability to pay will usually be resolved by some form of instalment arrangement, will add depth to your analysis.

The greatest impact of **Williams v Roffey Bros & Nicholls (Contractors) Ltd** is the distinction having to be made between the consideration provided for existing contractual duties to provide goods and services and that required to support the part payment of a debt.

✓ Make your answer stand out

- Consider the decision in *Re Selectmove*: in the absence of economic duress, payment by instalments would appear to provide a practical benefit to all parties to avoid a potential insolvency. This limitation to *Williams* v *Roffey* is interesting when compared to the more liberal approach taken recently where the defence of promissory estoppel has been relied upon to enforce a promise not to pursue a debt for which the defendant was originally jointly liable for having paid his portion of the debt (*Collier* v *P & M J Wright (Holdings) Ltd* [2007] EWCA Civ 1329).
- Note that Williams could not rely on the doctrine of promissory estoppel as he was bringing an action, not defending one.
- The decision has also challenged the principle that consideration must move from the promisee. This has led to some criticisms (see *South Caribbean Trading Ltd* v *Trafigura Beheever* [2005] 1 Lloyd's Rep 128) of the decision and its reasoning, particularly in the reliance on *Pao On* v *Lau Yiu Long* [1980] AC 614, a case where the pre-existing obligation was owed to a third party, which is capable of amounting to good consideration.
- Add some academic opinion to support your analysis: for example, Coote, B. (2004) Consideration and variations: a different solution, 120 *LQR* 19.

! Don't be tempted to . . .

- Describe the facts of *Williams* v *Roffey* in detail and forget to discuss in sufficient depth why this case has posed such a challenge to the current thinking on consideration.

❓ Question 6

Jacob has been commissioned by Stellaforic Ltd to landscape their rooftop garden, complete with a fountain water feature for a total contract price of £16,000. The weather has been particularly bad. Jacob's work van has frequent breakdowns, delaying him in transporting materials and himself to and from the site. Stellaforic Ltd are aware of this and also know that until Jacob is paid for this job he will not be able to replace the van. As a result Jacob has fallen behind schedule with the work. Stellaforic Ltd intends to hold their business launch party in the newly landscaped garden and promise Jacob an extra £4,000 if he completes the work by the originally agreed date. Jacob completes the work on time by working very long hours and not accepting any new work.

Stellaforic Ltd say they are only willing to pay Jacob the £16,000 originally contracted for and that they will only pay that in quarterly instalments. Jacob reluctantly agrees and takes the first instalment of £4,000, as he needs to put down a deposit on a new work van that evening. Jacob is now demanding the remaining balance of £16,000 in one lump sum immediately. Stellaforic Ltd say they no longer have the budget to pay Jacob immediately as they have stocked the water feature with 16 exotic carp which cost £1,000 each.

Advise Stellaforic Ltd as to whether they are obliged to pay Jacob the extra £4,000 they promised and whether they can insist Jacob takes payment of any monies owed to him by the agreed instalments.

Answer plan

→ Consider whether the promised additional payment of £4,000 is enforceable. Did Jacob provide fresh consideration, something beyond his existing contractual duty?

→ Establish the principle that part payment of a debt is not good consideration for the whole debt and evaluate whether an instalment payment will fall under this rule.

→ Discuss whether the defence of promissory estoppel is available to Stellaforic Ltd, preventing Jacob from going back on his promise to accept payment by instalments and a lesser sum of money.

Diagram plan

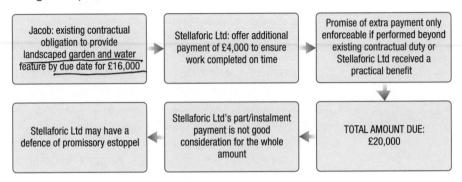

A printable version of this diagram plan is available from www.pearsoned.co.uk/lawexpressqa

Answer

Stellaforic Ltd will only be legally bound to their promise to pay the extra £4,000 if Jacob can establish that he provided fresh consideration for that promise beyond the performance of an existing contractual duty. Stellaforic Ltd will rely on the defence of promissory estoppel to any action by Jacob to recover the full £20,000 or to renege on the promise to accept payment by instalments.[1]

[1] The clear identification of key legal principles raised by the facts sets the work off to a strong well-structured start.

The traditional view of consideration is that to enforce a promise something must have been given in return for that promise. What amounts to sufficient consideration to support the original agreement is concerned with the law recognising its presence, more demonstrative of an intention to be bound than any interest in any economic value which might or might not attach to the bargain (*Chappell & Co. Ltd v Nestlé Co. Ltd* [1960] AC 87). The situation alters where the parties seek to vary the terms of the agreement but do not negotiate a completely new bargain.[2] In *Stilk v Myrick* (1809) 2 Camp 317 the promised extra wages for the increased work involved on a return sea voyage when the crew's complement was decreased by two was not enforceable. The crew were contractually obliged to make the voyage and had not done anything beyond their existing contractual duty that would amount to sufficient consideration in law for the promised extra payment. By contrast, in *Hartley v Ponsonby* (1857) 7 E & B 872 the return voyage with only

[2] A depth of knowledge is demonstrated to the marker from reflection on different standards required when dealing with variation to agreed terms.

half of the usual crew made the conditions of performance of the contract so different from the original agreement that it was held that the old contract had been terminated and a new one concluded on the new terms, including the promise to pay more. Stellaforic Ltd will view the situation as being very similar to **Stilk v Myrick** as regards their promise to pay more than contractually agreed. Jacob had a contractual obligation to complete the work by a due date; in working the extra hours and not taking on extra work, it could be argued that he had not actually done any more than his existing contractual duty. It is unlikely that Jacob's original contract would be deemed to be terminated and a new one negotiated as in **Hartley v Ponsonby**, as the changed conditions under which he is working are not so extreme.[3]

[3] The application here mirrors the terminology from the decided cases cited, amplifying your legal reasoning.

With the development of the doctrine of economic duress, the law has been able to refine and limit the application of **Stilk v Myrick**[4] and it is possible for the performance of an existing contractual duty to provide consideration for a fresh promise where the promisor has received some 'practical benefit'. In **Williams v Roffey** [1991] 1 QB 1 the defendants promised extra payment on the refurbishment of flats, work which the plaintiff was already contractually obliged to do. However, the promised extra payment by the defendants was enforceable as they had received some 'practical benefit' in that they had reorganised the way in which the work had been organised, conducted and paid for, as well as not having to find another contractor to complete the work, and perhaps most importantly, or at least where the judgments laid most emphasis, they would not have to pay a penalty to the main contractor for late completion of the work. Stellaforic Ltd will be able to have their launch party; if the work goes ahead on time, they will also not have the expense and disturbance in finding another contractor; and these, following **Williams v Roffey**, can amount to valuable consideration even though the promisor is only avoiding a detriment.[5] In addition, Jacob has also rearranged his work schedules and given more than planned hours to meet their needs. As such, it can be argued, that in the absence of any duress,[6] this would appear to be the case as it is Stellaforic Ltd's idea to offer an increased payment; Jacob has provided sufficient consideration to support the promise of the extra £4,000.

[4] This is an important point to raise as it helps understand the reasoning in *Williams v Roffey*, an analysis of which follows.

[5] Mentioning that merely avoiding a detriment can amount to consideration shows you have a sophisticated understanding of this much debated authority.

[6] *Stilk v Myrick* was very much concerned with the potential oppression of the promisor.

The rule in **Pinnel's Case** (1602) 5 Co Rep 117, as affirmed in **Foakes v Beer** (1884) 9 App Cas 605, provides that part payment

Pinnel's Case → confirmed
Foakes an Beer

of a debt cannot be good consideration for the whole debt, nor can an arrangement to pay by instalments which would when completed be equivalent to the full amount (**Re Selectmove** [1995] 2 All ER 531). In other words, paying part of the money owed will not discharge the whole debt unless it can be brought within one of the exceptions.[7]

Pinnel's case - promissory estoppel.

One of the exceptions to the rule in **Pinnel's Case** is the defence of promissory estoppel. This defence is available where a promise has been made that is unsupported by consideration but it would be inequitable to allow the promisor to go back on that promise.[8] The requirements and limitations of this doctrine were articulated by Lord Denning in **Central London Property Trust Ltd v High Trees House Ltd** [1945] KB 130, relying on the older case of **Hughes v Metropolitan Railway Co. Ltd** (1877) 2 App Cas 439. Both cases required that the promisor has adjusted their legal position promising not to enforce their strict legal rights. Jacob has promised not to enforce his rights to the full amount of payment, that is to say the extra £4,000 promised, and not to insist on immediate payment of the lesser amount.[9]

Secondly promissory estoppel cannot be used as a cause of action (**Combe v Combe** [1951] 2 KB 215). Stellaforic Ltd would satisfy this requirement as they would be defending an action by Jacob to recover the full amount of the monies owed immediately. It would appear that whether the effects are temporary or permanent will depend on the parties express or implied intentions to give up their rights permanently.[10]

The doctrine requires that the promisee should have relied on this promise. Stellaforic Ltd has used the extra money to stock the fountain. The question of reliance ties in with the core issue concerning promissory estoppel as to whether or not it would be inequitable for the promissory to go back on their promise (**D & C Builders Ltd v Rees** [1966] 2 QB 617).[11] Stellaforic Ltd may be prevented from relying on the defence if it is established that they secured the promise from Jacob knowing that he had no real alternative but to agree.

Stellaforic Ltd owes a total of £20,000 to Jacob; the defence of promissory estoppel is unlikely to be accepted in the circumstances.

[7] A practical benefit will not amount to consideration in these circumstances, as it would too easily allow a debtor to escape their contractual obligations.

[8] You should provide a good definition of fundamental requirements.

[9] The principle stated is followed by immediate application to the problem.

[10] Ask yourself whether there is a presumption that effects are suspensory unless contrary intention is shown.

[11] This raises an issue needing further judicial clarification. Does reliance have to also be detrimental, which it would not be here, or is it inextricably linked with the concept of it being inequitable to go back on the promise?

Make your answer stand out

- The answer has picked up on some of the complexities and contradictions surrounding this area: fully develop your analysis. The following academic authorities may help (citing them will gain extra marks):
  - Hird, N.J. and Blair, A. (1996) Minding your own business – *Williams* v *Roffey* revisited: consideration reconsidered, *JBL* 254.
  - Coote, B. (2004) Consideration and variations: a different solution, 120 *LQR*, p. 19.
  - Mitchell, P. and Phillips, J. (2002) The contractual nexus: is reliance essential? 22 *OJLS* 115.

! Don't be tempted to . . .

- Only answer half of the question: there are two basic issues.
  - (i) Do Stellaforic Ltd owe the extra £4,000? Do not panic if you are unsure if your application is accurate; you will get marks for your legal reasoning.
  - (ii) If you decide that the extra £4,000 is due, then you have the promise of acceptance of part payment of a debt. If you decide that the £4,000 is not owed, then the promise to accept payment by instalments is still part payment of a debt and your arguments will be the same, with greater emphasis put on the decision in *Re Selectmove*.

www.pearsoned.co.uk/lawexpressqa

Go online to access more revision support including additional essay and problem questions with diagram plans, You be the marker questions, and download all diagrams from the book.

Privity

How this topic may come up in exams

Usually the topic area is examined with an essay question surrounding the impact of the Contracts (Rights of Third Parties) Act 1999 and the effect on other common law mechanisms for avoiding the doctrine. Decisions concerning the interpretation and application of the Act have been made and the problem-style question given below will become more popular and familiar. A detailed knowledge of the Act and its interpretation will be required, together with alternative causes of action should the Act not apply or the third party wishes to have a choice as to how to enforce their rights.

Attack the question

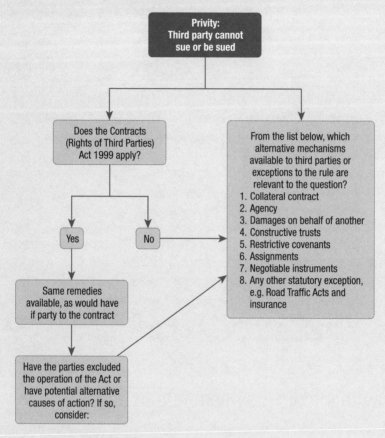

A printable version of this diagram is available from www.pearsoned.co.uk/lawexpressqa

 Question 1

Discuss the proposition that the Contracts (Rights of Third Parties) Act 1999 does not abolish the common law mechanisms for the avoidance of the doctrine of privity but merely coexists with them.

Answer plan

→ Define the doctrine of privity and the potential harsh repercussions of its application.

→ Discuss the effect of the 1999 Act, its ability to reinforce the express intentions of the parties, but no more than that.

→ Consider and define the common law mechanisms developed to avoid the privity rule. And their continued relevance.

Diagram plan

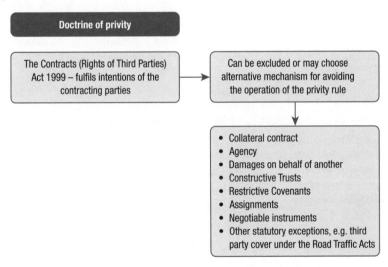

A printable version of this diagram plan is available from www.pearsoned.co.uk/lawexpressqa

Answer

The doctrine of privity provides that only a party to a contract can sue or be sued upon that contract. It would appear only logical that a party could only incur an obligation they have consented to. However, even where there is consent to a promised benefit, without consideration the promise will not be enforceable under the doctrine of privity.[1] Although a statutory means of avoiding the rule was not developed until 1999 the common law had developed mechanisms by which, where the parties truly intend for a third party to have actionable rights under a contract, those rights would be enforceable by them in spite of the doctrine of privity. It should be noted that the 1999 Act itself only provides an exception to the privity rule: it does not abolish it.

[1] This immediately focuses on the core issue raised by the question.

Beswick* v *Beswick [1968] AC 58 demonstrates the potential harshness of the doctrine of privity. Mr Beswick sold his business to his nephew in return for regular payments during his lifetime and an annuity payable to his wife after his death. As Mrs Beswick did not provide any consideration for the promise, and was not a party to the contract, even though there was a clear intention that she should benefit, she could not sue in her own right when the nephew refused to honour his promise. However, as the administratrix of the estate, she was able to get an order of specific performance against the nephew. This was fortuitous: had she not been the administratrix of the will, she would have had no cause of action.

The 1999 Act now allows a third party to a contract to enforce contractual rights in that contract where a contract expressly provides that they should be able to do so (s. 1(1)(a)) or when a term of a contract purports to confer a benefit upon them (s. 1(1)(b)).[2] Therefore Mrs Beswick would today have a remedy in her own name. The Act does not, however, render the doctrine of privity obsolete, as section 1(2) provides that the Act will not apply where the parties do not intend it to. The third party in that situation will have no cause of action under the Act but may be able to rely on one of the other common law mechanisms for the avoidance of the privity rule.

[2] Emphasising that the Act only applies where it is expressly intended to do so by the parties demonstrates your application of knowledge to the question set.

Purporting to confer a benefit can include any performance due under the contract, such as the provision of a service or payment of money. In ***Nisshin Shipping* v *Cleaves*** [2003] EWHC 2602 (Comm) the contract between the shipowners and the charterers provided that the brokers would be entitled to 1 per cent commission of the contract price for the work done in negotiating the contracts. Once it had been established that the contract did purport to confer a benefit, there was a rebuttable presumption that the parties intended the term to be enforceable by the brokers. There was no evidence to rebut this presumption and therefore the brokers could enforce that term.[3]

Without the intention to confer a benefit the doctrine of privity will still have an application and in spite of the broad interpretation taken of 'purporting to confer a benefit' the common law mechanisms will still have a role to play where the Act does not apply, or has been excluded.[4]

[4] This explains why you are now going to investigate the common law exemptions, keeping your answer relevant to the question set.

The finding of the existence of a collateral contract can avoid the operation of the doctrine of privity, as a bilateral contract is found to exist between the parties.[5] In **Shanklin Pier Ltd v Detel Products Ltd** [1951] 2 All ER 471 the painters of a pier purchased paint from the defendants on the specific instructions of the plaintiffs, who had been assured by the defendants that the paint would last seven years. The paint lasted three months and the plaintiffs sought to recover for the remedial work required. The pier owners were not party to the contract for the sale of the paint nor had the painters made any assertions as to the quality of the paint, but it was held that a collateral contract existed between the paint supplier and the pier owner. The consideration provided for the defendants' promise as to the durability of the paint was in the stipulation of the paint to be used by the contractor.

[5] Good use of technical language applied appropriately.

Collateral contracts have often been used as a device to give a third party the benefit of an exemption clause (**The Eurymedon** [1975] AC 154). Section 1(6) specifically covers the enforcement of the benefits in exemption or limitations clauses.[6] This mechanism for avoiding the doctrine of privity will still have an important role to play, as most commercial parties will resist the potential granting of rights to third parties, particularly as the 1999 Act only requires the third party to be identified as a member of a class or answering a particular description. The courts have implied that a constructive trust had been created where such an intention could be found even though the contract was silent on the matter (**Les Affreteurs Reunis SA v Walford** [1919] AC 801). **Nisshin Shipping v Cleaves** should negate the need to rely on such artificiality as there will be a strong presumption in favour of the application of the Act.

[6] As such the threshold consideration is low and the legal reasoning somewhat contrived. Marks will be given for recognising that the 1999 Act makes such legal gymnastics less necessary, but can still be of practical application.

Jackson v Horizon Holidays [1975] 1 WLR 1468 raised the possibility that damages could be recovered on behalf of another in spite of the doctrine of privity. This has also been found in a commercial context in **Linden Gardens Trust v Lenesta Sludge Disposals** [1994] 1 AC 85. These decisions will have an application even if the Act has not been excluded, as section 4 provides that a party to the contract can still enforce any term of a contract even if it applies to a third party who has the ability to sue in their own right.[7]

[7] Good recognition that the Act is providing additional rights.

Other common law exceptions to the privity rule are found in agency relationships where the agent is viewed as an intermediary rather than a party to the contract, negotiable instruments such as cheques where the Act is specifically excluded (s. 6), and assignments where the benefit of the contract can be assigned to a third party without the permission of the other party to the contract. Restrictive covenants would be unenforceable once a piece of land changed ownership were the rules of privity to apply. Both **Tulk v Moxhay** (1848) 2 Ph 774 and section 56(1) of the Law of Property Act 1925 allow the protection afforded by the restrictive covenant to pass down the chain of ownership. Other statutes also provide third-party rights: for example, the Road Traffic Acts provide the benefit of the contract to an unidentified injured third party.[8]

[8] Summarised succinctly and kept relevant to the question asked.

The Contracts (Rights of Third Parties) Act 1999 has not rendered the doctrine of privity obsolete nor the existing exceptions to it, as at heart it is just another means of evading the privity rule but only to the extent to which the parties intend it to so operate.

✓ Make your answer stand out

- Demonstrate a breadth of reading and make reference to some academic journals you have read, for example: MacMillan, C. (2000) A birthday present for Lord Denning: the Contracts (Rights of Third Parties) Act 1999, 63 *MLR* 887. This will allow you to make a link between *Beswick* v *Beswick* and the situation today.

- Consider reading Andrews, N. (2001) Strangers to justice no longer – the reversal of the privity rule under the Contracts (Rights of Third Parties) Act 1999, *CLJ* 353 to gain some depth of understanding of the topic.

- In addition, Roe, T. (2000) Contractual intention under section 1(1)(b) and section 1(2) of the Contracts (Rights of Third Parties) Act 1999, 63 *MLR* 887 will provide a starting point for your discussion on the interpretation of these sections using case law decided after this was written, again demonstrating currency of knowledge.

! Don't be tempted to . . .

- Mess up your timing in the exam. Privity essays tend to be broad in content. Some issues you can only be expected to have a general understanding of at this point in your studies. Keep relevant to the issues of privity and focus on the question.
- Agree with the question: it suggests that the only thing pertinent to the doctrine of privity post-1999 is the Act; establish from the outset that it is not so.

? Question 2

Sporting Choice Ltd and Black Box Ltd have negotiated a contract for the provision of an online game which emulates major sporting events with live interactive facilities. Some of the software developments were made possible as a result of research and trials undertaken by postgraduate students of the University of Middleshire. Sporting Choice Ltd and Black Box Ltd agree in their contract to donate 10 per cent per annum of their profits to the University as a reward for the works undertaken, with a view to assisting with the continued funding of postgraduate research students. The University are delighted by this and host an evening celebrating the successful collaboration. The University have received £1,000 to date; this represents only 1 per cent of the previous year's profits. The University have already allocated the promised funding to chosen research students. Sporting Choice Ltd and Blackbox Ltd assert that they have no contractual obligation to pay the money and furthermore they have a right to vary the terms of their own private agreement at will.

Advise the University of Middleshire if the doctrine of privity will prevent them having any legally enforceable rights as regards the terms agreed between Sporting Choice Ltd and Black Box Ltd.

Answer plan

→ Define the doctrine of privity and problems inherent in enforcing a benefit conferred on a third party.

→ Consider how the Contracts (Rights of Third Parties) Act 1999 avoids the privity rule where a contract purports to confer a benefit.

→ Evaluate the extent of those rights and discuss them in relation to the University's right to object to a variation in the terms.

→ Consider whether the Act applied and whether any alternative cause of action is available to the University.

Diagram plan

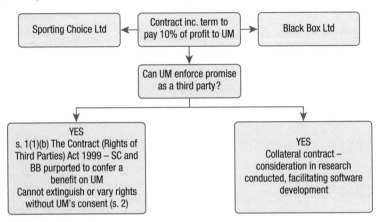

A printable version of this diagram plan is available from www.pearsoned.co.uk/lawexpressqa

Answer

The doctrine of privity provides that contractual burdens and benefits can only be claimed by those that are party to the agreement. Although it is reasonable not to impose a burden upon a third party that has not agreed to it, the result is harsh where a benefit was clearly intended but then cannot be enforced.[1] To a large extent, the provisions of the Contracts (Rights of Third Parties) Act 1999 have given a third party the right to enforce contractual terms aimed at providing them with a benefit.

Beswick v Beswick [1968] AC 58 demonstrates the harshness of the privity rule. Mr Beswick's nephew promised, as part of the purchase of his coal round, to pay a regular amount to Mr Beswick for life and an annuity to his widow following his death. The nephew refused to make payments to the widow even though it was the clear intention of both parties to the contract that this would take place. Although Mrs Beswick had provided no consideration for the contractual benefit to be received, it would appear unjust that the nephew will profit from his deliberate breach of contract with the uncle.[2] Sporting Choice Ltd and Black Box Ltd clearly intended to benefit the University of Middleshire but the doctrine of privity would prevent the University from enforcing that obligation to them in their

[1] Straight to the point, the legal issue is identified with a potential solution and this will impress an examiner.

[2] Confidence with the substantive point of law is evident in the emphasis on the fact that no action could be brought in her own name, although she won the case on other grounds.

own name. The Contracts (Rights of Third Parties) Act 1999 was passed which provides that in certain circumstances the doctrine of privity should no longer apply. It is broad in its application but still upholds the principle of the freedom of contract in allowing the parties to the contract to determine the extent to which the privity rule should be avoided and the third parties able to enforce their rights.

Section 1(1)(a) provides that a third party to a contract should be able to enforce a term of the contract if the contract expressly provides that they should be able to do so[3] or under section 1(1)(b) the term purports to confer a benefit on them. In **Nisshin Shipping v Cleaves** [2003] EWHC 2602 it was held that the promise of 1 per cent commission to the brokers that had negotiated the contract between a shipowner and his charterers was enforceable by the brokers, even though there was no term that expressly gave the right of enforcement as the contract 'purported' to provide such a benefit and therefore the claimants could enforce the term under section 1(1)(b).[4] The University of Middleshire would fall under section 1(1)(b) as the contract does not expressly provide that a term will be enforceable by them but does purport to confer a benefit in promising the annual donation.[5] Section 1(1)(b) will always be read in the context of section 1(2), whereby section 1(1)(b) will not apply if, on a proper construction of the contract, it was not intended by the contracting parties that the term would be enforceable. In **Nisshin Shipping v Cleaves** it was held that the contracting parties had purported to confer a benefit and that created a rebuttable presumption that the term was intended to be enforceable, with no evidence to rebut the presumption that the brokers were entitled to bring an action based on that term.[6] There are no indications that Sporting Choice Ltd and Black Box Ltd expressly looked to exclude the University of Middleshire from enforcing the term.

In **Prudential Assurance Co. Ltd v Ayres** [2007] 3 All ER 946 it was held that the 1999 Act could still apply even if the ultimate beneficiary of the promise would be someone other than the third party identified for the purposes of section 1(3).[7] Here the University of Middleshire are expressly identified and therefore could enforce the promise, even though it could be argued that the ultimate beneficiaries would be postgraduate research students.

[3] This is clearly and succinctly put. A good flow in the narrative will gain higher marks.

[4] Ensure you use up-to-date authorities supporting and mirroring the statutory provision.

[5] Focused application shows an examiner that you can use your legal knowledge, not just memorise it!

[6] Identifying the common law development of the rebuttable presumption in this context and the application of this will gain significant marks as your analysis has depth.

[7] Use of up-to-date knowledge and demonstrating wider reading will distinguish your answer from the many others a marker will be likely to see.

Sporting Choice Ltd and Black Box Ltd as the original contracting parties can exercise their freedom to cancel or vary the terms of their contract subject to the limitations in section 2. As such, the University of Middleshire as third parties cannot have their rights extinguished or varied without their consent where they have communicated their assent to the term to be relied on; the promisors are aware that the third party has relied on that promise or it would be reasonably expected for the promisors to have foreseen that reliance. Nothing suggests that the contract contained a term excluding the University's right to consent to a variation. In hosting the celebratory event, the University have communicated their assent to the promised share of the profits by conduct. It would be reasonable to expect Sporting Choice Ltd and Black Box Ltd to foresee that the University would in reliance on the promise allocate the funds to eligible students. Therefore, the University of Middleshire can enforce the full 10 per cent of profits promised.[8]

[8] Focused analysis and application on defence raised by SC and BB.

The 1999 Act is severely limited in its impact as nothing stops contracting parties from expressly preventing the enforcement of a term or the third party choosing an alternative cause of action. In such a situation the University would have to look to an alternative means of avoiding the privity rule.[9] A mechanism effective in such circumstances would be the finding of a collateral contract. In **Shanklin Pier Ltd v Detel Products Ltd** [1951] 2 All ER 471, the manufacturers had promised the plaintiff pier owners that a specified paint would last ten years. On the basis of that promise the plaintiff pier owners had instructed the decorators to purchase the paint from the defendant manufacturers. It was held that the plaintiffs had provided consideration for the promise as to the durability of the paint by specifying that the paint be bought from the manufacturers and a collateral contract had been created. The University, were the 1999 Act not to apply, could argue that a collateral contract had come into existence in their providing consideration in the research undertaken to facilitate the software development in return for the promise of 10 per cent of the profits.[10]

[9] Superior understanding of the topic is evident here by your awareness that the Act does not render other avoidance mechanisms obsolete.

[10] A really good analysis goes beyond the merely descriptive often encountered in this topic area.

Sporting Choice Ltd and Black Box Ltd have purported to confer a benefit upon the University of Middleshire. The 1999 Act, unless expressly excluded, will prevent the variation or rescission of the promise to pay 10 per cent of the profits, and as third parties the University will have the same remedies available to them as if they were parties to the contract (s. 1(5)).[11]

[11] This tight conclusion covers all issues raised by the question.

Make your answer stand out

- Consider discussing the avoidance of the doctrine of privity by the courts in finding that a constructive trust had been created – *Les Affreteurs Reunis SA* v *Walford* [1919] AC 801.
- Evaluate that the courts are always cautious in such an assumption unless there is a clear intention – *Green* v *Russell, McCarthy* [1959] 2 QB 226.
- Following the decision in *Nisshin Shipping* v *Cleaves*, many more such issues can be satisfactorily resolved through the Contracts (Rights of Third Parties) Act 1999.

! Don't be tempted to . . .

- Rely on your knowledge of the provisions of the Act only: ensure your knowledge is up to date, with a working knowledge of the more recent cases.
- Miss out on valuable marks by not picking up on the more sophisticated issues raised: for example, does it matter that the ultimate beneficiary of the promise is someone different from the third party enforcing the right?
- Forget any alternative cause of action: the Act can be easily excluded but the claimant third party also has a choice of how to bring their claim.

www.pearsoned.co.uk/lawexpressqa

 Go online to access more revision support including additional essay and problem questions with diagram plans, You be the marker questions, and download all diagrams from the book.

Express and implied terms

4

How this topic may come up in exams

This topic area requires you to be able to deal confidently with the sources and status of the terms of the contract. As terms of a contract, exclusion and limitation clauses have been dealt with in this section of the book but they tend to be stand-alone questions. Problem questions on this topic almost invariably have issues of incorporation and construction to deal with before dealing with the statutory regulation, in the Unfair Contract Terms Act 1977. Also consider the Unfair Terms in Consumer Contracts Regulations 1999 when dealing with a business-to-consumer transaction.

■ Attack the question

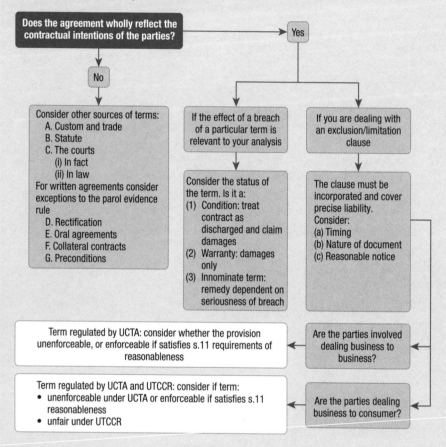

Does the agreement wholly reflect the contractual intentions of the parties? → **Yes**

No

Consider other sources of terms:
- A. Custom and trade
- B. Statute
- C. The courts
  - (i) In fact
  - (ii) In law

For written agreements consider exceptions to the parol evidence rule
- D. Rectification
- E. Oral agreements
- F. Collateral contracts
- G. Preconditions

If the effect of a breach of a particular term is relevant to your analysis

Consider the status of the term. Is it a:
(1) Condition: treat contract as discharged and claim damages
(2) Warranty: damages only
(3) Innominate term: remedy dependent on seriousness of breach

If you are dealing with an exclusion/limitation clause

The clause must be incorporated and cover precise liability. Consider:
(a) Timing
(b) Nature of document
(c) Reasonable notice

Term regulated by UCTA: consider whether the provision unenforceable, or enforceable if satisfies s.11 requirements of reasonableness

Are the parties involved dealing business to business?

Term regulated by UCTA and UTCCR: consider if term:
- unenforceable under UCTA or enforceable if satisfies s.11 reasonableness
- unfair under UTCCR

Are the parties dealing business to consumer?

A printable version of this diagram is available from www.pearsoned.co.uk/lawexpressqa

 **Question 1**

Discuss the extent to which the parol evidence rule is a presumption rather than a strict legal rule.

Answer plan

→ Define the parol evidence rule and the rationale for its existence.

→ Discuss rectification as a means of giving effect to parties' intentions.

→ Evaluate the extent to which the parol evidence rule is a presumption not strictly applied. To do this, analyse the courts' willingness to facilitate exceptions and incorporate additional express terms from outside of the written document by: reading oral terms alongside written agreements, collateral contracts, or recognising that no intention for a contract to come into operation existed.

→ Discuss implied terms as additional sources of terms to a written agreement found from the following sources: statute, the courts and custom and practice.

→ Concluding argument: the written agreement is often just the starting point in defining the terms of a contract.

Diagram plan

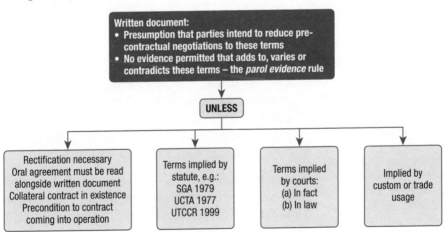

A printable version of this diagram plan is available from www.pearsoned.co.uk/lawexpressqa

Answer

The parties to a contract will potentially have been through a series of negotiations and discussions about their ultimate contractual agreement. These pre-contractual communications could include, inter alia, oral statements, draft contracts or letters. Some of these communications may have become express terms of the finalised agreement and some may only ever amount to representations or rejected proposals having been deliberately omitted from the contract. The law will presume that where the parties have gone to the trouble of putting their agreement in writing, then it is those terms that were intended to be binding and reflect the intentions of the parties to the contract regardless of any extrinsic evidence to the contrary. The refusal to look at extrinsic evidence which contradicts, seeks to vary or add to the written terms of the agreement is known as the parol evidence rule.[1]

The rationale for the existence of the parol evidence rule is to reinforce the objectivity and certainty in the law.[2] The objectivity of the law is maintained in adhering to the parol evidence rule as the parties are bound to the terms contained within the four corners of the document which represents their manifest if not their actual intentions. Equally, the parol evidence rule avoids uncertainty in that all interested parties, including the courts and third parties, know that the written agreement will be enforced and its terms upheld.

Although it is presumed that the written document is an accurate representation of the parties' agreement, mistakes can be made and an application can be made to the courts to have the document rectified. Extrinsic evidence is admitted to support the application to achieve what had been the true intentions of the parties.[3]

The rule cannot be applied where the contract is found to be partly written and partly oral. In *Gillespie Bros & Co.* v *Cheney, Eggar & Co.* [1896] 2 QB 59 it was held that, although there was a strong presumption that a written contract intended to contain all the relevant terms, it is possible for either party to allege and bring evidence to support the assertion that the written agreement had to be considered alongside a previous express term which it was intended should remain in force. Similarly the parol evidence rule had no application in *Couchman* v *Hill* [1947] 1 KB 554. In this

[1] Focused definition on the question set puts your marker on your side from the outset. The examiner is now looking for you to develop the arguments you have introduced. A good start will help you structure your answer.

[2] Clearly identifying the rationale for the existence of the rule demonstrates your depth of understanding of the law which goes beyond a repetition of bare principles and case names.

[3] Beginning with rectification of a document whereby an error can be put right to truly reflect the intentions of the parties is common sense but is also illustrative of the logical and strong structure to your work; start with a principle easy to reconcile with the legal rule under discussion.

case the standard terms for the auction of livestock applied and excluded liability for mistakes in the catalogue. However, the written terms had to be read alongside the verbal assurance by the vendor and auctioneers that the heifer was 'unserved', which formed a term of the contract. This term was breached when the heifer died calving. It would therefore appear that the parol evidence rule is presumed and applied only to the extent that a contrary intention cannot be demonstrated.[4]

[4] The application to the question here is moving you to the main thrust of your argument that the written document is the starting point for establishing the terms of a contract.

The finding of the existence of a collateral contract is an effective mechanism for avoiding the parol evidence rule (*Heilbut, Symons & Co. v Buckleton* [1913] AC 30). In *City and Westminster Properties v Mudd* [1958] 2 ALL ER 733 an oral promise that the defendant could sleep in the shop, in contradiction to a term of the written lease, was held to be a collateral contract. Consideration for the oral promise was provided in entering the main contract. The only limitations to defeating the parol evidence rule in this way are that there must be consideration and, to avoid being past consideration, it must be given before the conclusion of the main contract.[5]

[5] This is a point well made that the promise was made in return for entering the contract.

Extrinsic evidence can be used which will demonstrate that the parties only had the intention that the written agreement would come into operation dependent on the occurrence or non-occurrence of a given circumstance. In *Pym v Campbell* (1856) 6 E & B 370 the parties drew up an agreement for the purchase of a share in an invention that was only intended to be effective after an independent expert had approved the invention. Again, the presumption that the contract is operational can be rebutted by looking beyond the written document itself.[6]

[6] Well directed to the question; being relevant gains marks.

The parol evidence rule cannot be applied where the terms of the written document are subject to an implied term. The implied term can supplement or reconcile an express term in a written agreement where a conflict or inconsistency can be found.

Terms can be implied by statute, such as section 14(2) of the Sales of Goods Act 1979, and having statutory force will take precedence over the express terms of any contract to the contrary and cannot be excluded. Some statutory terms will provide a term where none has been agreed by the parties themselves as a default position in the absence of agreement to the contrary: for instance, section 18 of the Sale of Goods Act 1979.[7]

[7] This is a good point, but do not worry if you do not have a specific example.

Terms can also be implied as the facts of the situation demand it. These terms are necessary and, although sourced from outside of the written document itself, it is assumed that such a term would have been included had the parties thought about it. The implication of such a term is that it is only sparingly used and only where the contract could not operate without it (**Equitable Life Assurance Society v Hyman** [2000] 2 WLR 798).[8] Two tests are used which overlap: the officious bystander test (**Shirlaw v Southern Foundries (1926) Ltd** [1939] 2 KB 206) and the business efficacy test (**The Moorcock** (1889) LR 14 PD 64). Both these tests are subjective and ask what the parties to the contract would have agreed, not what a reasonable person in their situation would have agreed. The parol evidence rule has no role here as the courts will look at all the available evidence to adduce the intentions of the parties, not just the written document which had some crucial omission. The courts also imply terms because the very nature of the relationship demands it. These are terms implied in law and are commonly found in landlord and tenant relationships and employment contracts.

[8] By including a recent decision together with the more obvious cases, you demonstrate an up-to-date knowledge of the topic area and evidence of wider reading.

It is also possible to find that a term has been implied by custom, where that particular trade practice or custom would explain a written agreement, or add to it (**British Crane Hire Corp. Ltd v Ipswich Plant Hire** [1975] QB 303) but not contradict it (**Exxonmobil Sales and Supply Corp. v Texaco Ltd** [2004] 1 All ER (Comm) 435).[9]

[9] This is again good use of current case law for a topic area that is not normally considered by students to be very dynamic. By using very current materials, your answer has taken your analysis outside of the run-of-the-mill and usually rather dull answer.

The parol evidence rule has never had a strict application where the terms of the written agreement do not reflect the intentions of the parties, and this is consistent with recent decisions which enforce entire agreement clauses, confining terms to those in the written agreement (**Inntrepreneur Pub Co. v East Crown Ltd** [2000] 3 EGLR 31).

✓ Make your answer stand out

- Consider whether an entire agreement clause would prevent one party from arguing that an earlier written or oral statement is part of the written document (*Lloyd* v *Sutcliffe* [2007] EWCA Civ 153).

! Don't be tempted to . . .

■ Ignore a discussion on the rationale for the existence of the rule excluding parole evidence before launching into the means for avoiding its application.

■ Forget that parol evidence may be used in certain circumstances to support the use of an implied term or rebut its application.

[handwritten notes] Causation – Damages
m tryer – Knowledge
victim round

? Question 2

Nick is a supplier of eco home pods: mobile units providing living accommodation, manufactured entirely from sustainable and renewable sources. The wood used in his designs is locally sourced cedar and is decorated with plant-based paints and varnishes.

Tony sells wood for floors and cladding. Nick in his discussions with Tony explains how the whole of his business depends on his reputation as an ethical builder and any deviation from his environmental policies would destroy his credibility in the eco home pod marketplace. Nick is therefore adamant that all wood is locally sourced and all varnishes and paints are plant rather than chemical based. Tony promises that this is not a problem and that he will be able to comply.

Nick and Tony enter a written agreement which specifies that the contract will last five years, the delivery dates, amounts, price and wood type. The contract is silent as to sourcing and paint/varnish requirements.

Three months into the contract, Nick discovers that when the locally sourced cedar is not available Tony has been making up the order with cedar sourced from Canada, but not charging any more for it. It also comes to light that all the wood finishes supplied by Tony use the same chemical-based varnishes and paints.

Advise Nick, who wishes to terminate the contract and recover potential damages.

Answer plan

→ Discuss whether Nick can have additional terms read alongside the written contract; this involves a discussion of the parol evidence rule and the exceptions to it.

→ Explore the possibility that there has been the creation of a collateral contract.

→ Presuming Nick can rely on additional express terms as to the sourcing of the wood and the varnishes and paints, he will only be able to terminate the contract if the terms breached are conditions.

Diagram plan

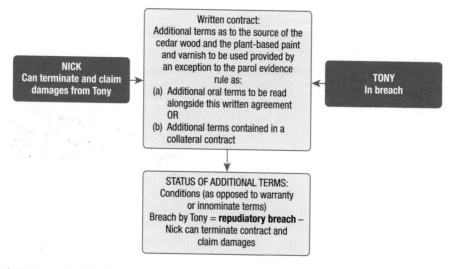

A printable version of this diagram plan is available from www.pearsoned.co.uk/lawexpressqa

Answer

Parties to a contract will determine certain terms between themselves. These terms are called express terms. During discussions and negotiations it can be hard to determine which parts of the negotiations were agreed to and which amounted to no more than representations, or which propositions were rejected as not being feasible for or desirable to one or other of the parties. Where the parties put their agreement in writing, the law presumes that it is the intention to be bound by those and no others. The refusal to consider extrinsic evidence to the written agreement is known as the parol evidence rule. This rule provides that the parties will be bound by the terms of the written agreement and no evidence will be admitted which purports to vary, add or contradict that document.[1] Exceptions to this have been developed where the document does not truly reflect the intentions of the parties. Unless Nick can rely on one of these exceptions, he will be bound by the written terms of the contract with Tony.

The parol evidence rule will not be applied where a term agreed orally is of such importance that it should be read alongside the written agreement.

[1] By articulating the general rule, which is bad news for Nick, the argument has a natural flow to find a way around the presumption.

In **Bannerman v White** (1861) 10 CBNS 844 the fact that sulphur had not been used in the production of hops purchased by the seller was held to be a term of the contract as it was known to both parties to be of importance. The courts accepted that, had the defendants informed the plaintiffs that the hops had been subjected to sulphur, they would not have entered negotiations, not even to ask the price. The situation with Nick and Tony has direct parallels with **Bannerman v White**.[2] Having the wood sourced from Canada and the paint and varnishes having a chemical base are not acceptable terms for Nick and he would never have agreed to them. Tony was fully aware of this situation and the importance of the sourcing of the wood and the ingredients of the paints and varnish.

[2] The similarities with the facts of the precedent used add weight to your argument.

An alternative argument available to Nick is that alongside the main written agreement was an oral collateral contract to the effect that the wood was locally sourced and the paints and varnishes plant-based. In order to find a collateral contract, Nick must have provided consideration for the promises as to sourcing and the paint and varnish. It is sufficient consideration that the other party entered the main contract (**Heilbut, Symons & Co. v Buckleton** [1913] AC 30).[3] The finding of a collateral contract will allow an exception to the parol evidence rule to add to, vary or even contradict the main written agreement (**City and Westminster Properties v Mudd** [1958] 2 All ER 733). The written lease in **City and Westminster Properties v Mudd** prohibited a tenant from sleeping on the premises. The defendant asked if he could continue his previous practice of sleeping on the property and the plaintiffs agreed on the understanding that he signed the lease. The plaintiffs ten years later sought to have the defendant forfeit the lease, on the grounds that he had breached the written agreement by sleeping on the premises. It was held that the collateral contract was a promise not to enforce that particular term as to forfeiture, which could be used as a defence to the action brought for breach of the covenant not to sleep in the shop. In finding a collateral contract, Tony would be in breach of contract in not sourcing the wood as promised and using paints and varnish contrary to the agreed process of manufacture, as the collateral contract would add to the terms of the main agreement. Nick has provided consideration in entering the contract with Tony, which he would not have done on any other basis.

[3] This point is well made. Consideration must be legally present even if it is not a very high threshold to meet. Again, this demonstrates the courts wishing to give effect to the true intentions of the parties.

Nick will be able to argue successfully either that the written agreement be read alongside the oral terms as to the sourcing of the wood and the plant-based paints and varnish to be used, or that there is an enforceable collateral contract in existence which contains those terms. It is, however, the status of those terms which will determine Nick's remedies for any breach.[4]

Terms are classified as conditions, warranties, or innominate terms. A condition is a fundamental term of the contract which if breached gives the innocent party the right to an option to terminate the contract and claim damages.[5] A warranty as a less important term will only give rise to an award of damages if breached. The difference can be illustrated by the following two cases. In **Poussard v Spiers and Pond** (1876) 1 QBD 410, missing the first week of a season's performances for a singer was a repudiatory breach of contract as the opening night has such significance. By contrast, in **Bettini v Gye** (1876) 1 QBD 183, missing three days of rehearsals before performances began was an ancillary to the main part of the contract and therefore amounted only to a breach of warranty, giving rise to an award of damages only and not a right to termination. If a term is not designated a condition or a warranty by operation of law or by interpreting the intent of the parties, it may be designated an innominate term, which will look at the consequences of the breach to determine whether or not that breach should be treated as a breach of warranty or condition (**Hong Kong Fir Shipping Co. Ltd v Kawasaki Ltd** [1962] 1 All ER 474).

From the facts given, both Nick and Tony were aware of how important the sourcing of the wood and the materials used to decorate that wood were to the eco home pod business, and therefore the courts would have no problem in determining these requirements as conditions. The breach of these conditions would entitle Nick to repudiate the contract with Tony and claim any damages arising from that breach.

Confining the parties to the written agreement they have made can create certainty and maintain the objectivity of the law. In situations such as that with Nick and Tony, it can also fail to give effect to the true intentions of the party.[6] The courts would therefore in this situation give effect to Nick's very clear requirements as to the quality and characteristics of the wood, paint and varnish, recognising them as terms of the agreement or terms of a collateral contract: in either case having the status of conditions, breach of which will allow Nick to terminate the contract and claim any losses.[7]

[4] This is well structured reinforcing that, unless these terms are enforceable against Tony, Nick would have no cause of action, and introducing the issues surrounding the status of a contractual term.

[5] By defining all three possibilities with supporting case law, which clearly articulates the differences, knowledge and understanding is demonstrated by explaining why the additional terms would be classified as conditions.

[6] A good depth of analysis is achieved here by defining the rationale for the general rule and the justification of the deviation from it.

[7] Drawing together all your deliberations into a clear application of the law to the problem set will give the work an effective and neat conclusion.

Make your answer stand out

- Ensure you fully develop your analysis by defining the alternatives to the classification of the terms as to the sourcing of the wood, paint and varnish as conditions.
- Consider adding some academic authority into your discussion on the classification of terms, such as Bojczuk, W. (1987): 'When is a condition not a condition?' *JBL* 353.

! Don't be tempted to . . .

- Lose marks by not having a logical structure to the answer; start from the premise that the parties are bound to the terms of their written agreement and then see whether there is any possible rationale to justify a deviation from that standpoint.
- Miss the point of the question and concern to Nick: which is, can he terminate the contract? This will involve an evaluation of the status of the terms concerned as conditions, warranties or innominate terms.

Question 3

Implied terms give effect to the reasonable expectations of the parties. Discuss the veracity of this statement.

Answer plan

→ Identify sources of implied terms.

→ Discuss the implication of a term on the grounds of custom/trade usage in the absence of express agreement to the contrary.

→ Appraise how terms implied by statute often create a floor of rights/obligations, often redressing inequalities of bargaining power.

→ Demonstrate your understanding of the justification of terms implied by the courts:

(i) In fact, using the officious bystander/business efficacy tests. Implication is necessary because the facts of the situation demand it.

(ii) In law, the nature of the relationship requires such implication of a term, predominantly found in landlord/tenant and employment relationships.

Diagram plan

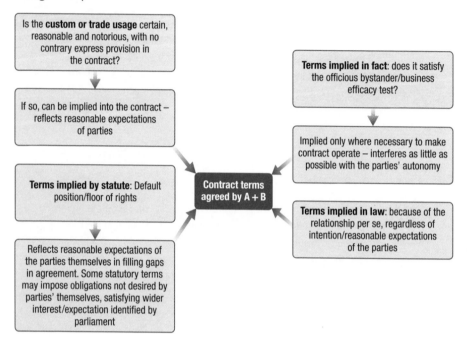

Is the **custom or trade usage** certain, reasonable and notorious, with no contrary express provision in the contract?

If so, can be implied into the contract – reflects reasonable expectations of parties

Terms implied by statute: Default position/floor of rights

Reflects reasonable expectations of the parties themselves in filling gaps in agreement. Some statutory terms may impose obligations not desired by parties' themselves, satisfying wider interest/expectation identified by parliament

Contract terms agreed by A + B

Terms implied in fact: does it satisfy the officious bystander/business efficacy test?

Implied only where necessary to make contract operate – interferes as little as possible with the parties' autonomy

Terms implied in law: because of the relationship per se, regardless of intention/reasonable expectations of the parties

A printable version of this diagram plan is available from www.pearsoned.co.uk/lawexpressqa

Answer

Terms determine respective rights and obligations of contracting parties. Terms can be expressly agreed between the parties or they can be implied by custom, statute or the courts. Freedom of contract is an important principle of English contract law and any term implied from another source has the potential to limit the autonomy of the contracting parties. As such, it might appear that implying any term into a contract might not be fulfilling the reasonable expectation of the parties, as the term may be contrary to what was expressly agreed. However, implied terms often redress any inequalities of bargaining power or fill necessary gaps in that agreement to ensure the contract can operate.[1]

An important source of terms in commercial contracts is found in custom and trade usage. ***Cunliffe-Owen v Teather & Greenwood***

[1] Always target your analysis on the question. This is the core argument which will be picked up throughout the analysis. Introducing it here gives your work direction and focus.

[1967] 1 WLR 1421 held that in order for a term to be implied into a contract, its usage must be 'notorious, certain and reasonable'. Being notorious requires that the custom or trade usage must be known in the trade or market in which the parties are operating. It is not essential that the parties themselves knew of the custom but that an outsider making enquiries would hear of it (**Kum v Wah Tat Bank Ltd** [1971] 1 Lloyd's Rep 439). The certainty in the definition refers to the custom or trade usage being clearly established. It must be more than practice or habitual behaviour. A term implied by custom has a presumption that the parties intended to contract in a manner consistent with that commercial environment and would view compliance as a legal obligation. The presumption that such a custom is a term of the contract is defeated by an express term to the contrary. Where the express term contradicts the implied custom, then the express term will prevail as it would be unreasonable to imply such an inconsistent term. **Exxonmobil Sales and Supply Corp. v Texaco Ltd** [2004] 1 All ER (Comm) 435 concerned an entire agreement clause which the court concluded was effective to prevent an implication of a term based on custom or usage.[2] The courts when implying a term on the grounds of custom and usage are satisfying the reasonable expectations of the parties, as they only do so where there is no contrary intention of the parties.

[2] Using the traditional definition of a custom has demonstrated its limitations in a modern commercial environment.

Terms are also implied by statute. The aim and effect of the individual statutory provision can vary. A statute may aim to give effect to the intention of the parties, or to provide a default rule if the parties have not decided for themselves as to a particular term, or provide a floor of rights redressing an inequality of bargaining power. Statutes such as the Unfair Contract Terms Act 1977 are illustrative of this in that the provisions seek to regulate exclusion or limitation clauses: for example, the 1977 Act renders an exclusion clause void in a business-to-consumer contract which purports to exclude section 14(2) of the Sale of Goods Act 1979, which itself implies a term that goods will be of satisfactory quality. By way of contrast, the purported exclusion of section 14(2) in a business-to-business transaction will be acceptable if it satisfies section 11 of the Unfair Contract Terms Act 1977 as to reasonableness.[3] This balanced approach satisfies the expectations of those most vulnerable in the marketplace, leaving a greater degree of autonomy to others where the allocation of risk is part of a legitimate commercial transaction.

[3] This is a smart use of an implied statutory term regulating another implied statutory term.

The courts can also imply terms which have not been expressly included in the contract, but as a question of fact the parties must have intended such a term to be incorporated in their agreement. The courts can be viewed as satisfying the expectation of the parties, but it should be noted that the courts do not rewrite bad bargains. Terms implied in fact are done so infrequently and only where necessary to the operation of the contract.[4] Two tests are used by the courts to determine the intention of the parties: the officious bystander test (**Shirlaw v Southern Foundries (1926) Ltd** [1939] 2 KB 206) and the business efficacy test (**The Moorcock** (1889) LR 14 PD 64). Both tests are subjective as they try to ascertain what the parties to this agreement would have agreed to and as such seek to satisfy the reasonable expectation of those particular parties.[5] The officious bystander test poses the question that if, at the time the bargain was made, a third party (the officious bystander) had suggested an express provision, would the answer be so obvious as they would answer 'of course'. The business efficacy test looks at the implication of a term that if not included the contract could not operate. In the **Moorcock** case the mooring for the boat was unsuitable and damage was suffered. The contract did not specifically provide that the mooring was safe; however, the courts were willing to imply such on the grounds of necessity. The contracting parties could not have intended to contract for an unsuitable mooring.

The courts can also imply terms in law. These terms are implied into a particular type of contract regardless of the intentions of the parties.[6] This type of implied term has been found with increasing frequency in employment contracts (**Malik v Bank of Credit and Commerce International** [1998] AC 20). Although such an implied term cannot contradict an express term, it can regulate the way in which such a term is operated (**United Bank v Akhtar** [1989] IRLR 507).[7]

Terms are implied on the grounds of custom or trade usage only where there is no express term to the contrary and the custom is so established as to raise a presumption of inclusion. To this extent, such implied terms reflect the expectations of the parties.[8] Terms implied by statute can fill gaps, providing default provisions in the absence of agreement to the contrary. This is reflective of the intention of the parties; however, statutes can also provide terms which cannot be contracted out of. This may not satisfy the reasonable expectations of the parties, but often does satisfy the expectations of

[4] This is the most important factor to remember when looking at implication in fact.

[5] Relating the analysis directly to the question emphasises the ability to apply knowledge directly to relevant issues. Do not forget to do this: if you do, the work will drift and become woolly and possibly irrelevant.

[6] Draw a parallel with some statutory terms which frequently create minimum rights. This term in employment law has raised the standard of acceptable behaviour between the parties.

[7] Having examples supports your analysis. You may well be versed in alternatives such as landlord and tenant, *Liverpool City Council v Irwin* [1976] 2 All ER 39.

[8] The conclusion draws on the essence of each issue raised and focuses it on the 'reasonable expectation' of the question. This will reinforce the examiner's awareness of your ability to use your knowledge effectively.

a wider society that needs protection from a better informed or more powerful party to a contract. Terms implied in fact are narrow in their application and are only used where absolutely necessary and interfere with the parties' agreement as little as possible. Terms implied in law by contrast apply simply by virtue of the fact that the relationship exists and, as such, regulate that relationship regardless of the expectations of the parties.

✓ Make your answer stand out

- Consider the inclusion of some academic authority to support your arguments and demonstrate wider reading and research, for example:
  - Peden, E. (2001) Policy concerns behind the implication of terms in law, 117 *LQR* 459
  - Kramer, A. (2004) Implication in fact as an instance of contractual interpretation, 63 *CLJ* 384.

! Don't be tempted to . . .

- Be too descriptive; ensure the analysis is focused on the question. Ask yourself whether that method of implication satisfies the reasonable expectations of the parties or whether those terms are implied in spite of them.
- Forget any of the potential sources of implied terms; ensure you cover custom and practice as well as terms implied by statute and the courts, but bear in mind the extent to which the parties can override such a term by express agreement and the use of entire agreement clauses.

Question 4

Ugolin has contracted with Blodwen for the hire of a large open animal shelter adjacent to a national cycleway in the heart of the Belleshire National Park.

Ugolin intends to use the shelter for his bike hire business. A hosepipe connection to the mains water supply on Blodwen's land is the only source of water and without it Ugolin will be unable to wash and carry out on-site maintenance of his bike stock in preparation for rides.

The written contract is for the months of June to October inclusively and is silent as to the water supply.

Blodwen has disconnected the hosepipe following the water authority installing a meter and charging her by the amount used. Ugolin is new to the area but has been told by local farmers that it is unheard of for these animal shelters to be supplied without access to water. This has always been the case, as without water their livestock would die.

The first month of business for Ugolin has been disastrous. Those not put off by the bikes being dirty complain of grinding gears, the seat and handlebars being almost impossible to adjust, and slow punctures.

Advise Ugolin whether Blodwen is in breach of any contractual term that could be implied on the grounds of custom or necessity.

Answer plan

→ Consider the usual presumption that the written contract between Ugolin and Blodwen contains whole agreement.

→ Mention alternative sources of terms but focus on the question which asks you only about the possibility of a term being implied on the grounds of custom or necessity.

→ Investigate whether the tradition of providing a water supply could be a term implied on the grounds of custom or trade usage. Unlikely here, as the different use for the shelter means it is no longer for livestock.

→ Evaluate the possibility of a term being implied on the grounds of necessity. This is possible as it would fulfil the unexpressed intention of Blodwen and Ugolin.

Diagram plan

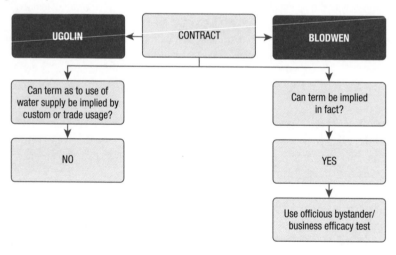

A printable version of this diagram plan is available from www.pearsoned.co.uk/lawexpressqa

Answer

Ugolin and Blodwen have put their contractual agreement in writing, so the law will presume that it is those terms that were intended to be binding and no others. It is, however, possible for terms to be incorporated from extrinsic sources such as statute, an oral agreement that should be read alongside the written terms, or terms that are implied by the courts on the grounds of custom, by necessity, or in law as a result of the nature of the relationship itself. The two potential sources of implied terms to be considered in relation to Ugolin and Blodwen are on the grounds of custom and practice and whether the facts of the situation necessitate the implication of a term.[1]

[1] Focusing on the question set will avoid the inclusion of irrelevant material and digression from issues that will gain marks, although you have also demonstrated you know alternative sources.

In **Hutton v Warren** (1836) 1 M & W 466 extrinsic evidence of custom could be used to supplement terms of a written agreement where the written agreement was silent on those issues. The key principle drawn from this case is that such a term can be implied, but only where the written agreement is silent on the matter. This is because, where such a trade usage or custom exists, it is presumed that the parties intended to adhere to that custom or trade usage unless they demonstrate a contrary intention by an express term in the contract. Ugolin and Blodwen's written agreement is silent as to the water supply.

A term implied on the grounds of custom or trade usage must be 'notorious, certain and reasonable' (**Cunliffe-Owen v Teather & Greenwood** [1967] 1 WLR 1421). The requirement that the custom is notorious means that the custom must be known in the trade or market in which the parties are operating. Here the local farmers know that it is customary to provide a water supply; it is not essential that Ugolin knew of the custom when he made the contract[2] (**Kum v Wah Tat Bank** Ltd [1971] 1 Lloyd's Rep 439). The element of certainty refers to the custom being clearly established: it must be more than practice or habitual behaviour. **Cunliffe-Owen v Teather & Greenwood** goes further in that the custom must be complied with, not just as a mere courtesy but in the sense of it being a legally binding obligation. Ugolin may struggle to establish that the term as to the water supply should be implied into his contract by custom, as the custom applied to the supply of water to support livestock, not

[2] Extra marks will be awarded for identifying the non-issue of Ugolin's ignorance of the custom.

the cleaning of items stored there.[3] It is unlikely that the custom would apply to the letting of all such structures for whatever purpose on farm land.

Terms can be implied by the courts into contracts on the grounds of necessity where the contract could not operate without the implication of such a term. It should be noted that the courts do not rewrite bad bargains and the situations in which terms will be implied on these grounds have been narrowly construed. These terms are implied because the facts require the courts to do so and the parties themselves would have intended such a term to have been included in their contract.[4] Two overlapping tests are used to determine the unexpressed intention of the parties: the business efficacy test and the officious bystander test.

[4] As we will see, giving effect to intentions can be shown as necessary.

The business efficacy test was put forward by Bowen LJ in **The Moorcock** (1889) 14 PD 64. The test is based on necessity, not reasonableness. In other words, without the implication of this term the contract will not operate. In **The Moorcock** the plaintiffs had contracted for a mooring on the Thames. The mooring was unsuitable as the bed at that part of the river was rock rather than sand. The presumed intention of the parties must have been to provide a mooring suitable for the ship in question and that was necessary to give efficacy to the contract: in other words, to make it work a term had to be implied as to the mooring being suitable, and the risk of taking reasonable steps to do so had to lie with the defendant. The contract to allow Ugolin the use of the animal shed does not need a term as to the provision of a water supply to make the contract work. It can be argued that the bike hiring business does need a water supply to make the business run more effectively.[5] It can be argued that if the intention to carry on with the water supply existed at the time the contract was made, then it is necessary to give effect to that intention.

[5] This raises a complex issue: how far can the business efficacy test be stretched before it merely becomes a means of rewriting a bad bargain?

The second test used is the officious bystander test (**Shirlaw v Southern Foundries (1926) Ltd** [1939] 2 KB 206). Using this test, a term will be implied if the parties were asked at the time they were making their bargain by an officious bystander whether a suggested express provision was included, and the parties would answer but 'of course' as its inclusion is so obvious. Blodwen only appears to have changed her mind about the hosepipe after the method of billing changed. If Ugolin and Blodwen had been asked at the time if they expected the continued use of the water supply to be used, both of them would have answered 'of course'. The officious bystander test does appear to be of greater effect in giving effect to a common intention if that common intention can be evidenced.

[6] Many cases blend the tests. The focus of the analysis here has rightly been that the courts would fulfil the clear intentions of the parties.

Both tests are subjective, aiming to fulfil the intentions of the parties at the time the contract was made; and where evidence is produced that at the time both parties had this intention, then whichever test is used the courts are willing to give effect to that intention[6] (*Greaves (Contractors) Ltd* v *Bayham Meikle & Partners* (1975) 4 BLR 56). Ugolin will be unable to rely on custom or trade usage to imply a term as to the provision of a water supply, as it would appear that the supply in the past has been for livestock rather than applied to any user of the shelters. However, as there is strong evidence to suggest that both parties had the tacit intention to continue the supply of water at the time the contract was made, the courts would imply that term in fact as part of what was agreed.[7]

[7] The conclusion directly provides a solution to the facts of the problem: this will gain marks.

✓ Make your answer stand out

- Discuss how the officious bystander test and business efficacy test raise judicial and academic argument as to whether they are blended or an 'either/or' requirement.
- Consider that the solution to the problem does not require such an in-depth analysis of this issue but an awareness of it would gain marks.
- Use the following articles to evidence your wider reading and research on the topic area: Lord Steyn (1997) Contract law: fulfilling the reasonable expectations of honourable men, 113 *LQR* 433 and Hibbert, T. (2009) Sovereignty of the contract, 9 *JIBF* 524 may help with this and your general understanding.

! Don't be tempted to . . .

- Miss the directions of the question; you only have to worry about custom and trade usage and terms implied in fact.
- Worry about the narrowness of the question; just ensure that the application of the analysis to the problem is logical.

Question 5

Discuss the means of defining the classification of a contractual term, the effect that status has on the remedies available and whether it is appropriate to determine those effects after the breach has occurred.

Answer plan

→ Define types of term and potential consequences of breach:

   (a) condition, breach of which can lead to termination of the contract and damages

   (b) warranty, breach of which has damages only as a remedy

   (c) innominate terms, the consequences of a breach of which depend on the effect of the breach.

→ Consider how the courts determine the status of a term by looking at the:

   (a) parties' intentions determined at the time the contract was made

   (b) statutory provisions in force at the time the contract was made.

→ Discuss and evaluate the courts' use of innominate terms.

Diagram plan

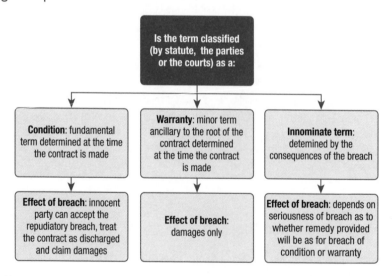

A printable version of this diagram plan is available from www.pearsoned.co.uk/lawexpressqa

Answer

Contracts contain terms, whether expressly agreed or implied from whatever source.[1] The consequences of a breach of a term will depend on whether a term is classified as a condition, a warranty, or an innominate term. The effects of a breach of a condition or a warranty are determined at the time the contract was made as the status of the term is defined at that point. The consequences of a breach of an innominate term are defined only after the seriousness of the consequences of the breach is known. This provides flexibility and may produce a 'fair' result, but it is at the expense of certainty and focus on the nature of the term breached.[2]

A condition is a fundamental term of the contract. It is the significance of the term itself rather than any consideration of the consequences of the breach that is analysed. The breach of a condition is a repudiatory breach which gives the innocent party the choice of accepting that repudiation, which terminates the contract releasing the innocent party from further performance of the contract. The innocent party can also claim damages, or affirm the contract and just claim damages.[3]

A warranty is a term which is defined to be a minor term of the contract, ancillary to the main 'root' of the contract. A breach of warranty only gives the innocent party the right to recover damages; they cannot elect to terminate the contract. The two cases of ***Poussard v Spiers and Pond*** (1876) 1 QBD 410 and ***Bettini v Gye*** (1876) 1 QBD 183 illustrate the difference between the two species of term.[4] In ***Poussard v Spiers and Pond*** an actress had missed a week of performances of a play. A substitute was engaged and her contract terminated. The breach of contract in arriving a week late was a breach of condition, even though the play was to run for a whole season, as the opening night was regarded to be of fundamental importance and as such the contract could be lawfully terminated. By contrast, in ***Bettini v Gye*** the contract required the performer to arrive six days before opening night for rehearsals; in fact he arrived three days before. The term was ancillary to the main part of the contract and as such amounted to a warranty, therefore a right to damages only arose.

Innominate terms look at the consequences of the breach rather than the status of the term at the time the contract was made to

---

[1] This really brings home the point that these principles apply to ALL terms.

[2] This provides a good focus on the issues raised by the question.

[3] Use technical language accurately and with meaning and you will gain marks.

[4] Comparing the two illustrates and emphasises your analysis of the difference between the two classifications.

determine the remedies available. If the consequences of breach are serious, then the breach will be treated as a breach of condition and the innocent party will have a right to terminate the contract and claim damages. If the effects of the breach are minor, then the court will treat the breach as having been a breach of warranty. This can make contractual planning and the appropriate reaction to a breach difficult, as there is an element of uncertainty in predicting a judge's view of the breach being sufficiently serious to allow termination of the contract.[5] In ***Hong Kong Fir Shipping Co. Ltd v Kawasaki Ltd*** [1962] 1 All ER 474 the loss of twenty weeks in a ship's charter as a result of unreliable engines and staff breached a term as to being seaworthy. It was held that the effect of the breach had to be considered, not the nature of the term as a condition or warranty. The breach in this case did not deprive the charterers of substantially the whole benefit and therefore there was no right of termination.[6]

The difficulty arises in defining which terms are significant enough to give rise to a right of termination derived from the nature of the terms itself, and when the courts will introduce an innominate term to look at the effects of the breach.[7]

Contract law tries to give effect to the intentions of the parties and therefore it may be that a particular term is of importance to those parties. To a large extent, the courts look to give effect to the intentions of the parties at the time they made the contract, where they have attempted to classify the terms themselves as conditions. However, they will look for evidence that the parties intended the term to be interpreted in its strict legal sense, particularly where the interpretation of a term as a condition would lead to unreasonable results (***Schuler AG v Wickman Machine Tool Sales*** [1974] AC 235). Making a term 'of the essence' has proved effective in demonstrating the intention that a term be classified as a condition (***Lombard North Central plc v Butterworth*** [1987] QB 527).

Parliament can legislate to determine the classification of a term. Sections 13–15 of the Sale of Goods Act 1979 imply terms as to goods having to correspond to their description, being of satisfactory quality and fit for purpose, and having to correspond to any sample provided. The Act further provides that breach of these implied terms gives a right of rejection. In other words, they are breaches of condition. This is always the case with consumer sales; however, where

[5] This reinforces your introductory point that the remedial flexibility is at the expense of certainty. Drawing threads of an argument through the analysis demonstrates not only a strong structure but also a depth of understanding of the topic.

[6] The innocent party to the breach had, therefore, wrongfully repudiated the contract.

[7] This articulates the complex issue of when it is appropriate to look at the effects of breach rather than the intentions of the parties at the time the contract was made.

the breach is so slight that the right of rejection would be unreasonable, then in a business-to-business transaction such a breach will be treated as a warranty with only damages being available as a remedy (s. 15A Sale of Goods Act 1979). Determining what is slight and reasonable does still focus on the right to terminate rather than the reasons for the termination.[8] Section 15A of the Sales of Goods Act 1979 very much aims to prevent the termination of contracts on technicalities insisting on precise performance, as encountered in cases such as ***Arcos Ltd v E.A. Ronaasen & Sons Ltd*** [1933] AC 470. It is interesting to note that prior to the enactment of section 15A the finding of an innominate term had this effect (***The Hansa Nord*** [1976] QB 44).[9]

[8] Delivering an extra level of depth to the analysis precisely focused on the question set will greatly enhance marks.

[9] Pulling together threads of argument demonstrates understanding which a marker will be looking for.

The courts will be compelled to define status according to the intentions of the parties and the requirements of Parliament. They are also bound by precedent in interpreting an identical term. The remedial flexibility of an innominate term has to be balanced against the need for commercial certainty and, therefore, although the innominate term is firmly established in UK contract law, there is caution in giving it too broad an application (***The Mihalis Angelos*** [1971] 1 QB 164).[10]

[10] This may appear a rather equivocal statement, but so is the law on this point.

✓ Make your answer stand out

- Consider a third alternative put forward by Professor Brownsword (1992) Retrieving reasons, retrieving rationality? A new look at the right to withdraw for breach of contract, 5 *JCL* 83, in determining the status of a term.

- Currently the courts look at either the nature of the term at the time of its agreement or the effect of the breach as to remedies that will be available. What about a consideration of the reasons behind the termination?

! Don't be tempted to . . .

- Be over-descriptive; ensure you give depth to your analysis by addressing the pointers given in the question as to definition, remedies and critique of a post-breach approach.

- Miss out on potential marks by not fully expanding your analysis: for example, evaluating the inherent difficulties in the finding that the term is an innominate one, and how determining the effect at breach defeats good contractual planning.

4 EXPRESS AND IMPLIED TERMS

❓ Question 6

Malcolm is attending an annual sci-fi convention held in the Planetarium Hotel in Greenwich. He has attended this event for the last ten years.

Malcolm arrives early at the hotel. He is informed by reception that his room is not ready. Malcolm decides to leave his luggage at the left luggage office, as he has done every year previously and go for a swim in the hotel pool. At the luggage office he is given a small ticket with a number on the front which he presumes is to allow identification of his property on his return. He puts the ticket in his wallet to add to the other nine he has at home as part of his convention scrapbook and heads off to the pool. In actual fact on the back of the ticket in very small letters is written 'for terms and conditions please see the notice at the main reception desk', which is ten metres from the left luggage office. The notice at the hotel reception desk declares that luggage is left at the owners' risk and any damage arising out of the hotel's negligence will be limited to £50. Malcolm's costume for the convention, as an original piece used in the filming of his favourite sci-fi film, is worth at least £800.

On returning to claim his luggage, Malcolm is told that the hotel is very sorry but his luggage has been lost and they offer him £50 cash. Malcolm is very upset and wishes you to advise him as to the legality of the hotel limiting their liability in this way.

Answer plan

→ Initial discussion needs to focus on incorporation, as unless the limitation clause is incorporated into the contract the hotel will not be able to rely upon it.

→ Consider incorporation by reasonable notice and incorporation by a previous course of dealings.

→ Consider whether, as a matter of construction, the clause covers the loss that Malcolm is claiming for.

→ Presuming the clause is incorporated, discuss how and why section 11 of the Unfair Contract Terms Act 1977 will apply to the hotel's limitation clause.

→ Extra marks could be gained for an analysis of the 1999 Unfair Terms in Consumer Contracts Regulations and whether it would be applicable to the hotel's unnegotiated term limiting their liability to Malcolm as a consumer.

Diagram plan

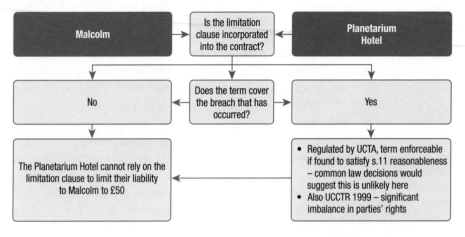

A printable version of this diagram plan is available from www.pearsoned.co.uk/lawexpressqa

Answer

[1] This clear and direct introduction starts by identifying the issues of law and immediately applies these to the question asked. The examiner immediately has a strong indication that the answer addresses the core issues and will develop the analysis with depth and understanding. Getting your marker thinking positively about your work from the outset is good exam technique.

[2] Notice has to be *reasonable* and *before* the contract is concluded. Dealing with the timing first is logical. A strong flowing structure will ensure you communicate your analysis effectively and achieve higher marks.

Limitation and exemption clauses aim to restrict or avoid the liability of one party to the other. The ability to do this is limited both by common law and statutory rules. The limitation clause which the Planetariun Hotel are seeking to rely on will be governed by the common law rules on incorporation and interpretation. The enforceability of the clause will depend on its compliance with the Unfair Contract Terms Act 1977 and the Unfair Terms in Consumer Contracts Regulations 1999.[1]

The Planetarium Hotel will have to establish that the term limiting their liability to £50 had been incorporated into their contract with Malcolm to store his luggage. Incorporation can be effected by giving reasonable notice of the term.[2] Notice has to be given at the time or before the contract was made. In *Olley v Marlborough Court Ltd* [1949] 1 All ER 127 a notice purporting to exclude liability for theft situated in a hotel bedroom was not incorporated into the contract, as the contract was concluded downstairs in the lobby before the notice was seen. The Planetarium Hotel's notice was situated in the main reception area which was fairly close to the luggage office and was visible to Malcolm when he checked into the hotel and before he deposited his luggage. Attention to this notice was also purportedly drawn by the ticket. In **Parker v South Eastern Railway Co.** (1877) 2 CPD 416 the test was found to be objective in having to take reasonable steps to bring the clause to the attention of the other party. Doing this by reference to another document is acceptable (**O'Brien v MGN Ltd** [2001] EWCA Civ 1279), but not if the document is not of the type usually considered to have contractual force. In **Chapelton v Barry UDC** [1940] 1 KB 532 the giving of a ticket for the hire of a deck chair did not amount to a contractual document but merely a receipt or voucher and, as such, could not incorporate the exclusion clause for damage or injury alluded to on the back of the ticket.[3] Similarly, here the ticket would be regarded as a means by which to identify the left property rather than one including important terms of the contract. However, in checking in to his room at the reception desk, the notice concerning left luggage was visible before the contract to leave the luggage was concluded. The timing may therefore arguably be before the contract, but the more unusual or onerous the term the greater the degree of notice required for incorporation (**Interfoto Picture Library v Stiletto Visual Programmes Ltd** [1989] QB 433).

Malcolm has been attending this convention for ten years: it is possible that the limitation clause could be incorporated into the contract by a previous course of dealing. Malcolm has used the left luggage office before. In **McCutcheon v MacBrayne** [1964] 1 All ER 430 the previous course of dealings could not incorporate the exclusion clause, as usual steps to incorporate the term had not been applied consistently. Malcolm has checked in every year at the convention and been given a ticket for his luggage in the same way year on year. In **Hollier v Rambler Motors (AMC) Ltd** [1972] 2 QB 71 four occasions in five years was held to be insufficient to establish a course of dealings.[4]

The courts in looking at issues of incorporation and construction of the clause itself are looking to redress the potential inequality of bargaining power and have an emphasis on protecting the consumer. To this end they will construe an exclusion clause or limitation clause against the party relying on it, *contra proferentem*, particularly where there is ambiguity (**Hollier v Rambler Motors**). The limitation clause in the foyer of the hotel is not ambiguous. Therefore, if it is found that the clause has been incorporated into the contract, Malcolm will have to rely on the operation of statutory protection

[3] Effective use of case law to reinforce and build your application in this way demonstrates that you have understood the principles but also updated your knowledge to go beyond the basic key cases of this topic area.

[4] The detailed knowledge of the case law is evident here and an examiner will be impressed to see an answer dealing with the finer detail beyond the fact that if you have been there before, the notice will have been seen and therefore incorporated.

[5] Don't worry if your answer
seems equivocal as to
whether or not the clause
is incorporated; that is a
question of fact. Treat it as if
it is incorporated and you still
have two further opportunities
to look at limiting its
enforceability through
the statutory regulation,
further demonstrating your
knowledge of the topic area.

to prevent the Planetarium Hotel being able to rely on their
exclusion clause.[5]

UCTA 1977 provides differing protection in certain sections of the
Act, depending on whether the contract concerned is dealing business to business or business to consumer. One party must be
acting in the course of a business. The Act covers both exclusion
and limitation clauses. The contract between Malcolm and the
Planetarium Hotel is business to consumer and is therefore subject to
the provisions of UCTA. Depending on the infringement, the operation
of the Act will render an exclusion or limitation clause either totally
ineffective, or effective only if found to be reasonable under section 11.
The hotel in losing Malcolm's luggage are in breach of contract and
they may only exclude or limit their liability under section 3 of UCTA if
they can satisfy the reasonableness requirement. Section 11 refers to
Schedule 2 to UCTA which provides general guidance in determining
reasonableness. Section 11(4) specifically discusses limitation clauses
and a consideration of the resources putting forward the term and
the practicality of insuring against loss.[6] The common law has a
wide discretion in determining reasonableness, as the term is not
specifically defined in the Act. ***George Mitchell Ltd*** v ***Finney Lock
Seeds Ltd*** [1983] 2 AC 803 found that the limiting of liability of
defective seed to the contract price was unreasonable; as they had
in the past made ex gratia payments, the breach was serious: the
defendants had been careless and it was easier for the seller than
the buyer to insure. The hotel here have been negligent, the breach
is serious and it is the kind of risk you would reasonably expect the
hotel business to insure against. Furthermore, in ***Smith*** v ***Eric S.
Bush*** [1990] 1 AC 831 the court held that the greater the complexity
of the task the more likely is the clause to be found to be reasonable.
Minding luggage is not complex.[7]

[6] The build-on analysis here,
from the general aim of the
protection to the specifics
related to the problem
question, has clarity and
introduces the common law
definition of 'reasonableness'
in this context.

[7] Reinforcing the language
used in the main reasoning
of the decided cases cited,
'serious breach' and
'complexity of task', ensures
that your application cannot
miss the target and your
rationale is explicit.

The 1999 Regulations overlap with UCTA and would also apply to
Malcolm's situation, as he is a consumer and the term was not
individually negotiated. Malcolm would have to establish that the
term was unfair and the regulations provide guidance including the
term causing a significant imbalance in the parties' rights and
obligations. If found to be unfair, the term would be unenforceable
against Malcolm.

The sum of £50 is a rather small one and would not cover the costs
of the average contents of a suitcase, even the suitcase alone. The

[8] The conclusion focuses on the statutory regulation, as without the incorporation the legislation would not apply.

limitation clause is therefore unlikely to satisfy the requirement of reasonableness for UCTA and is probably unfair under UTCCR. As such, the limitation would not apply and Malcolm could recover to the full extent of his losses.[8]

 Make your answer stand out

■ Consider further development of your analysis as regards what will amount to satisfaction of the requirement of reasonableness under UCTA and what will amount to being unfair under the 1999 Regulations, using academic authority and analysis: for example, Brown, I. and Chandler, A. (1993) Unreasonableness and the Unfair Contract Terms Act, 109 *LQR* 41; MacMillan, C. (2002) Evolution or revolution? Unfair terms in consumer contracts, *CLJ* 22.

! Don't be tempted to . . .

■ Panic that the facts are equivocal as to whether or not a term has been incorporated. The examiner is looking for analysis of your understanding of the law on the topic and logical conclusions drawn from that analysis. A tip is that without incorporation you have no need to discuss the legislation. It is unlikely that your examiner would miss the opportunity to challenge your knowledge on at least UCTA as well.

Question 7

Evaluate whether the common law and statutory protection afforded parties to contracts containing an exclusion clause have achieved the appropriate balance between control and the freedom of contract.

Answer plan

→ Consider the role of exclusion clauses in a contract.

→ Consider how the common law rules on incorporation and the *contra proferentem* rule provide an effective control mechanism on the use of all exclusion clauses.

→ Discuss the role of UCTA and the UTCCR in regulating exclusion clauses and explain the differing levels of protection afforded a consumer contract.

Diagram plan

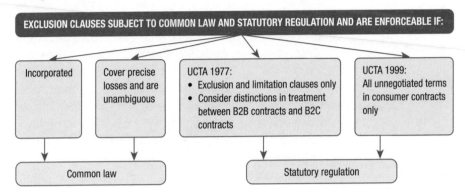

EXCLUSION CLAUSES SUBJECT TO COMMON LAW AND STATUTORY REGULATION AND ARE ENFORCEABLE IF:

| Incorporated | Cover precise losses and are unambiguous | UCTA 1977:
• Exclusion and limitation clauses only
• Consider distinctions in treatment between B2B contracts and B2C contracts | UCTA 1999:
All unnegotiated terms in consumer contracts only |

| Common law | Statutory regulation |

A printable version of this diagram plan is available from www.pearsoned.co.uk/lawexpressqa

Answer

[1] Immediately focusing on the question will gain marks.

[2] An identification of the rationale for the use of exclusion clauses is illustrative of a depth of understanding.

[3] The structure of your evaluation has been mapped out clearly whilst demonstrating an identification of the key issues.

Exclusion clauses reinforce the principle of freedom of contract and allow a party to determine the extent of potential liabilities.[1] This is good contractual planning and can encourage parties to take practical steps by way of reflecting the cost of the absorption of such a risk in the price paid, resources allocated to the avoidance of the perceived loss, and often insurance.[2] However, their use is of particular concern in consumer contracts where often terms are not negotiated and the business side of the transaction is much more powerful. An exclusion clause to be enforceable must be incorporated into a contract and cover the loss suffered. If an exclusion clause is validly incorporated and covers the precise loss covered, then it will be subject to the regulation of the Unfair Contracts Terms Act 1977, which from a business perspective can be more restrictive with regard to consumer contracts than commercial ones. Further protection is afforded to consumers only by the Unfair Terms in Consumer Contracts Regulations 1999.[3]

An exclusion clause is incorporated into a contract by giving reasonable notice at the time or before the contract is made (**Thornton v Shoe Lane Parking Ltd** [1971] 2 QB 163). Reasonable notice requires that the more unusual or onerous the term, the greater the steps required to bring it to the other party's attention (**Spurling v Bradshaw** [1956] 1 WLR 461). The courts have not required a higher standard when dealing with consumers on this point (*O'Brien v MGN Ltd* [2001] EWCA Civ 1279). Any document directing the contracting party to the exclusion clause must be of a type that a reasonable person would consider might contain such terms (*Chapelton v Barry UDC* [1940] 1 KB 532). The rules on incorporation look only to a limited extent at the substance of the clause to determine if sufficient attention was drawn to it. This reinforces the principle of the freedom of contract as the law is not concerned with the content if the other party had knowledge of its existence. Such a principle does not take account of the situation where one party cannot negotiate that term and presupposes an equality of bargaining power.[4]

[4] The question requires evaluation and you will gain marks for doing this.

A previous course of dealings is sufficient evidence of reasonable notice to incorporate an exclusion clause (*Spurling v Bradshaw* [1956] 2 All ER 121). The clause must have been brought to the attention of the other party in a consistent manner and would not appear to apply where the dealings have been on a few occasions over a substantial period of time (*Hollier v Rambler Motors (AMC) Ltd* [1972] 2 QB 71). Incorporation will also be effective if a written document is signed, even if not read (*L'Estrange v Graucob* [1934] 2 KB 394).

The common law rules on incorporation preserve the freedom of the parties to strike whatever bargain they choose. Provided the clause was brought to the attention of the other party it will be enforceable regardless of fairness or any inequality of bargaining power.[5] If an exclusion clause does not cover the breach complained of or is ambiguous the courts will interpret the clause against the person seeking to rely on it. This is the *contra proferentem* rule and applies to both consumer and commercial contracts. Prior to statutory regulation the common law used rules of interpretation somewhat artificially to limit the enforceability of some clauses (*Hollier v Rambler Motors (AMC) Ltd*). With statutory regulation now regulating the fairness of exclusion clauses, only where a term is ambiguous will the *contra proferentum* rule apply (*Internet Broadcasting Corporation v MAR LLC* [2009] 2 Lloyd's Rep 295).[6]

[5] This point keeps coming through as you are emphasising that the common law preserves the freedom of contract whereas the legislation deals with unfairness, creating the requisite balance.

[6] This builds to your consideration of the statutory regulation and the authority used shows your knowledge is up to date.

The common law does not effectively regulate the fairness of an exclusion clause. UCTA 1977 concerns the enforceability of all exclusion and limitation clauses in both business-to-consumer and business-to-business contracts. The Act differentiates between the two, providing greater protection to consumers in specified areas.[7]

[7] This paragraph adds emphasis to your argument and provides an introduction to your narrative on the statutory regulation.

UCTA 1977 renders all exclusion clauses void under section 2(1) for the purported exclusion of liability for death or personal injury caused by negligence. Other clauses will be enforceable only if they satisfy the section 11 test of reasonableness, for example section 2(2) for harm caused as a result of negligence short of death or personal injury. Both these provisions apply regardless of whether the transaction is between two commercial parties or where one is dealing as a consumer. Dealing as a consumer can include companies operating outside of their usual main business (*R & B Customs Brokers Co. Ltd v United Dominions Trust Ltd* [1988] 1 WLR 321).[8]

[8] A sound knowledge of the topic area is evident here.

The distinction is paramount in section 6 where terms implied by sections 13–15 of the Sales of Goods Act 1979 cannot be excluded when one party deals as a consumer, but is subject to the section 11 test of reasonableness when dealing business to business. This maintains the principle of freedom of contract to commercial parties to allocate such risk between them, but recognises that such transference would be inappropriate in a consumer context.[9]

[9] Good point: you are emphasising that in a commercial context a greater freedom of contract may be more appropriate.

Section 11 reasonableness refers to Schedule 2 to the Act which suggests issues for consideration in determining reasonableness, the first of which is an inequality of bargaining power.[10] This has been key particularly between a business's dealing with a consumer and two commercial parties (*Granville Oil & Chemicals Ltd v Davies Turner & Co. Ltd* [2003] 1 All ER (Comm) 819). The *Granville* case puts great emphasis on the freedom of commercial parties to determine their own terms. However, in *Britvic Soft Drinks Ltd v Messer UK Ltd* [2002] 1 Lloyd's Rep 20 the defendants could not enforce a term shifting the risk of a flaw in their own production process to the claimants. The case demonstrates that even where the parties are both of equal bargaining power and in a commercial context a substantively unfair clause will not be enforceable.[11]

[10] This reinforces your previous point.

[11] Focusing on the question shows the marker you can accurately apply your knowledge.

UTCCR 1999 applies to terms not individually negotiated in consumer contracts. The Regulations only apply to terms which have not been negotiated (*Bryen & Langley Ltd v Boston* [2005] EWCA Civ 973). Therefore the protection does not exist where the consumer has some freedom of contract in being able to negotiate beyond core

[12] You have fully developed the analysis here, so where the consumer has been able to negotiate he will still have some statutory protection.

terms, but the consumer would still have the protection of the common law and UCTA.[12]

Within the context of the statutory regulation and the common law the freedom of contract is still preserved. However, this is balanced by the law requiring that the other party have reasonable notice of the clause; it covers the loss specifically excluded; that it is not of a type which is automatically deemed to be unfair and in the circumstances of the case it is reasonable.[13]

[13] A summation of your arguments will gain marks.

 ## Make your answer stand out

- Read and assimilate Lord Denning's view of the 'idol' of the freedom of contract as regards the abuse of power in the use of exclusion clauses prior to the legislation in *George Mitchell (Chester Hall) Ltd* v *Finney Lock Seed Ltd* [1983] QB 284.

- L. Rutherford and S. Wilson in their article Signature of a document, (1998) 148 *NLJ* 380 consider the effect of UCTA on the rule of incorporation in *L'Estrange* v *Graucob* [1934] 2 KB 394, which could add depth to your analysis on this point.

- H. Beale, (2005) An unfairly complex law, 153 *NLJ* 318 considers whether UCTA goes far enough in affording protection to small businesses contracting with larger players in the market. This may provide an opportunity to add depth to your discussion on the comparison between the approaches in *Granville Oil & Chemicals Ltd* v *Davies Turner & Co. Ltd* [2003] 1 All ER (Comm) 819 and *Britvic Soft Drinks Ltd* v *Messer UK Ltd* [2002] 1 Lloyd's Rep 20.

- Consider analysing the complexity created by the overlapping provisions contained in UCTA and UTCCR. Beale (2005) considers whether reform is needed and if small businesses require similar protection to consumers.

! Don't be tempted to . . .

- Forget to focus your analysis on the question set: the balance the law has achieved in the regulation of exclusion clauses beyond just consumer protection.

- Be too descriptive: the question is open and directs you to move through the means by which exclusion clauses are controlled. The higher marks will be achieved by moving beyond the descriptive to the evaluative.

❓ Question 8

Lakeland Water Explorations Ltd have purchased a glass viewing porthole and fittings for the bottom of their boat, *The Happy Pike*, from Fenster Ltd. Lakeland Water Explorations Ltd will install the glass bottom themselves.

John the CEO of Lakeland Water Explorations Ltd placed the order for the porthole in person at Fenster Ltd's office. Fenster Ltd completed an order form which they gave to John, asking him to check the details of the contract. The order form had the following clause on the back:

> Fenster Ltd does not accept any liability for any defects in their products which are reported later than 10 days after delivery.

John did not read the print on the back of the form. He took notice only of the price, details of the item purchased and delivery date which were printed on the front. At the very bottom of the order form in bold red letters was written: 'Please see over for our standard terms and conditions'.

The porthole was delivered in February, as agreed, in plenty of time for installation and the commencement of the tourist season on 1 March.

On 10 March a latent defect in the glass porthole caused it to crack and let in water. *The Happy Pike* sank very slowly. The passengers were rescued by another boat. However, the boat remained out of commission for four weeks waiting for a replacement bottom.

Advise Fenster Ltd as to whether or not they will be able to rely on their exclusion clause to avoid any liability to Lakeland Water Exploration Ltd, who are claiming both the cost of the porthole replacement and the loss of profits.

Answer plan

→ The first issue to consider is if the exclusion clause is incorporated into the contract.

→ Discuss whether the term is particularly unusual or onerous and if so whether Lakeland Water Exploration Ltd had reasonable notice of the clause.

→ Establish that the clause does cover the loss that has occurred.

→ Consider the application of the Unfair Contract Terms Act 1977 and whether the exclusion clause satisfies section 11 reasonableness.

Diagram plan

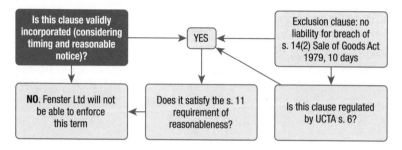

A printable version of this diagram plan is available from www.pearsoned.co.uk/lawexpressqa

Answer

Commercial parties often allocate risk and plan for potential liabilities through express terms including exclusion and limitation clauses. The law recognises that particularly commercial parties should be left to negotiate any bargain they think fit without interference (*Glanville Oil & Chemicals Ltd v Davies Turner & Co. Ltd* [2003] 1 All ER (Comm) 819). However, even between commercial parties bargaining power can be unequal and the common law regulates the use of exclusion clauses through rules on incorporation and construction. There is statutory regulation of exclusion clauses through the Unfair Contract Terms Act 1977, which will only permit certain terms to be enforced if capable of satisfying the requirement of reasonableness in section 11.[1]

[1] Clearly laying out the legal issues you are going to deal with in an introduction will help maintain a structure and logical flow to your work.

A contract between Lakeland Water Exploration Ltd and Fenster Ltd was agreed. The first issue to determine is whether the exclusion clause on the order form is incorporated into the contract. In order to be incorporated the other party must have reasonable notice of the term on or before the contract is made (*Olley v Marlborough Court* [1949] 1 All ER 127). The document was given to Lakeland Water Exploration Ltd at the time the contract was made and, as there was no signature to be bound by the exclusion clause, Fenster Ltd must have given reasonable notice of that term. If incorporated, Lakeland Water Explorations Ltd will be bound by the exclusion clause even if unread by John. An unsigned document will only form part of a contract if the nature of the document was the kind that you would expect to have such an effect (**Chapelton v Barry UDC** [1940] 1 KB 532). The test is an objective one: would a reasonable person have assumed that the document in question contained terms of the agreement? As this document had the core terms as to price, delivery and content included, the answer to that question has to be yes. It is normally sufficient notice where terms are prominently set out or referred to on the face of the document (**Thompson v LMS Railway** [1930] 1 KB 41). The exclusion clause here is on the back of the document but is referred to.[2] However, the more unusual or onerous the clause, the greater the steps that have to be taken to incorporate the term. It may not be sufficient just to hand them over. In **Interfoto Picture Library v Stiletto Visual Programmes Ltd** [1989] QB 433 a delivery note containing very onerous terms for the late return of photographs required the party relying on the terms to ensure the other party knew of it. In **J. Spurling v Bradshaw** [1956] 2 All ER 121 Lord Denning held that some clauses were so unusual or onerous that they would have to be printed in red ink with a red hand pointing at them. The reference to the terms being on the back of the document given to Lakeland Water Exploration Ltd was in red and the salesman at Fenster Ltd did ask John to check the details: this would probably be sufficient to incorporate the exclusion clause.[3]

Once incorporation is established, in order for the exclusion clause to be relied on it must cover the breach that has occurred. Here the porthole would appear not to be of satisfactory quality or fit for purpose under section 14(2) of the Sale of Goods Act 1979. Fenster Ltd is purporting to exclude its liability for this after 10 days.

Fenster Ltd's exclusion clause will be subject to the Unfair Contract Terms Act 1977. As both Lakeland Water Exploration Ltd and Fenster Ltd are operating business to business, the purported exclusion of liability under section 14(2) of the Sales of Goods Act 1979 will be under section 6 of UCTA, enforceable if found to satisfy the requirement of reasonableness under section 11.[4]

Section 11(2) refers to Sched. 2 of UCTA and puts forward issues which the courts may take into consideration in determining if an exclusion clause is reasonable for the purposes of section 6, including an inequality of bargaining power, or an inducement to accept the term, knowledge of the term, whether the goods were adapted or

[2] A good logical flow to the analysis using the facts of the problem to build in depth demonstrates a deeper level of understanding.

[3] If you found the clause not to be incorporated, the answer would end here; it is unlikely your examiner will miss the opportunity to test you on UCTA.

[4] If Lakeland Water Exploration Ltd had been dealing as a consumer, then the term would be unenforceable under section 6.

made to special order, or the clause only came into operation because another condition was not fulfilled.[5]

[5] Remember this is not a finite list but the courts do tend to justify their findings of reasonableness by reference to it.

There is nothing to suggest an inequality of bargaining power between Lakeland Water Exploration Ltd and Fenster Ltd. Recent case law suggests that where the two businesses concerned are of equal bargaining power the courts should be reluctant to interfere (*Watford Electronics Ltd v Sanderson CFL Ltd* [2001] EWCA Civ 317). However, in *Britvic Soft Drinks Ltd v Messer UK Ltd* [2002] 2 All ER 321 these two parties were of equal bargaining power. In this case the carbon dioxide supplied for the claimants' business had too much benzene present. This was not a health risk but the claimants removed the contaminated drinks stock to maintain consumer confidence in their products. Britvic sought to rely on section 14(2) of the Sale of Goods Act 1979. Messer argued that their exclusion clause was enforceable under section 6 of UCTA 1977 and satisfied the requirements of reasonableness. The court found the exclusion clause to be unreasonable, as at the time of making the contract the parties would not have expected the buyer to carry the risk of a flawed manufacturing process.[6] Fenster Ltd's exclusion clause would put the risk of the glass porthole being manufactured to a satisfactory quality on to Lakeland Water Exploration Ltd and, as such, will not be reasonable.

[6] The analysis here is therefore going against the courts' current trend for a non-interventionist approach.

In *R.W. Green Ltd v Cade Bros Farm* [1978] 1 Lloyd's Rep 602 the requirement to give notice of defects within three days of delivery was found to be an unreasonable exclusion clause, as although it might be reasonable as to obvious defects this would not be the case in relation to a hidden defect. The glass porthole had a latent defect and also Fenster Ltd would be aware of the seasonal operation of the boats, the time required for installation, and that any defects would not be apparent until the boat was in the water. These facts were known to both parties at the time the contract was made, and therefore the time to report the defects is unlikely to be viewed as reasonable.[7]

[7] The paragraph above dealt with the unreasonableness of the clause as regards excluding section 14(2) in these circumstances; this paragraph also attacks the clause's reasonableness as being too short a time limit for latent defects.

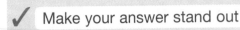

✓ Make your answer stand out

- Consider arguing that Fenster Ltd's clause is a limitation rather than an exemption clause.

- The courts tend to apply the *contra proferentem* rule less rigorously to limitation clauses than exemption clauses (*Ailsa Craig Fishing Co. Ltd* v *Malvern Fishing Co. Ltd* [1983] 1 WLR 964 *and Photo Production Ltd* v *Securicor Transport Ltd*) [1980] AC 827.

- It could be argued that rather than trying to exclude liability Fenster Ltd are merely trying to limit that liability to 10 days.

- This is not unusual and the courts are not averse to commercial parties putting a final limitation on their liability (*Whitecap Leisure Ltd* v *John H. Rundle Ltd* [2008] All ER (D) 383 (Apr)). However, following the decision in *R.W. Green Ltd* v *Cade Bros Farm* it is unlikely to be a successful argument even if accepted; as a limitation clause, the reasoning concerning its unreasonableness would be the same.

 Don't be tempted to . . .

- Miss out on marks by failing to develop your analysis fully; for instance, correctly recognising the pertinent sections of UCTA would be correct application and will get you an average pass grade. However, being able to move beyond that in recognising the current trend to let business-to-business transactions define their own limits of liability, and further to where the allocation of risk as to flawed manufacture is unreasonable, will take you into the much higher grades.

www.pearsoned.co.uk/lawexpressqa

Go online to access more revision support including additional essay and problem questions with diagram plans, You be the marker questions, and download all diagrams from the book.

Misrepresentation

How this topic may come up in exams

Misrepresentation questions will require you to identify whether a statement made is potentially actionable, the type of misrepresentation involved and the remedies available. The structure is formulaic but the topic throws up current issues surrounding statements as to law, exaggerated pre-contractual promises and the duty of disclosure. Examiners are keen that students can deal with the complexities of the differences in the types of misrepresentation and which might be most appropriate to a given situation. Watch out for the detailed points on exclusion clauses and the effect of having the opportunity to verify the truth of a statement.

Attack the question

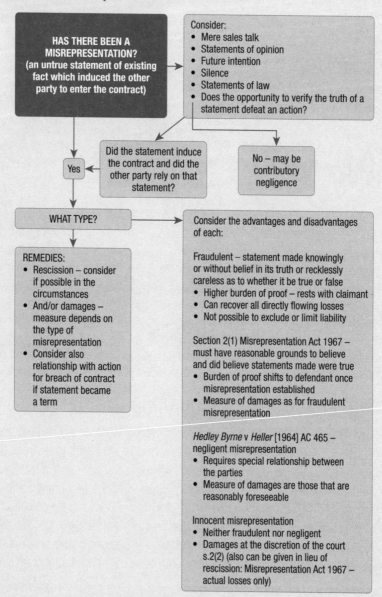

HAS THERE BEEN A MISREPRESENTATION?
(an untrue statement of existing fact which induced the other party to enter the contract)

Consider:
- Mere sales talk
- Statements of opinion
- Future intention
- Silence
- Statements of law
- Does the opportunity to verify the truth of a statement defeat an action?

Yes

Did the statement induce the contract and did the other party rely on that statement?

No – may be contributory negligence

WHAT TYPE?

Consider the advantages and disadvantages of each:

Fraudulent – statement made knowingly or without belief in its truth or recklessly careless as to whether it be true or false
- Higher burden of proof – rests with claimant
- Can recover all directly flowing losses
- Not possible to exclude or limit liability

Section 2(1) Misrepresentation Act 1967 – must have reasonable grounds to believe and did believe statements made were true
- Burden of proof shifts to defendant once misrepresentation established
- Measure of damages as for fraudulent misrepresentation

Hedley Byrne v *Heller* [1964] AC 465 – negligent misrepresentation
- Requires special relationship between the parties
- Measure of damages are those that are reasonably foreseeable

Innocent misrepresentation
- Neither fraudulent nor negligent
- Damages at the discretion of the court s.2(2) (also can be given in lieu of rescission: Misrepresentation Act 1967 – actual losses only)

REMEDIES:
- Rescission – consider if possible in the circumstances
- And/or damages – measure depends on the type of misrepresentation
- Consider also relationship with action for breach of contract if statement became a term

A printable version of this diagram is available from www.pearsoned.co.uk/lawexpressqa

❓ Question 1

Lillabeth places the following advertisement in the local paper:

> For Sale: Artists' Refuge Café, turnover of £100,000 p.a. Includes resident artists' rented work spaces. The café is situated in the picturesque hamlet of Little Butte, on the main tourist route between Stonehenge and the historic city of Bath.

Rufus is interested in purchasing the café. He is not interested in the rental income from the artists as he will use this space for additional seating, but does want to continue selling their work.

Rufus visits the premises. The café is crowded with tourists but the outside space is empty. He asks Lillabeth how much of the £100,000 turnover is down to the café business, the art sales, and rentals. Lillabeth tells him that £65,000 of the income is derived from the café sales, £30,000 from art sales and £5,000 from rentals. Lillabeth invites Rufus to see her account books which are stored in an outhouse. He goes with Lillabeth but decides he will take her word for it as the books are covered in mouse droppings and the outhouse is very dirty.

Lillabeth has not told Rufus that 'her artists' have all now hired space in the local village hall. They still buy food and drink from Lillabeth and supply her with their work.

Between seeing the café and signing the contract the planned bypass has been built around Little Butte. This has caused a substantial fall in the amount of passing trade. Rufus also finds out that the total turnover of the business had never been more than £50,000.

Advise Rufus if he has any potential claim against Lillabeth on the grounds of misrepresentation.

Answer plan

→ Define misrepresentation.

→ Identify which statements are of existing fact (the turnover), which are half-truths, or potential change of circumstance (the bypass and rented space outside).

→ Consider if the misrepresentations identified above induced Rufus to enter the contract, and if having the opportunity to verify the truth of the statement as to the turnover but choosing not do so will affect any potential action brought.

→ Decide which type of misrepresentation is the most appropriate and the possible remedies, in this instance section 2(1) Misrepresentation Act 1967.

Diagram plan

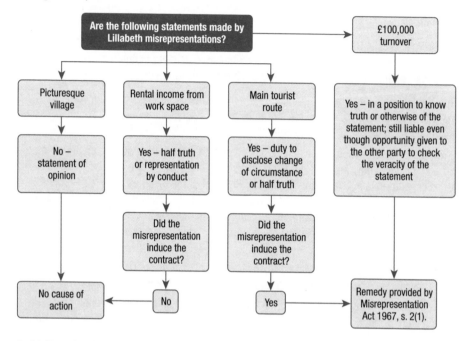

A printable version of this diagram plan is available from www.pearsoned.co.uk/lawexpressqa

Answer

A misrepresentation is a false statement of existing fact which induces the other party to enter into a contract. As such, Lillabeth in inducing Rufus to enter a contract for the purchase of her café has made several representations which later turn out to be untrue and may be actionable on the grounds of misrepresentation, even though they do not become terms of the contract per se. Potentially, if Rufus can establish misrepresentation, he may be able to rescind the contract with Lillabeth and/or claim damages for his losses.[1]

[1] Establishing the structure of your answer with immediate application to the problem set demonstrates to a marker immediately that you understand the core issues.

A misrepresentation is a false statement of existing fact and not merely a statement of opinion or just sales talk. The description of the hamlet as 'picturesque' could be a 'mere puff' (***Dimmock* v *Hallett*** (1866) LR 2 Ch App 21). A statement of opinion, where the maker of the statement is in no better position to know the truth or otherwise of the statement than the recipient, is also not actionable

[2] Misrepresentation problem questions often require students to establish why something will not be actionable as well as why a statement could result in liability. There is a good build of the principles involved here, demonstrating an in-depth knowledge of the issues and case law.

(*Bisset* v *Wilkinson* [1927] AC 177).[2] However, if the maker of a statement knows that the opinion proffered is untrue or is in a better position to know the truth, as they have some specialist skill or knowledge, then an action in misrepresentation will be possible (*Esso Petroleum Co. Ltd* v *Mardon* [1976] 2 All ER 5). In *Smith* v *Land & House Property Corporation* (1884) 28 Ch D 7 the description of the tenant of a property as a 'most desirable tenant' amounted to a misrepresentation, as the maker of the statement knew the tenant to be in arrears. Similarly, here, Lillabeth is in a position to know the true turnover of her business. This she mis-represents twice, once in the newspaper advertisement and then again orally when showing Rufus around. The fact that she offered Rufus the opportunity to verify her statement will not protect her from an action in misrepresentation (*Redgrave* v *Hurd* (1881) 20 Ch D 1). The failure to take such an opportunity could, however, be consid-ered contributory negligence and result in a reduction in damages if the representee could be seen to be at fault (*Gran Gelato Ltd* v *Richcliff (Group) Ltd* [1992] Ch 560). This is unlikely here as the opportunity to look at the books was in an unpleasant environment and Rufus's caution justified.[3]

[3] Depth of analysis gains marks. Here an above average mark would be given for recognising that not taking an opportunity to check the veracity of a statement will not defeat an action, but the highest grade will be achieved by going one step further in articulating a potential consequence of not doing so.

Silence will not usually amount to a misrepresentation. An exception to this is where the statement in itself appears to be true but what is not said may amount to a misrepresentation. In *Dimmock* v *Hallett* the statement that the farms were tenanted was true but the vendor failed to mention that the tenants were about to leave. Omitting this information so altered the situation that it amounted to a misrepre-sentation. Lillabeth not mentioning that her rented spaces were no longer used may be liable for this half-truth. In *Spice Girls Ltd* v *Aprilia World Service* [2002] EWCA Civ 15, by presenting a pop group for a photo shoot session a representation was made that the band was to remain together during the currency of the promotion, or certainly a split was not in their contemplation. In actual fact the band already had the intention of splitting up at that time.[4] The out-side space was shown to Rufus and the presumption would be that it was still used for rental income. Additionally, when asked about the proportions of income, Lillabeth does not mention that the situation has changed.

[4] Two cases are used here, showing an extensive knowledge of case law, but the *Spice Girls* case on its own develops the key point that silence of itself is not normally a misrepresentation, but that partial disclosure or statements made by conduct can be actionable.

There is no overriding general duty to disclose information in UK contract law unless a special duty exists, as for example in insurance contracts. An exception to this rule exists where a statement was true when made but subsequently owing to a change of circumstance has become false. If the maker of the statement does not inform the other party of the change of circumstance, then there may be grounds for an action in misrepresentation (**With v O'Flanagan** [1936] Ch 575). Presuming Lillabeth did not know of the bypass at the time she made the representation of the café being situated 'on the main tourist route', she has a positive obligation to tell Rufus of the change and the impact on the business. If Lillabeth did know of the proposed bypass at the time she made the representation, she would still potentially be liable for the misrepresentation in only revealing part of the circumstances, a so-called half-truth (**Dimmock v Hallett**).[5]

[5] There is good linkage to the previous analysis in the paragraph before as to partial disclosure, but it also gives the opportunity to discuss potential liabilities in the event of a change of circumstances. In doing this a solid understanding of the topic area is evident and shows an ability to deal with more than one potential line of argument.

Rufus will need to establish that Lillabeth's misrepresentations induced the contract. The misrepresentation does not have to be the sole reason why the representee entered the contract but it must be 'an' inducement (**Edgington v Fitzmaurice** (1885) 29 Ch D 459). As Rufus had no interest in the rental space, that misrepresentation would not be actionable. The statements as to the turnover of the business and the silence as to the bypass would be misrepresentations, as they would induce a reasonable person to enter the contract (**Downs v Chappell** [1996] 3 All ER 344).[6]

[6] The statement must induce the contract; the test you articulate is the modern interpretation of the arguments surrounding materiality.

Rufus will be able to rely on section 2(1) of the Misrepresentation Act 1967 to provide him with a remedy for Lillabeth's misrepresentations. The immediate advantages of relying on this as a cause of action are: the burden of proof is less than for an action in fraudulent misrepresentation; there is no need to establish the existence of a special relationship required under **Hedley Byrne & Co. Ltd v Heller & Partners** [1964] AC 465; the burden of proof once misrepresentation is established shifts to the defendant, Lillabeth, to show that she had reasonable grounds to believe and did believe up until the contract was made that her statements were true; the remedies available are comparable to other types of misrepresentation. Rescission is available and the contract for the sale of the café can be set aside unless Rufus decides to affirm the contract, innocent third party rights will be affected or there has been a lapse of time. The damages available under section 2(1) satisfy reliance rather than expectation interest but are the same measure as available under the tort of deceit (**Royscot Trust Ltd v Rogerson**

[7] This paragraph shows knowledge of the remedy provided by the Misrepresentation Act 1967, but also provides an in-depth analysis as to the advantages the Act provides to Rufus, and as a consequence marks will be gained for knowing the potential alternatives.

[1991] 2 QB 297) and therefore potentially as generous as a claim under any other form of misrepresentation.[7]

[8] Concluding with directed advice to the subject of the question demonstrates clarity of understanding and knowledge.

Rufus has a claim for misrepresentation against Lillabeth for the statements regarding the business turnover and location. The Misrepresentation Act 1967 provides a procedural advantage once the misrepresentation is established and, as the innocent party, the choice of whether to affirm or rescind the contract, with a measure of damages equal to that of an action in the tort of deceit.[8]

 Make your answer stand out

- Consider expanding your analysis of what amounts to a material inducement and how this test has developed in recent years, being applied in cases such as *County NatWest* v *Barton* [2002] 4 All ER 494.

! Don't be tempted to . . .

- Miss the opportunity to gain higher marks by discussing why something is or is not a misrepresentation.
- Stop your analysis before you have fully discussed all the possible lines of argument.
- Miss the plenty of opportunities the question gave you to develop depth in your answer: for example, the consequences of not checking the truth of a statement made when given the opportunity to do so.

Question 2

Evaluate how section 2(1) of the Misrepresentation Act 1967 provides a potentially superior remedy for parties induced into a contract by a misrepresentation, whether that representation becomes a term of the contract or not, and even if that misrepresentation is a statement of law.

Answer plan

→ Discuss recent case law and liability for misrepresentations and statements of law and the requirement that the statement induced the contract.

→ Define section 2(1) of the Misrepresentation Act 1967 and its procedural advantages.

→ Evaluate remedies available in relation to other types of misrepresentation.

→ Compare the potential remedies for any breach of contract if the statements made became a term of the contract and not just an inducement.

Diagram plan

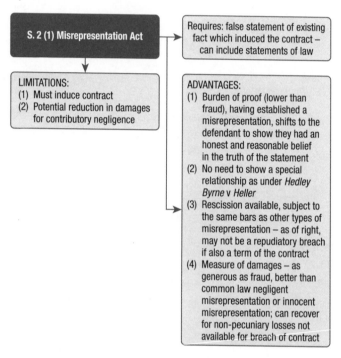

A printable version of this diagram plan is available from www.pearsoned.co.uk/lawexpressqa

Answer

[1] The accurate use of technical language will enhance any answer.

All actionable misrepresentations render a contract voidable.[1] Any claimant must initially prove that the statement complained of was a false statement of existing fact which induced the contract. Recent judicial decisions have confirmed that statements of law can be misrepresentations, but may amount to no more than statements of opinion which may not be actionable. Section 2(1) of the Misrepresentation Act 1967 has provided procedural advantages as well as the most generous measure of damages in comparison to other types of misrepresentation.

[2] Introducing the concept of statements of opinion not being actionable will build depth into your final analysis on this point.

[3] This point is specifically raised in the question; directing your analysis to relevant issues gains marks.

[4] This demonstrates a currency of knowledge and the ability to reconcile this decision with the long-established principles concerning statements of opinion.

[5] Higher grades are achieved by candidates who develop their arguments fully. It is impressive to identify the potential direction that the law may take.

[6] The question hints at the need to discuss inducement, but it is important to emphasise that only misrepresentations leading to a contract will incur potential liability under section 2(1).

[7] This demonstrates that you understand not only why an action under section 2(1) would be preferable but also the actual test required for fraudulent misrepresentation.

Any claim for misrepresentation must first establish that the statement made was a false statement of existing fact which induced the contract, not mere opinion[2] (*Bisset* v *Wilkinson* [1927] AC 177). Until the decision in **Kleinwort Benson Ltd** v **Lincoln City Council** [1999] 2 AC 349 it was understood that a statement of law could not be actionable as a misrepresentation.[3] In the **Kleinwort Benson** case it was held that distinguishing between payments made under mistakes in law and mistakes in fact would no longer be made. The natural repercussion of this would be that such a distinction should also not exist with regard to misrepresentations. This was confirmed in the case of **Pankhania** v **Hackney London Borough Council** [2002] EWHC 2441 (Ch). The contract was induced in the belief that the tenant was a contractual licensee rather than a business tenant. This legal distinction made obtaining vacant possession of the premises much more costly and difficult. The distinction between statements in law and fact, therefore, will not defeat an action in misrepresentation if the maker of the statement had specialist knowledge or was in a better position than the other party to know the truth or otherwise of the statement.[4] The courts have not yet had to consider the situation where the maker of the statement did not have specialist knowledge or was not in a position to know the truth or otherwise of the statement of law. Arguably such a statement may amount to no more than a statement of opinion and is not actionable.[5]

For section 2(1) to be applicable the statement must have induced the contract.[6] It does not have to be the only reason that the contract was made but it must be 'a' reason (*Edgington* v *Fitzmaurice* (1885) 29 Ch D 459). The misrepresentation must be important enough that it would have influenced a reasonable person to have entered the contract (*JEB Fastners Ltd* v *Marks Bloom & Co.* [1983] 1 All ER 583). The test therefore appears to be objective but it must also be shown that the person to whom the statement was made did actually rely on that misrepresentation (*Attwood* v *Small* (1838) 6 Cl & Fin 232). This introduces a subjective element into the concept of inducement.

There are four potential types of misrepresentation. Fraudulent misrepresentation requires the claimant to prove that the maker of the statement knew it was false or had no belief in the truth of the statement or was recklessly careless as to its truth (*Derry* v *Peek* (1889) 14 App Cas 337).[7] This is a high burden of proof for the claimant.

5 MISREPRESENTATION

Negligent misrepresentation under the common law was established in the case of **Hedley Byrne & Co. Ltd v Heller & Partners** [1964] AC 465. This widened the potential claims to statements that were negligently made, but the claimant has to establish that a special relationship and a duty of care exists between the parties (**Caparo Industries plc v Dickman** [1990] 1 All ER 568), or that the defendant had voluntarily assumed responsibility for the veracity of the statement (**Spring v Guardian Assurance plc** [1995] 2 AC 296).[8] Under section 2(1) of the Misrepresentation Act 1967 the claimant merely has to establish that there has been a misrepresentation: there is no need to prove a special relationship, merely that it led to the formation of a contract. It is for the defendant to show that they had reasonable grounds to believe and did believe up to the time the contract was made that facts represented were true.[9] As such, under section 2(1) the burden of proof shifts to the maker of the statement. If an action should fail because the defendant had reasonable grounds to believe and did believe the statement made to be true, then a claimant can still claim innocent misrepresentation (**Thomas Witter Ltd v TBP Industries Ltd** [1996] 2 All ER 573).

An innocent misrepresentation is neither fraudulent nor negligent, the remedy for which is usually rescission and an indemnity representative of costs incurred in performance only.

All four types of misrepresentation provide the remedy of rescission, although with innocent misrepresentation the court can use its discretion to give damages in lieu of this right under section 2(2) of the Misrepresentation Act 1967. Apart from section 2(2), the rights to rescission are limited in the same way regardless of the type of misrepresentation being claimed – that is, by affirmation, lapse of time or where it is impossible to restore the parties to their pre-contractual position: for example, because the goods have been consumed or third party rights have been acquired.[10]

If a misrepresentation has become a term of the contract, a claim for breach of contract is possible. The status of the term will determine whether the breach is a repudiatory one or not. By contrast, the right to rescission puts no emphasis on the importance of the pre-contractual statement and section 1(a) of the 1967 Act provides that the remedy of rescission is available in spite of the fact that the representation has become a term of the contract per se.[11]

[8] Depth of knowledge and understanding is shown here as you identify the current debates surrounding the basis of liability for negligent misrepresentation at common law.

[9] Emphasis is given here to the procedural advantage of the burden of proof being shifted, while articulating the defence needed to escape liability.

[10] This has made good use of an opportunity to demonstrate the breadth of knowledge by briefly outlining the bars to rescission.

[11] The question was tricky as it demanded detailed knowledge on specific points of law; this has been done well here in dealing with the potential advantage of an action in misrepresentation as opposed to an action for breach of contract.

Section 2(1) refers to liability in damages to be as if the misrepresentation had been made fraudulently. This was confirmed in **Royscott Trust Ltd v Rogerson** [1991] 2 QB 297, which will allow damages to be recovered for all consequential losses as for the tort of deceit. This principle has been referred to as the 'fiction of fraud'. The measure is more generous than that for a claim under the common law for negligent misrepresentation, which will only allow for the recovery of foreseeable losses, and innocent misrepresentation, which has no right to damages but where awarded in lieu of rescission will be only actual losses. Potentially, the measure is also more generous than an action for breach of contract, which does not allow for the recovery of non-pecuniary losses.[12]

[12] The analysis here picks up the greatest advantage to an action under section 2(1) – the amount that potentially can be recovered.

Section 2(1) provides procedural and remedial advantages to other types of misrepresentation or an action for breach of contract. However, it only applies where the representation induced a contract. Where there is no resulting contract another type of misrepresentation must be relied upon.

✓ Make your answer stand out

- Consider that an action for misrepresentation will not be available if the misrepresentation is a term of the contract but was not made prior to the contract being entered into: in other words, it did not induce the contract (*Leofolis SA v Lonsdale Sports Ltd* [2008] All ER (D) 87 (Jul)). Using such up-to-date authorities demonstrates your currency of knowledge and breadth of reading.

- Add a minor disadvantage and give your analysis greater depth: the use of section 2(1) raised in *Gran Gelato Ltd v Richcliff (Group) Ltd* [1992] 1 All ER 865 the issue that damages can potentially be reduced under section 2(1) for contributory negligence which cannot be done for fraud.

! Don't be tempted to . . .

- Miss the focus of the question; it specifically directs you to a discussion on statements of law and statements that become terms of the contract as well as the advantages of an action under section 2(1).

❓ Question 3

Promoting a new Italian cooking course, La Bella Toscana Ltd, describes the course as 'Promising to be the best Italian cooking course in the UK'. It also says 'This intensive weekend takes place in the comfort of top quality hotel spa accommodation' and 'is suited to all levels including current professional chefs'. It also mentions that La Bella Toscana Ltd is planning to run courses for national franchised chains headed up by three well-known celebrity chefs. Potential applicants are invited to check out the hotel's website as the brochure purports to accept no liability for the standard of accommodation in which their courses take place.

Elena, who runs a small Italian deli/café, reads the brochure and signs up to the £2,000 fee. She hopes to expand her repertoire of dishes and is also looking forward to some down time from her business. She is so busy before her planned trip that she does not check the hotel's website, which shows it has only got a one star rating.

From the first day of the course Elena realises that the level of tuition is aimed at beginners. In addition the hotel is cold and noisy. The kitchens are old fashioned and ill-equipped for a professional chef. There are no spa facilities. One of the instructors tells her that 'All that stuff about training chefs for well-known franchises is a load of rubbish'.

Elena is upset as she has learnt nothing and had to stay at a second rate hotel. In addition, during the weekend that she was at the course, she did not work and so lost £500 profit.

Advise Elena whether there has been a misrepresentation and what remedies she will be entitled to if she sues La Bella Toscana Ltd successfully.

Answer plan

→ Identify why the standard of the accommodation, level of tuition, and future delivery of courses may amount to misrepresentation.

→ Consider the enforceability of the exclusion clause.

→ Discuss what amounts to inducement.

→ Consider the effect of the opportunity to verify the truth of a statement made.

→ Identify a cause of action and the remedies available.

Diagram plan

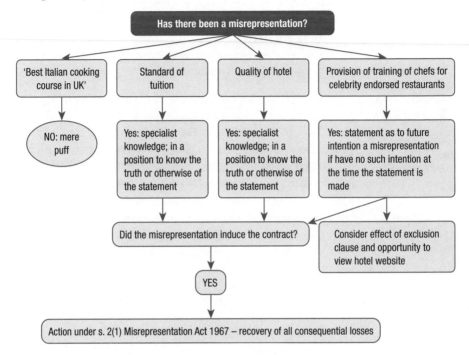

A printable version of this diagram plan is available from www.pearsoned.co.uk/lawexpressqa

Answer

To bring an action for misrepresentation against La Bella Toscana Ltd, Elena will have to establish under the common law that there had been an unambiguous false statement of existing fact which induced her to enter the contract.[1] Once it is established that a misrepresentation has been made Elena will be looking for a potential remedy under the Misrepresentation Act 1967.

A 'mere puff' (***Dimmock v Hallett*** (1866) LR 2 Ch App 21) or statement of opinion does not amount to a misrepresentation (***Bissett v Wilkinson*** [1927] AC 177). As such, describing a course as being the 'best Italian cooking course in the UK' will not be grounds for a cause of action in misrepresentation.[2] However, La Bella Toscana Ltd would be in position to know of the standard of the tuition offered (***Smith v Land & House Property Corp.*** (1884) 28 Ch D 7) and

[1] Excellent definition directly applied to the question maintaining the succinctness required for a strong introduction.

[2] The question included the phrase, obviously intending the student to explain why such a claim would not be a misrepresentation.

127

indeed have the specialist knowledge and skills to know if that tuition is suitable for clients such as Elena and whether the kitchen is adequate for the running of such a course (**Esso Petroleum Co. Ltd v Mardon** [1976] 2 All ER 5). The course advertised as being suitable for 'current professional chefs' is a misrepresentation of existing fact which induced Elena's contract.[3]

[3] This question has a tricky structure so good planning to allow you to build your analysis in this way.

The brochure describes the course as being held in 'top quality hotel spa accommodation': although 'top quality' can appear to be a mere statement of opinion,[4] on reflection in having a one star rating it is unlikely that anyone would describe such a hotel as 'top quality'. As the providers of the course La Bella Toscana Ltd would be expected to be in a position to know the truth or otherwise of the statement made (**Smith v Land & House Property Corp.**). Moreover, it would be expected that the providers of the course would have specialist knowledge of the venue chosen (**Esso Petroleum Co. Ltd v Mardon**). Even if the description 'top quality' could be considered a 'mere puff', having spa facilities could not.[5]

[4] Good, referring back to the first point made that a statement of opinion per se is not a misrepresentation.

[5] Good application, as is applying the same principles outlined in the previous point but in a more subtle context.

By the use of an exclusion clause La Bella Toscana Ltd purport to exclude liability for any misrepresentations made as regards the accommodation and venue of the course.[6] Section 3 of the Misrepresentation Act 1967 as amended by section 8 of the Unfair Contract Terms Act 1977 permits the exclusion or limitation of liability for misrepresentations made if the term satisfies the test of reasonableness under section 11. The courts are not overly sympathetic to the exclusion or limitation of liability for statements made which have induced the contract (**HIH Casualty and General Insurance Ltd v Chase Manhattan Bank** [2003] 2 Lloyd's Rep 61). Although it was not the only reason Elena entered the contract, the statement made as to the spa facilities was 'an' inducement (**Edgington v Fitzmaurice** (1885) 29 Ch D 459). **JEB Fastners Ltd v Marks Bloom & Co.** [1983] 1 All ER 583 articulates the objective element[7] of determining whether the innocent party was induced by the statement made and that is to ask if the statement would be considered important enough to influence a reasonable person to enter the contract. If that is the case then it is for the representee, here La Bella Toscana Ltd, to demonstrate that Elena was not actually induced into the contract by the promise of top quality hotel spa facilities.[8] This is unlikely to be the case.

[6] Good identification of the issue.

[7] Excellent analysis, succinctly done but demonstrating an ability to explore fully the issue of inducement in the context of the added complication of an exclusion clause.

[8] You pick this point up below using *Museprime* as your authority. A well-structured answer will gain marks.

La Bella Toscana Ltd may further argue that Elena was invited to check the truth of the statement as to the quality of the hotel and spa facilities, and as such should be prevented from bringing a claim in misrepresentation.[9] The case of **Redgrave v Hurd** (1881) 20 Ch D 1 provides that simply having an opportunity to check the truth of a statement will not prevent a claimant bringing an action based on that misrepresentation.

[9] Only the best candidates would have picked this up.

A statement as to future intention cannot be a misrepresentation unless the person making the statement has no such intention at the time the statement is made (**Spice Girls Ltd v Aprilia World Service** [2002] EWCA Civ 15).[10] The statement as to the course being used for the training of chefs for chains of celebrity-endorsed restaurants is untrue at the time it was made in the brochure and therefore is an actionable misrepresentation provided that it was an inducement to Elena to enter the contract. Knowing that you are being trained by the same institution as well-known restaurants would be an incentive to take the course as well as potentially adding credibility to her business. It would be for La Bella Toscana Ltd to show that even if a reasonable person would have been induced by such a claim[11] Elena was not so induced (**Museprime Properties Ltd v Adhill Properties Ltd** (1991) 61 P & CR 111).

[10] Often *Edgington v Fitzmaurice* is used here: good to show knowledge of alternative authority making the same point.

[11] Again, point made earlier but reinforced by supporting authority.

Under section 2(1) of the Misrepresentation Act 1967 the damages awarded for negligent misstatement would be the same as if an action in the tort of deceit were taken (**Royscott Trust Ltd v Rogerson** [1991] 3 All ER 294). This means that Elena will be able to recover all consequential losses, including her loss of profits. Additionally, under the Act once the misrepresentation has been established it is for the other party, here La Bella Toscana Ltd, to demonstrate that they had an honest belief in the statements made and reasonable grounds for holding such a belief. By contrast, if Elena were to bring an action for fraudulent misrepresentation the burden of proof would remain with her. However, if the exclusion clause were found to be enforceable if would have no application in an action for fraudulent misrepresentation. Under the Misrepresentation Act 1967 there is no need to prove the existence of a special relationship, as there is with an action under **Hedley Byrne & Co v Heller & Partners** [1963] 2 All ER 575.[12]

[12] Succinctly put as you have added depth to your analysis demonstrating why using section 2(1) would be advantageous to Elena.

Having established that there has been a misrepresentation as to the facilities of the hotel, the standard of the tuition on the course and

Excellent conclusion drawing all the application together.

potential future applicants, and that those statements induced the contract, it would appear that Elena's best cause of action would lie under the Misrepresentation Act 1967.[13]

✓ **Make your answer stand out**

- Demonstrate your up-to-date knowledge: the case of *Raiffeisen Zentralbank Osterrich AG* v *Royal Bank of Scotland* [2011] 1 Lloyd's Rep 123 reinforces the principle that where personal knowledge or skill has been relied upon and has induced the contract purporting to exclude liability for such statements will be difficult to enforce.

- Consider if in not taking the opportunity to check the truth of the statements as to the standard of the hotel Elena may have her damages reduced for contributory negligence, *Gran Gelato Ltd* v *Richcliff (Group) Ltd* [1992] Ch 560.

- Build depth by establishing that an action for fraudulent misrepresentation will preclude reliance on a term of the contract: *BskyB Ltd* v *HP Enterprise Services UK* [2010] All ER (D) 05 (Jul).

- Read Hooley, R. (1991) Damages and the Misrepresentation Act 1967, 107 *LQR* 547 to enhance your understanding of damages awarded under section 2(1).

❗ **Don't be tempted to . . .**

- Write your answer before carefully considering the issue raised; the question of the standard of the accommodation raised here is tricky.

- Forget to give the rationale for relying on the Misrepresentation Act 1967.

 Question 4

Consider the extent to which silence can amount to a misrepresentation and situations in which a positive duty of disclosure of pertinent facts exists.

Answer plan

→ Examine the general rule that silence of itself is not a misrepresentation.

→ Evaluate the exceptions to this rule and when a positive duty of disclosure exists in relation to a change in circumstances, conduct and half-truths.

→ If the change of circumstance, conduct or half-truth has induced the contract, examine why the Misrepresentation Act 1967 may provide the best cause of action.

→ Consider the positive obligation of disclosure in insurance contracts and fiduciary relationships.

Diagram plan

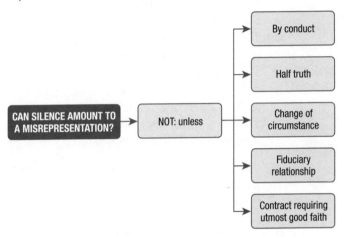

A printable version of this diagram plan is available from www.pearsoned.co.uk/lawexpressqa

Answer

A misrepresentation is an unambiguous false statement of existing fact which induces the party misled to enter a contract. Conduct is capable of amounting to a misrepresentation: however, whether silence is a misrepresentation can depend on the limited circumstances in UK law where disclosure is a positive obligation.[1] The effect of a misrepresentation is to render a contract voidable which gives the innocent party the option to rescind the contract. Rescission is available for all types of misrepresentation, but this right can be lost if too much time has lapsed, third parties have acquired rights, or restitution is impossible. Damages are also available in lieu of or in addition to rescission. The measure of damages depends on the type of misrepresentation claimed.

The law of misrepresentation recognises that in contractual negotiations each party will emphasise the positives in the bargain they are

[1] Identifying the core issue raised by the question in the introduction will put your marker in a positive frame of mind as they begin to assess your work.

[2] This shows understanding of the commercial tension that exists which the law must balance.

[3] Simply and clearly put and is built on in the following exceptions to the rule.

[4] Drawing on the issue that the general rule is that silence is not a misrepresentation: when does a positive obligation of disclosure exist?

[5] Another exception building a logical flow to the analysis, demonstrating the ability to structure a complex argument.

[6] This point relates back to the balance the law needs to achieve.

proposing while remaining silent about any weaknesses.[2] English law does not require, as a general rule, a party to disclose information which might hamper their deal (*Fletcher v Krell* (1872) 42 LJQB 55). This follows the traditional Latin maxim of caveat emptor, whereby it is the responsibility of the purchaser to ask apposite questions. As such, silence of itself is not a misrepresentation.[3]

The case of *With v O'Flanagan* [1936] Ch 575 provides an exception to the general rule against having to make a positive disclosure. If a statement is made which is true at the time but a change of circumstances renders it untrue, then remaining silent about the change can amount to a misrepresentation.[4] In this case the statement as to the turnover of a doctor's practice was true when made, but his subsequent illness dramatically changed the income, and there was a positive duty to disclose this change. In not doing so the respondents were liable in an action for misrepresentation.

Conduct is also capable of being a statement of existing fact and although not vocalised is not silence in spite of there being no positive duty to disclose pertinent facts and no fiduciary relationship in existence.[5] This was demonstrated in the case of *Spice Girls Ltd v Aprilia World Service* [2002] EWCA Civ 15. A successful action was brought under section 2(1) of the Misrepresentation Act 1967. The group had represented themselves in a photo shoot as having five members whereas it was known before the agreement was signed that one of them had the intention of leaving.

The courts are equally unsympathetic to partial revelations, where the statement made is literally true but what is left unsaid misrepresents the whole situation.[6] This again is an actionable misrepresentation. In *Dimmock v Hallet* (1866) LR 2 Ch App 21, the vendor of land described all the tenancies as being let but failed to mention that all the tenants were about to leave.

Where an action for misrepresentation lies because of an undisclosed change of circumstance, the conduct of the maker of the statement, or a partial truth, the remedies available will depend on the type of misrepresentation claimed. All types of misrepresentation have the potential restitutionary remedy of rescission and the possibility of damages for additional losses. Where possible a claimant will be advised to use the Misrepresentation Act 1967, as the burden of proof once misrepresentation is established shifts from the claimant

[7] The advantages of the Act are usually pertinent to answers on this topic area; although brief, this summarises the key issues and also leads neatly into the special contracts and relationships where the situation is different.

[8] The question neatly falls into two parts, so here is a mini introduction to the second part.

[9] A very broad obligation.

to the respondent to show that they honestly held such a belief. The measure of damages is also potentially higher than an action under *Hedley Byrne & Co Ltd* v *Heller Ltd* [1964] AC 465 and is equal to an action under the tort of deceit (*Royscott Trust Ltd* v *Rogerson* [1991] 2 QB 297).[7]

The nature of a contract or the relationship of the parties involved can impose a duty of disclosure and, as such, silence can result in liability or the ability of the other party to renege on all contractual obligations owed.[8]

Some contracts to be entered into require *uberrimae fidei*, utmost good faith. This is most often encountered in insurance contracts. If the person to be insured fails to disclose facts which would affect the insurance company's decision to accept the risk or the amount of premium payable, then the contract is voidable.[9] In *International Management Group UK Ltd* v *Simmonds* [2004] Lloyd's Rep IR 247, the IMG took out insurance against the risk of a cricket tournament being cancelled while not declaring that they had received information from reliable sources that India might well refuse to allow Pakistan to play in the light of the political tensions existing at the time.

As such, there is no legal obligation to pay out on a claim where pertinent facts were not disclosed even if the facts not disclosed had no bearing on the claim, and it is irrelevant whether the non-disclosure was merely a slip or downright dishonesty. An example would be life insurance taken out without declaring a heart condition but a claim being made on an unrelated cause of death. The type of misrepresentation is irrelevant. This duty is the subject of a Law Commission (2007) paper, 'Insurance contract law: misrepresentation, non-disclosure and breach of warranty by the insured', which looks at reducing the duty on consumers to disclose but instead having a duty to answer questions honestly, and reasonably placing the onus on the insurers to ask the pertinent questions: in the event of a misrepresentation, the remedies available to the insurer would depend on the type of misrepresentation.[10]

[10] Much higher marks will be gained by recognising how this situation is different from misrepresentations by conduct, partial truths and changes in circumstances, and how potentially the law needs reform to create a similar approach.

Rather than the type of contract involved imposing a duty of disclosure, it can be demanded by the relationship involved. The relationships which require such disclosure are called fiduciary relationships and include solicitor and client, trustee and beneficiary, and agent and principal. The class is not a closed one and it is open to a party to demonstrate that such a relationship exists. The fiduciary will be the one in whom the higher standards of behaviour are required.

It can be argued that no remedy is available in UK law for non-disclosure or pure silence; that there has to be something more, such as conduct, or some half-truth which distorts the truth of a statement, or that a change in circumstance creates an ongoing obligation to maintain the veracity of representation.[11] Outside of these limited circumstances, there is a requirement that a fiduciary relationship or a species of contract demanding *uberrimae fidei* exists. However, such duties of disclosure can overly favour the stronger party in certain circumstances. A modern approach appears to be developing suggesting that perhaps damages should be available for 'dishonest' non-disclosure (**Conlon v Simms** [2008] 1 WLR 484).

[11] This conclusion pulls together the key components of the point-by-point analysis into one succinct point.

✓ Make your answer stand out

- Use a modern example to illustrate the principle that silence alone cannot give rise to an action in misrepresentation: *Hamilton* v *Allied Domeq* [2007] UKHL 33.
- Note that it is possible voluntarily to assume responsibility for remaining silent, although this will be rare and difficult to establish: *Banque Fiancière de la Cité* v *Westgate Insurance* [1991] 2 AC 249.
- Consider that legislation can impose a duty of disclosure, particularly in a consumer context: for example, it is a criminal offence not to disclose certain information to consumers under the Consumer Protection from Unfair Trading Regulations 2008.

! Don't be tempted to . . .

- Partially develop your analysis: for example, fully develop and explain why the duty on consumers to disclose with regard to insurance contracts is potentially in need of reform, and how the proposals would mean those disclosures would be treated much more in parallel with other areas of misrepresentation.

✒ Question 5

Jed is the owner of a new wine bar, Lizard Street, which specialises in live and high-tech entertainment. During negotiations with Cyber Blue Ltd, Jed is told that the technical infrastructure and systems will be completed and ready for his planned New Year's Eve opening, with three months to spare. This means that the work will be completed a whole six months before any of the contractors Jed spoke to could promise. The promise that the work will be completed quicker was the deciding factor in Jed entering a contract with Cyber Blue Ltd. In actual fact the work is not completed on time and the system is full of glitches. Cyber Blue Ltd insist that such 'snagging' is normal in the industry. The computer system controls many functions of the business from the tills to lighting, as well as video, tweet and sound systems, and the planned opening has to be cancelled as nothing works. The contract is silent as to a completion date.

Jed has taken out insurance against the cancellation of his opening night. However, he never told the insurers, Protectaplan plc, when taking out the policy that he was appealing a decision by the licensing authorities to refuse a late night liquor licence. The insurance company are refusing to pay out on these grounds.

Advise Jed if he has any potential cause of action against Cyber Blue Ltd for their misrepresentation as to the time the work would take, and whether by Jed keeping silent as to the uncertainty surrounding the licence the insurance company can avoid paying out for covered losses.

Answer plan

→ Discuss the limitations of liability for misrepresentation for pre-contractual statements as to when the work could be finished. The statements made to Jed must be more than just sales talk, opinions or statements as to future intentions.

→ Establish that the statements made by Cyber Blue Ltd did induce Jed to make the contract.

→ Consider which type of misrepresentation would be the most appropriate, any possible defences available to Cyber Blue Ltd and the remedies available, including any bar to rescission, in making precise restitution to Cyber Blue Ltd.

→ Evaluate the extent of the duty of disclosure as regards insurance contracts and the possibility that Protectaplan plc may not have to pay out even though the claim and non-disclosure concern different subject matter.

Diagram plan

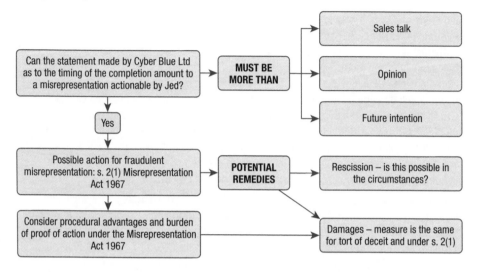

A printable version of this diagram plan is available from www.pearsoned.co.uk/lawexpressqa

Answer

[1] Focus and pertinence is achieved by the traditional definition being worked into the application to the specific question here.

For an action in misrepresentation Jed must establish that Cyber Blue Ltd made an unambiguous statement of existing fact which induced him to enter the contract.[1] Jed may be able to rescind the contract with Cyber Blue Ltd and claim damages, the measure of which will depend on the type of misrepresentation claimed. There was a duty on Jed to disclose all facts to Protectaplan plc which would be material to their decision as to providing insurance or the premium they would charge. This duty of disclosure goes beyond that normally required in English law and if breached would mean that the insurance company could rescind the contract.

To have an action for misrepresentation, the statement as to the completion of the work must be considered more than a 'mere puff' (*Dimmock v Hallet* (1866) LR 2 Ch App 21). The statements as to the timing are very specific and therefore likely to amount to more than just sales talk. Jed must also establish that the statement is more than a statement of opinion (*Bisset v Wilkinson* [1927] AC 177). In *Esso Petroleum Co. Ltd v Mardon* [1976] 2 All ER 5 the forecast as to the potential throughput of a petrol station was held not to be a statement of opinion but a misrepresentation, as the makers of the statement had specialist skill and knowledge in the provision of such information. Cyber Blue Ltd operates in this particular field and therefore must exercise reasonable skill and care in representing timescales for such work. In **BSkyB Ltd v HP Enterprise Services UK Ltd** [2010] All ER (D) 05 (Jul) a claim for misrepresentation was successful as the defendant had failed to complete work within timescales and to standards set in pre-contractual negotiations.[2] A statement as to future intention is not usually a misrepresentation, but if at the time of making the statement there was no such intention or the maker of the statement knew that such a promise could not be carried out, then that will amount to a misrepresentation of existing fact (**Edgington v Fitzmaurice** (1885) 29 Ch D 459).

[2] Up-to-date knowledge will impress the examiner: applying the traditional cases to an issue which is the subject of a plethora of current substantial claims and which may result in changed commercial behaviour.

The misrepresentation must be one of the reasons which induced Jed to enter the contract (**Edgington v Fitzmaurice**). The misrepresentation must also be important enough to induce a reasonable person to enter the contract (**JEB Fastners Ltd v Marks Bloom & Co.** [1983] 1 All ER 583). The timing of the work was important to Jed as it needed to be before his planned opening and he chose Cyber Blue Ltd over other contractors in reliance on this statement. Without reliance there can be no action for misrepresentation (**Attwood v Small** (1838) 6 Cl & Fin 232).[3] Having established that there is an actionable misrepresentation, two possible categories of misrepresentation are open to Jed: the possible remedies of rescission and a measure of damages which will allow the recovery of all consequential losses. Fraudulent misrepresentation requires the claimant to show that the maker of the false statement did so 'knowingly or without belief in its truth or recklessly careless as to whether it be true or false' (**Derry v Peek** (1889) 14 App Cas 337). Alternatively, under section 2(1) of the Misrepresentation Act 1967, it would be for Cyber Blue Ltd to establish that they believed their statement as to the timing of the completion of the work to be true and had reasonable grounds for that belief. Procedurally, this is easier for Jed as the burden of proof has shifted to Cyber Blue Ltd once a misrepresentation has been established.[4]

[3] Good identification of issues: here the assurances/promises as to the completion time for the work were of fundamental importance to Jed.

[4] This returns us once more to a question of balance and protects a contracting party from wide assertions of what can be done just to secure a contract when in reality there is no such prospect; it also ensures that, if such assertions were made honestly, only an action in breach of contract would be possible.

Both types of misrepresentation have the remedy of rescission, which will put the parties back in the position they were in before the contract was made and discharges any further contractual obligations between them. This remedy is available if it is possible to return the subject matter of the contract. Computer systems are complex and therefore more may be involved than the simple return of hardware and cable. At common law the courts have insisted on precise restitution; however, in equity a party who can make substantial restitution may return the subject matter together with an allowance for any deterioration in the product (**Erlanger v New Sombrero Phosphate Co.** (1878) 3 App Cas 1218). In this situation it could be argued that it is the misrepresentor that has changed the subject matter of the contract, and the right to rescind should not be lost because of his wrongdoing.[5]

[5] This is a complex point, and extra marks would be given for raising the possible approaches. It would not be expected to go any further than this.

With regard to fraudulent misrepresentation, the innocent party can recover damages whether or not they rescind the contract under the tort of deceit. Similarly, under section 2(1) of the Misrepresentation Act 1967 the decision to affirm the contract will not prevent a right to damages; however, recovery for the same loss cannot be made twice. The measure of damages for fraudulent misrepresentation under the tort of deceit is for damages 'directly flowing' from the fraudulent misrepresentation (**Doyle v Olby (Ironmongers) Ltd** [1969] 2 QB 158). For a claim under section 2(1) of the Misrepresentation Act 1967, the measure is the same (**Royscott Trust Ltd v Rogerson** [1991] 2 QB 297). This provides another advantage for Jed in pursuing an action under the Act rather than for fraud.[6]

[6] It is very important for Jed to know the most advantageous route for this claim.

There is no general duty of disclosure under English law and silence of itself is not a misrepresentation (**Fletcher v Krell** (1872) 42 LJQB 55). An exception to this is an insurance contract where there is a duty of disclosure of any fact known which would affect the insurers' decision to take the risk or the premium to charge (**International Management Group UK Ltd v Simmonds** [2004] Lloyd's Rep IR 247). A failure to disclose any such facts renders the contract voidable, and there will be no obligation to pay out against a claim even if the claim has no bearing on the undisclosed fact. Jed would be aware that not having a liquor licence on New Year's Eve would be disastrous for his opening; although it may not have led to a cancellation, it would have been a material consideration for Protectaplan plc. It is irrelevant that the cancellation was due to technical difficulties and not the lack of a licence.[7]

[7] Neatly and succinctly put, moving from the general rule to the specific with regard to insurance contracts and the potential severe consequences of non-disclosure.

Jed will have an action in misrepresentation against Cyber Blue Ltd and it would be procedurally to his advantage to use section 2(1) of the Misrepresentation Act 1967, as the remedies available would be the same. Protectaplan plc can refuse to pay on any claim Jed may make as a result of his non-disclosure of his licensing problem.

 Make your answer stand out

- Expand your answer by explaining why an action under *Hedley Byrne* v *Heller* [1964] AC 465 would not really benefit Jed.
- Read Would I lie to you? by A. Mayfield (2010) 160 *NLJ* 970 for a very clear and easy to follow discussion on *BSkyB Ltd* v *HP Enterprise Services UK Ltd*.
- Consider the review being undertaken by the Law Commission (2007) as regards insurance contracts and the principle of *uberrimae fidei*: Insurance contract law: misrepresentation, non-disclosure and breach of warranty by the insured (Consultation Paper No. 182).

! Don't be tempted to . . .

- Be frightened off by the insurance part of the question; it is only asking if silence can be a misrepresentation.
- Worry if you do not have the detail of the most current precedents in this area; it is topical but the principles you know apply.

Question 6

Discuss whether the law has achieved the correct balance between the maker of a statement trying to secure a contract and the recipient of that statement being misled by pre-contractual promises as to standards which may or not become part of the eventual contract.

Answer plan

→ Discuss what amounts to a misrepresentation and potential statements which fall short of this in pre-contractual promises as to standards.

→ Consider the types of misrepresentation, any defences and the remedies available.

→ Analyse how an action in fraudulent misrepresentation might prove advantageous in these circumstances, particularly where the contract purports to limit liability.

→ Evaluate whether the law has achieved the correct balance looked at in the light of recent decisions.

Diagram plan

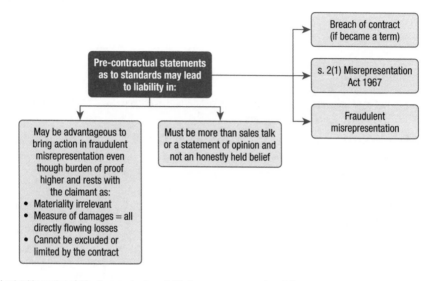

Pre-contractual statements as to standards may lead to liability in:	Breach of contract (if became a term)
	s. 2(1) Misrepresentation Act 1967
	Fraudulent misrepresentation

May be advantageous to bring action in fraudulent misrepresentation even though burden of proof higher and rests with the claimant as:
- Materiality irrelevant
- Measure of damages = all directly flowing losses
- Cannot be excluded or limited by the contract

Must be more than sales talk or a statement of opinion and not an honestly held belief

A printable version of this diagram plan is available from www.pearsoned.co.uk/lawexpressqa

Answer

[1] The introduction highlights the potential liability that may arise if promises as to standards are made, and allows the answer then to develop on the balance between sales talk and misrepresentation.

A misrepresentation is an unambiguous statement of existing fact which has induced the other party to enter a contract. The effect of a misrepresentation is to render the contract voidable, giving the innocent party the potential remedy of rescission and/or damages. It is prudent in negotiations for parties not to get carried away in closing the deal by making extravagant claims or promises which they cannot later fulfil.[1]

[2] This practical articulation of the problem faced in negotiations demonstrates to the marker an understanding of the legal principles in their real world context.

The definition of misrepresentation given above limits an action to statements of existing fact. This would preclude liability for mere 'sales talk' (***Dimmock v Hallet*** (1866) LR 2 Ch App 21). Care has to be taken by the maker of the statement that claims about the product are not precise enough to be misrepresentations of fact. This dividing line can be difficult to draw at times, as can be the distinction between a statement of fact and a mere statement of opinion.[2] Venturing an opinion on subject matter beyond the usual experience and expertise of the maker will not amount to a misrepresentation (***Bisset v Wilkinson*** [1927] AC 177). However, if the maker of the statement has substantial experience and skill in a particular field, then it is probable that the court would find that the statement made is one of fact. In **Esso Petroleum Co. Ltd v Mardon** [1976] 2 All ER 5 the forecast as to the potential petrol sales from a newly situated forecourt did amount to misrepresentation, as they had superior skills and knowledge in this area and had failed to exercise reasonable care and skill in the preparation of the forecast. This would also apply to exaggerated claims made in pre-contractual negotiations as to standards which could be achieved or, indeed, time-frames in which work could be completed (**BskyB Ltd v HP Enterprise Services UK Ltd** [2010] All ER (D) 05 (Jul))[3] There is also a positive obligation to remedy what may have been a true representation at the time made but which owing to a change in circumstances has become untrue (**With v O'Flanagan** [1936] Ch 575). With regard to pre-contractual negotiations this could apply to changes in potential revenues but also to changes in circumstances which could affect promises such as representations made as to completion of task, and also changes in personnel which may have an impact on the decision to enter a contract (**Fitzroy Robinson Ltd v Mentmore Towers Ltd** [2009] EWHC 1552 (TCC)).[4]

The statements made must have induced the contract, and unless there has been reliance there will be no liability under any type of misrepresentation (**Attwood v Small** (1838) 6 Cl & Fin 232). It must be an inducement, although it does not have to be the only reason the innocent party entered the contract (**Edgington v Fitzmaurice** (1885) 29 Ch D 459). Outside of fraudulent misrepresentation, the misrepresentation must have induced a reasonable person to enter into the contract (**County NatWest v Barton** [2002] 4 All ER 494). Someone making a fraudulent misrepresentation will not be allowed to argue that the representation was immaterial.[5]

Liability for fraudulent misrepresentation will be established if pre-contractual standards and promises were made in the absence of a true belief in their being achievable, or the maker of the statement is reckless as to whether the representation is true or false (**Derry v Peek** (1889) 14 App Cas 337). Alternatively, liability can be established under section 2(1) of the Misrepresentation Act 1967. The burden of proof shifts to the maker of the statement to show that they had reasonable grounds to believe and did believe that the pre-contractual statements made were true.[6]

[3] A strong development in the flow of your arguments demonstrates your depth of knowledge around the subject area. Using a very current example of the point further emphasises this, as well as your ability to research beyond the main textbooks.

[4] A good answer would discuss the principle with a traditional supporting authority; here the analysis goes further in relating a relatively recent authority of direct relevance to the question set.

[5] Most textbooks and questions focus on the advantages of an action under section 2(1) of the Misrepresentation Act 1967; here the thread of an argument is developing as to where fraudulent misrepresentation may be of greater benefit to the claimant.

[6] Laying out this definition demonstrates the balance achieved in having the defence that the statements made as to standards were made believing them to be true.

The measure of damages under section 2(1) and the tort of deceit, under which damages would be claimed for a fraudulent misrepresentation, appear to be the same. Damages under section 2(1) creates the 'fiction of fraud' and allows all losses which directly flow from the misrepresentation (**Royscott Trust Ltd v Rogerson** [1991] 2 QB 297). This is often purported to be an advantage for a party bringing an action under the 1967 Act.

Perhaps it is worth bearing in mind that only with an action for fraudulent misrepresentation will the misrepresentor be unable to rely on any contractual limitation to their liability. This removes a potential cap on the amounts which may be recoverable by the innocent party. It is also possible that such an action can be worth far more than the contract itself.[7]

[7] Again, this demonstrates a real understanding of the topic area being able to give real substance and practical application to your analysis.

Section 1 of the Act also provides that, where representations have become terms of the contract, an action can lie in both misrepresentation and breach of contract.[8] If a term of a contract has been breached, then it will depend on the nature of the term as to whether or not the innocent party can repudiate the contract. Misrepresentation does not consider the relative importance of the term. Often the innocent party to a contract will consent to variations and remedial action before finally losing patience, and may find the only recourse left is an action in misrepresentation relating back to early days of the negotiations. This may also potentially mean that the remedy of rescission which is available alongside damages has been lost, as the contract has been affirmed or it is impossible to put the parties in the position they would have been in before the contract was made. Damages for breach of contract will not allow for recovery of non-pecuniary losses and may also be limited by terms of the contract itself; therefore an action in misrepresentation will for the claimant potentially provide a better remedy.[9]

[8] This is an extremely incisive point to make, and the question does raise the issue of the term becoming part of the contract per se.

[9] Emphasising the preferential course of action for the innocent party and the reason will gain higher marks.

The law of misrepresentation does achieve a balance between the maker of a statement who does so in the full belief that their pre-contractual statements as to standards are achievable and the party that, in order to secure a deal, makes extravagant claims they could never hope to fulfil. If the defendant has an honest belief in those claims, they will not be liable. Recent litigation has highlighted how an action in fraudulent misrepresentation, where contractual limitations or exclusion clauses are contained in the contract, can prove more fruitful than an action under the 1967 Act or an action for breach of contract.[10]

[10] The conclusion relates directly back to the question and has drawn the issues raised together.

Make your answer stand out

- Expand your answer to include an explanation as to why an action under *Hedley Byrne* v *Heller* [1964] AC 465 would not yield any additional benefits in these circumstances, as the need to prove a special relationship would be an additional burden and the measure of damages is less generous.

- Consider, in *Thomas Witter Ltd* v *TBP Industries Ltd* [1996] 2 All ER 573, that where an action would not lie under section 2(1) of the Misrepresentation Act 1967 because of the innocence defence, then the claimant could still claim under innocent misrepresentation successfully with the requisite remedies.

! Don't be tempted to . . .

- Be too general in the analysis by not focusing on the question as to pre-contractual promises regarding standards.

- Miss out on higher marks; demonstrate the practical consequences and current difficulties encountered in this area.

- Avoid some discussion of the potential for an action in breach of contract if the statement made has become a term of the contract.

www.pearsoned.co.uk/lawexpressqa

 Go online to access more revision support including additional essay and problem questions with diagram plans, You be the marker questions, and download all diagrams from the book.

Mistake

How this topic may come up in exams

Common mistake and unilateral mistake as to identity are the most popularly examined issues in this topic area. The decisions in *Great Peace Shipping Ltd* v *Tsavliris Salvage (International) Ltd* [2002] EWCA Civ 1407 and *Shogun Finance Ltd* v *Hudson* [2004] 1 AC 919 have provided the opportunity for renewed discussion of the limits and scope of the application of the doctrine, particularly with regard to mistakes as to quality, mistakes in equity and arm's length transactions. An in-depth knowledge of the case law is required for this subject area.

Attack the question

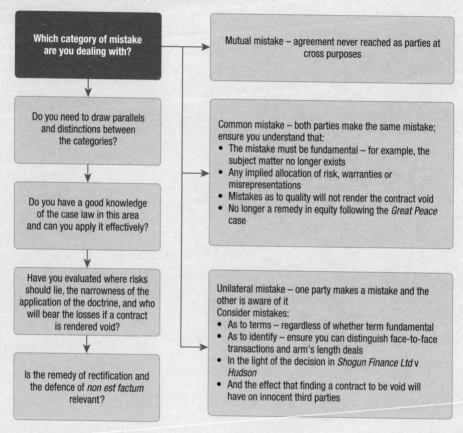

Which category of mistake are you dealing with?

Do you need to draw parallels and distinctions between the categories?

Do you have a good knowledge of the case law in this area and can you apply it effectively?

Have you evaluated where risks should lie, the narrowness of the application of the doctrine, and who will bear the losses if a contract is rendered void?

Is the remedy of rectification and the defence of *non est factum* relevant?

Mutual mistake – agreement never reached as parties at cross purposes

Common mistake – both parties make the same mistake; ensure you understand that:
- The mistake must be fundamental – for example, the subject matter no longer exists
- Any implied allocation of risk, warranties or misrepresentations
- Mistakes as to quality will not render the contract void
- No longer a remedy in equity following the *Great Peace* case

Unilateral mistake – one party makes a mistake and the other is aware of it
Consider mistakes:
- As to terms – regardless of whether term fundamental
- As to identify – ensure you can distinguish face-to-face transactions and arm's length deals
- In the light of the decision in *Shogun Finance Ltd* v *Hudson*
- And the effect that finding a contract to be void will have on innocent third parties

A printable version of this diagram is available from www.pearsoned.co.uk/lawexpressqa

 Question 1

Consider the rationale behind, and demonstrate using case law, the consistent narrow application of the doctrine of mistake.

Diagram plan

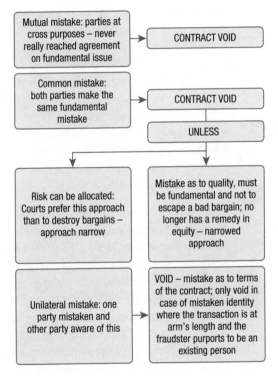

A printable version of this diagram plan is available from www.pearsoned.co.uk/lawexpressqa

Answer plan

→ Discuss the balance required between the need to enforce a bargain struck and one party realising they have not got what they were expecting.

→ Consider the traditional classifications of mistake:

   (i)   Mutual mistake – no agreement actually made.

   (ii) Common mistake – limited application if risk cannot be allocated between the parties. Can apply only to a fundamental mistake and is unlikely to apply to a mistake as to quality. A softer approach no longer given in equity.

(iii)   Unilateral mistake – if face to face, there is a presumption that you intended to deal with the person in front of you. Doctrine may operate in arm's length transactions where the fraudster is purporting to be an existing person.

Answer

The doctrine of mistake can allow for a contract to be set aside where a party discovers that the agreement they have entered is fundamentally different from that which was intended to be entered into. The effect of this is that the contract is void and treated as though it had never existed. The law requires that the doctrine be applied narrowly as it hits at the root of an objective approach to agreement and certainty in commercial transactions. If the doctrine of mistake is too readily applied, it will allow a party to escape from what has become a bad bargain or push potential losses on to an innocent third party by preventing them gaining good title to goods. Mistakes are traditionally categorised as mutual, common or unilateral.[1]

[1] Demonstrating an understanding of the context of the doctrine and not just the general rules as applied to each category of mistake gives depth to the analysis.

Mutual mistake is defined as being where both parties have made a mistake but they have each made a different mistake. The case of **Raffles v Wichelhaus** (1864) 2 H & C 906 is illustrative of this. The parties had agreed to the purchase and sale of a cargo of cotton which was to be delivered from the ship, *Peerless*, arriving from Bombay. Unfortunately there were two ships called *Peerless*, one sailing in October and one in December. The parties were operating at cross purposes and as such had never really reached agreement. The courts adopt an objective approach as to whether or not a contract has been formed, in finding that there has been an offer that has been accepted. To apply the doctrine of mistake in these circumstances, it must be impossible to determine that the parties intended to be bound by one set of terms rather than another. It is arguable that no contract was ever formed as there never was *consensus ad idem*, a meeting of minds, leading to an actual agreement.[2]

[2] The point as to the objectivity required in finding that a contract has been formed adds depth to the analysis.

Common mistake is where the parties both make the same mistake and it renders the contract void. Both parties being mistaken as to the existence of the subject matter can have this effect, as in **Couturier v Hastie** (1856) 5 HL Cas 673 where both parties were unaware that the cargo of corn had deteriorated before the contract was made and had been sold elsewhere. This situation is now covered by section 6 of the Sale of Goods Act 1979. The doctrine is, however, applied narrowly as in **McRae v Commonwealth Disposals Commission** (1951) 84 CLR 377: here it was held that the risk of the existence of a wreck, and the reef on which it was supposed to be, was on the defendants as they had contracted on the basis that the subject matter existed.[3] In **Associated Japanese Bank (International) Ltd v Credit du Nord SA** [1989] 1 WLR 255 the guarantee of a lease of machinery was found to contain an implied undertaking that the machinery in question was in existence and, as such, when found not to be the guarantee could not be enforced. Lord Steyn in the **Associated Bank** case stressed that the doctrine of mistake would only be available where the risk of mistake could not be allocated, and he suggested that this would cause many pleas of mistake to fail or be unnecessary. He also stressed that courts should attempt to hold up rather than destroy contracts.

[3] A structured development to the argument will gain marks and allows depth to be built into the analysis.

The judgment of Lord Atkin in **Bell v Lever Bros Ltd** [1932] AC 161 demonstrates the narrowness of the doctrine, particularly where to render the contract void would have the effect of allowing one party to escape what had become a bad bargain.[4] The judgment puts emphasis on the fact that the mistake made must be a fundamental one. This opened up the question as to what would amount to fundamental, and whether a mistake as to quality could operate as a ground to have a contract set aside. The answer to this again comes down to the allocation of risk. Lord Atkin gave the example of a painting being sold which both parties believe to be by a great master. It later turns out to be a fake. The contract cannot be set aside on the grounds of mistake, as the root of the contract was the sale of a painting which has been achieved; the mistake is only as to the quality of that painting.[5] Prior to 2002, equity had provided a softening of such a narrow approach to common mistake; however, in **Great Peace Shipping Ltd v Tsavliris Salvage (International) Ltd** [2002] EWCA Civ 1407 it was held no such separate rules existed for common mistake.

[4] Using the wording of the question demonstrates focus on the question set.

[5] Using the name of the judge where the principles derive from a particular judgment shows research/knowledge beyond that given in a main textbook.

A unilateral mistake is frequently relied on where one party has been misled as to the identity of the person they are contracting with. This often means that if the doctrine of mistake operates, a third party now innocently in possession of the property concerned would never

[6] Good emphasis here that, often, who bears the loss in cases where the doctrine of mistake operates is as innocent as the party relying on it.

have acquired good title to it and will be the one to bear the losses.[6] The courts will presume that the parties intended to contract with each other where a contract is concluded face to face (**Phillips v Brooks** [1919] 2 KB 243). The courts have held that the mistake is not as to identity but as to the person's attributes, in many of these cases their creditworthiness. Ostensibly the courts have been more willing to set aside a contract on the grounds of mistake where the transaction is at arm's length (**Cundy v Lindsay** (1878) 3 App Cas 459). However, this is not the case where the party being dealt with has provided an alias (**King's Norton Metal v Edridge Merrett & Co.** (1897) 14 TLR 98), rather than pretended to be another existing person (**Shogun Finance v Hudson** [2004] 1 AC 919), particularly where the creditworthiness of the existing person has been checked.[7]

[7] Logical build to the analysis, and succinctly draws together the established principles developed in the case law.

[8] This conclusion draws together the analysis of the different categories of mistake and the balance achieved in the limitations of the doctrine's operation.

The doctrine of mistake is necessarily narrow. The courts will accept the operation of the doctrine if no agreement was actually reached, as the parties were at cross purposes. The courts will not allow a party to escape what has become a bad bargain because what was contracted for is not of the quality expected. To widen the application of the doctrine would transfer risk from parties involved in a transaction on to a potentially innocent third party who has gained possession of the goods but not good title if the original contract is void. However, the doctrine is available to those in cases where there is a unilateral mistake of identity and everything was done in an arm's length transaction to check the truth of claims made by a fraudster.[8]

✓ Make your answer stand out

- Consider the limited remedy of rectification, where a written document may not reflect the true intentions of the parties, and the defence of *non est factum*, where a party believes the document signed was fundamentally different, the signature was induced by a trick or fraud and they were not careless in signing it.
- Read Chandler, A. and Devenney, J. (2004) Mistakes as to identity and the threads of objectivity, 1 *JOR* 7 to add some academic authority to support your analysis.

? Question 2

Following the death of her estranged father, Felicity has inherited his artist's studio and some of what she believes to be his completed works. Felicity's father, 'Clarky', worked in stained glass and his work was considered radical and progressive in the 1960s, particularly among 'A' list celebrities of the time. Unfortunately, owing to the fragility of the work, not much has survived to the present day. His recent death and the originality of his creations have rendered Clarky's work very valuable. Felicity invites Reah to have a look round with a view to purchasing any items she may be interested in. She sees a large panel depicting a dragon. She offers Felicity £50,000 for the piece. Felicity accepts her offer and will deliver on receiving payment in her bank. Reah immediately goes to her insurers to secure adequate cover in the event of an accident. The specialist valuer tells her that what she has is probably work done jointly by Clarky's evening beginner class students whom he would provide with a template of a dragon to fill in, to demonstrate and learn technique. Although attractive, the piece would at most be worth £5,000.

Reah is very upset and wants to know if she has to proceed with the contract, as she has not bought what she thought she was buying. Advise Reah as to the application of the doctrine of mistake.

Diagram plan

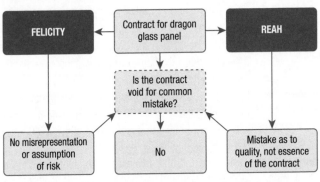

A printable version of this diagram plan is available from www.pearsoned.co.uk/lawexpressqa

Answer plan

→ Identify the relevant category of mistake (here, common), and the effect such a finding may have on the contract between Reah and Felicity.

→ Discuss the narrowness of the application of the doctrine, particularly with regard to mistakes as to quality; in essence, Reah has what she contracted for: the glass-dragon panel.

→ Evaluate whether Reah would have any relief in equity.

Answer

The operation of the doctrine of mistake renders a contract void: that is to say that it will mean that the contract will be treated as though it never existed. If applied, this would mean that Reah would not have a contract with Felicity and, as such, would not have to proceed with the purchase of the glass panel. However, the doctrine of mistake has a very restricted scope of operation and it will not allow a party to a freely entered bargain to escape easily from that agreement simply because the deal struck has not turned out to be as beneficial as anticipated. Reah will have to establish that her mistake was a fundamental one to have the contract set aside on the grounds of mistake. If she cannot do so, then the contract will be enforceable and she will have to pay Felicity £50,000.[1]

Traditionally, the doctrine of mistake under the common law falls into three categories: common, mutual and unilateral. Common mistake is where both parties have made the same mistake, mutual mistake is where both parties have made a mistake but a different mistake, and unilateral mistake is where one party has made a mistake and the other party is aware of this.[2] In this situation both Felicity and Reah are mistaken about the creator of the dragon glasswork. They both hold an honest belief that the artwork was created by Clarky. They have both made the same mistake and therefore Reah will argue that the contract should be set aside on the grounds of common mistake.[3] Felicity being estranged from her father probably knew no more about the work than Reah. There is no misrepresentation, nor could it be assumed that she assumed the risk of the authenticity of the authorship of the artwork.[4]

The doctrine of common mistake will apply only if the mistake is a fundamental one. The mistake must render the contract essentially

[1] Pointing out from the outset an understanding of what is at stake shows the examiner knowledge and application beyond the repetition of learnt principles.

[2] Never miss an opportunity to demonstrate breadth of knowledge, but ensure that you stay relevant.

[3] Clear confident application will gain marks.

[4] The identification of more complex principles gives depth to the analysis which a marker will credit.

and radically different from what the parties had supposed it to be. The House of Lords in **Bell v Lever Bros Ltd** [1932] AC 161 provides the leading authority on common mistake and what can amount to a fundamental mistake.[5] In this case, following a company merger, the chairman and vice-chairman of the company were surplus to requirements but still had five years on fixed-term contracts to run. By way of settlement for the early termination of the contract, the company paid them a total of £50,000 in compensation. The company later discovered that both men had been in breach of their contracts and could have been dismissed without paying for the privilege. The men themselves were not fraudulent as they had forgotten about the breaches and believed their contracts to be valid.[6] The company sought to have the contracts set aside on the grounds of common mistake, that is to say both parties believed the contracts to be valid whereas in actual fact they were voidable as a result of the breaches. The court held that the mistake was not sufficiently fundamental as to render the contract void. Lord Atkin in his judgment concluded that the company and the directors got exactly what they had bargained for in an early release from their contractual obligations.[7] Lord Atkin went further in discussing what would amount to being fundamental for the purposes of a common mistake, the first point being that both parties must be mistaken as to the fundamental assumption the contract was based on. However, Lord Atkin articulates his test for this in terms of quality.[8] The mistake of both parties must be as to some quality, without which the subject matter of the contract is rendered essentially different from what it was believed to be. Lord Atkin goes on to give the example of a painting believed to be the work of a great master which later turns out to be a fake. Reduced to its fundamental purpose, the contract is for the sale of a painting. A painting is what has been purchased; the mistake as to the quality of that painting or indeed its value is not sufficient for the doctrine of mistake to operate. Lord Atkin's hypothetical example became a reality in **Leaf v International Galleries** [1950] 1 All ER 693, whereby the claimants had no remedy in the absence of a warranty or representation when the purchased Constable painting turned out to be a modern copy.[9] Similarly, here the dragon glass is not of the quality in the terms of its creator being a renowned artist in the field, but Reah has got essentially what she contracted for: the glass dragon panel.

[5] There is no harm in reinforcing that the mistake must be a fundamental one; the key question is what will amount to a fundamental mistake?

[6] The facts help explain the legal principle that is being applied, so are worth detailing.

[7] This is further developed in the judgment with the analogy of the purchase of a painting believed to be by an old master — the flow of the work here develops the analysis in the same way.

[8] Excellent point, as it this that has led to so much legal debate as to whether a mistake as to quality is possible.

[9] Reinforcing the arguments already raised, and the work picks up the point made earlier (end of paragraph 2) that there was no misrepresentation or assumption of risk as to the creator of the work.

In *Great Peace Shipping Ltd* v *Tsavliris Salvage (International) Ltd* [2002] EWCA Civ 1407, Lord Phillips revisited the criteria needed to establish common mistake as to quality. First, there must be a common assumption as to the existence of a state of affairs. Both Felicity and Reah believed the artwork to be by Clarky. Secondly, neither party must give a warranty that a certain state of affairs exists. Neither Felicity nor Reah provide such a warranty or assume the risk. Thirdly, the non-existence of the state of affairs is not the fault of either party. Neither Felicity nor Reah appear to be at fault. The non-existence of the state of affairs must render performance of the contract impossible. The fact that the glass dragon is by a different artist does not prevent the contract being performed. Finally, the state of affairs may be the existence, or a vital attribute of the consideration to be provided. Successful claims in common mistake have often been where there has been a total failure of consideration (*Couturier* v *Hastie* (1856) 5 HL Cas 673). Reah has the glass panel she freely negotiated for.[10]

[10] Taking the criteria one by one and applying them to the problem demonstrates confidence with the subject matter, as well as giving clarity to the application and reasoning.

The *Great Peace* case put an end to the possibility of a separate doctrine of common mistake in equity which could be used to soften the approach taken by the common law. Reah will therefore not have an alternative remedy in equity.

The narrow application of the doctrine of common mistake will mean that Reah is obliged to pay the contract price for the panel. Her mistake was merely as to the quality of her purchase, not its core subject matter.[11]

[11] Direct and to the point, clear in the conclusion and application.

✓ Make your answer stand out

- Consider *Nicholson and Venn* v *Smith Marriott* (1947) 177 LT 189, which is often discussed in relation to mistakes as to quality. Although the claim for breach of contract was successful as the Carolean napkins purchased turned out to be Georgian, it was suggested in the judgment that the contract could have been treated as void by the buyer on the grounds of mistake.

- Read Dabbs, D. (2002) The risk of mistake in contract, 152 *NLJ* 1654 to add some academic opinion to your answer.

Don't be tempted to . . .

- Forget your application to the question by giving a general run-through of the courts' reluctance to allow the doctrine to operate where there has been a mistake as to the quality of the subject matter of the contract, not its essence.
- Miss out on the higher marks by missing the points on allocation of risk.

Question 3

'. . . a mistake will not affect assent unless it is a mistake of both parties and is as to the existence of some quality which makes the thing without the quality essentially different from the thing it was believed to be' per Lord Atkin in *Bell* v *Lever Bros* [1932] AC 161 p. 218. Evaluate whether this statement by Lord Atkin regarding common mistakes as to quality could also apply to a unilateral mistake as to identity where one party is mistaken as to the other party's attributes.

Answer plan

→ Discuss the narrowness of the application of the doctrine to a mistake as to the quality of the subject matter.

→ Consider the restricted approach of the courts to mistakes as to identity, particularly where that transaction has taken place face to face.

→ Analyse whether a mistake as to an individual's attributes is no more than a mistake as to their 'quality'.

→ Evaluate the similarities in approach taken in common mistake and mistake as to identity where the substance/identity does not exist.

Diagram plan

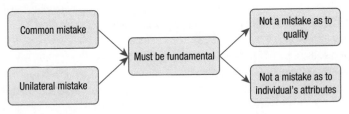

A printable version of this diagram plan is available from www.pearsoned.co.uk/lawexpressqa

Answer

The operation of the doctrine of mistake renders a contract void. The courts do not view themselves as the destroyers of bargains and therefore the doctrine operates within narrow parameters with regard to mistakes as to quality and identity.[1]

[1] A strong introduction recognising the complex level of analysis demanded by the question.

Common mistake occurs where both parties have made the same mistake. The doctrine, however, will not apply if the mistake is as to the quality of the subject matter. In the quote from **Bell v Lever Bros Ltd** [1932] AC 161 Lord Atkin stressed that for a contract to be void on the grounds of common mistake there must be missing some quality which makes the contract essentially different. It is clear from this that the mistake made must be a fundamental one.[2] The judgment goes on by way of illustration to define what would amount to being essentially different and gives the example of the purchase of a painting believed by both parties to be by a master, but which later turns out to be a fake. In essence what was bought was a painting. The mistake is as to the quality of the painting, not the subject matter itself. In the absence of misrepresentation or a warranty as to the authenticity of the painting, the contract will not be set aside on these grounds.[3] Subsequent cases such as **Leaf v International Galleries** [1950] 1 All ER 693 further illustrate this.

[2] Succinct summary of the quotation articulating that the mistake cannot be a minor or ancillary issue.

[3] This demonstrates a depth of knowledge recognising that the courts will always consider if the risk was assumed or should be implied to one party rather than the other.

In **Great Peace Shipping Ltd v Tsavliris Salvage (International) Ltd** [2002] EWCA Civ 1407 this issue was revisited. Could the mistake as to distance, an issue of quality, which the two parties believed the vessels to be apart, render the contract essentially different from that which had been agreed? It was held that the distance between the vessels did not render the provision of those services contracted for fundamentally different.[4] The judgment focuses not on a difference between substance and quality but on the possibility of performance. In the example of the painting the doctrine of mistake will not operate using an impossibility test, as the unaltered painting still exists and is the correct subject matter of the contract.[5]

[4] The facts in the *Great Peace* case are illustrative of the principle laid out in the quotation from *Bell* v *Lever Bros*.

[5] Again confirming the narrowness of the application of the doctrine.

A unilateral mistake is often sought to be relied on where one of the contracting parties is mistaken as to the identity of the other. The courts have drawn a distinction between where the party intended to contract with someone else, where the contract would be void, and where the party is mistaken as to the attributes of that individual

[6] The introduction of the key
issues here gives a structure
from which the analysis can
develop logically.

rather than their actual identity.[6] In **Phillips v Brooks** [1919] 2 KB
243 the plaintiffs were seeking to set aside the contract for the sale
of a piece of jewellery. They thought the purchaser to be Sir Geoffrey
Bullough. The cheque paid was dishonoured. The ring was pledged
to the defendants who acted in good faith. The court held that, in
spite of the plaintiffs checking the address of Sir George Bullough,
they intended to contract with the person present in the shop. They
were mistaken, not as to the identity of the person they wished
to contract with but merely as to his attributes, in other words his
creditworthiness. Similarly in **Lewis v Averay** [1972] 1 QB 198 the
contract for the sale of a car could not be set aside on the grounds
of mistake when the sellers accepted a cheque from a purchaser
they believed to be a television actor. Both **Phillips v Brooks** and
Lewis v Averay would appear to suggest the principle that, if you
are dealing face to face in a contractual negotiation, it will be presumed that you intend to contract with that person and this will not
render the contract void on the grounds of mistake.[7] A parallel exists
here with common mistake that, if at the root of the contract you
have who or what you intended, then you will be bound by the contractual obligations. Being mistaken as to the quality of a thing or the
attributes of a person is insufficient for the doctrine to operate.[8]

[7] By summarising the clarity
of the point being made is
ensured.

[8] This direct focus on
the question asked has
demonstrated the ability
to evaluate complex issues
appropriately.

Arm's length transactions provide a greater opportunity to establish
that the person you are dealing with is not who you intended to
contract with.[9] In **Cundy v Lindsay** (1878) 3 App Cas 459 a contract was concluded in such a way that the plaintiffs believed they
were dealing with a company of a similar name and similar address.
The contract was set aside on the grounds of mistake, as the plaintiffs intended to deal with a reputable company they had knowledge
of, not the actual party they did contract with, whom they had never
heard of. By contrast, in **King's Norton Metal v Edridge Merrett
& Co.** (1897) 14 TLR 98 the contract was not void where the contract was set up with a party using an alias rather than pretending to
be an existing person/company. Here, it was held that the plaintiffs
intended to deal with the party they had written to: they were mistaken as to his attributes not the identity of the party they wished to
contract with. The identity of the other party, for the doctrine of
mistake to operate, has to be fundamental to the contract.[10]

[9] Picking up on the earlier
point as regards face-to-face
transactions creates a strong
structured flow to the work.

[10] This recognises that just
being at arm's length will not
be sufficient for the doctrine
to operate.

Shogun Finance Ltd v Hudson [2004] 1 AC 919 considered
the issues of mistakes as to identity and laid to rest some of the

uncertainties created by cases such as ***Ingram v Little*** [1960] 3 All ER 332, which appear to contradict the reasoning in both ***Philips v Brooks*** and ***Lewis v Averay***. In this case, Hudson had been sold a car by a third party who had arranged finance while in the dealership on hire-purchase terms with Shogun. Shogun had been contacted by the dealership to arrange the finance and therefore were not transacting face to face. The client in the dealership had said his name was Patel and had given details which were verified as creditworthy. Shogun was able successfully to claim that the HP agreement was void on the grounds of mistake as they had only intended to contract with Mr Patel and no one else.

[11] A strong conclusion drawing together the analysis from the main body of the work and addressing the core elements to the question.

Common mistake and unilateral mistake share the same characteristic, as the mistake has to be a fundamental one. The issue of a mistake as to quality being insufficient for the doctrine to operate has similar reasoning to a mistake as to attributes with regard to identity. The doctrine has to have narrow application, as the losses will be borne by innocent third parties.[11]

✓ Make your answer stand out

- Add depth to your analysis by demonstrating the developments of the decision in the *Great Peace* case as regards common mistake as to quality.

- Consider the restriction put on the potential to consider a common mistake in equity following the *Great Peace* case. Pawlowski, M. (2002) Common mistake: law v equity, 152 *NLJ* 132 will assist in your understanding of this point.

- Read MacMillan, C. (2004) Mistake as to identity clarified?, 120 *LQR* 369. This academic article will support your analysis on the effect of the *Shogun* case, adding depth to your analysis.

- Consider that, although the identity of the other party will only render the contract void if it is fundamental to the contract, this will not be the case for a unilateral mistake as to terms of the contract (*Hartog* v *Colin & Shields* [1939] 3 All ER 566).

! Don't be tempted to . . .

- Be too descriptive by writing all you know about common mistake and then all you know about mistakes as to identity. The question requires you to think about parallels.

📋 Question 4

Justin is a car dealer. He has the Video Cinque Conceptor on his forecourt hot from the
Paris Motor Show. A limousine arrives outside and drops off someone whom he believes
to be the star of a popular TV show which featured the old-style 1980s' Video Cinque. To
his delight, the customer places an order for the Video Cinque Conceptor priced at £60,000,
and also a small run-around from the Zsa Zsa range for £12,000 for his assistant. To
Justin's surprise he asks for details of the hire-purchase terms available on the Video
Cinque Conceptor, as he says that their deal of 0 per cent interest for six months is too
good to miss. He intends to pay for the Zsa Zsa by cheque and the deposit of 10 per cent
for the Video Cinque Conceptor by cash. Justin rings the finance company, Performance
Car Finance Ltd. A finance search is done against James Dockherty, supposedly the actor's
real rather than stage name, on the address given on the driving licence produced. The
finance company then fax through the documentation for the customer to sign. As the
deposit has been paid Justin allows him to take the Video Cinque Conceptor. He also
allows the assistant to drive away in the Zsa Zsa.

No payment is made to the finance company. Ted purchased the Video Cinque Conceptor
from a private seller in good faith. Stella similarly purchased the Zsa Zsa. The private
seller involved in both sales was the rogue Justin sold the cars to, whose real identity is not
known. Suffice to say he is not the famous actor Justin thought. James Dockherty does
exist but his driving licence and cash were stolen during a robbery at his jewellery store.

Advise Ted and Stella on how the operation of the doctrine of mistake will determine
whether or not they can keep the cars they have purchased.

Answer plan

→ Discuss the concept of unilateral mistake and the potential for a contract to be void on the
grounds of mistaken identity.

→ Distinguish the sale of the Zsa Zsa as a face-to-face transaction which cannot be set
aside on the grounds of mistake (ultimately giving Stella good title to the car), and the HP
agreement with Performance Car Finance Ltd for the Video Cinque Conceptor as an arms'
length transaction which can be set aside (and preventing good title passing to Ted).

→ Evaluate whether *Shogun* has rectified the uncertainties in this area in the context of the
problem set.

Diagram plan

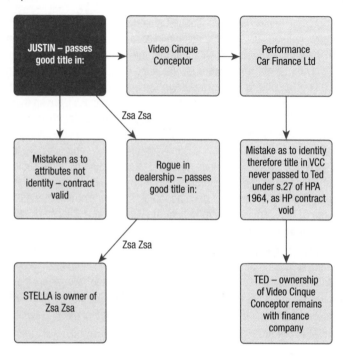

A printable version of this diagram plan is available from www.pearsoned.co.uk/lawexpressqa

Answer

[1] Clear identification of the legal issues and the delicate balance the law has to achieve in the operation of the doctrine as to which of the duped innocent parties should bear the losses.

A unilateral mistake is where one party makes a mistake which the other party is aware of. Unilateral mistake is often relied on in situations where one party to a contract thought they were contracting with someone else. Justin and Performance Car Finance Ltd thought they were contracting with 'Jack Dockherty'. The operation of the doctrine of mistake will render a contract void. If no contract existed, then property in the cars never passed from Justin or Performance Car Finance Ltd to the purchaser. If property did not pass, then under the *nemo dat* rule the rogue could not pass good title to anyone else. This could have harsh repercussions for bona fide purchasers such as Ted and Stella. The law therefore has to provide rules by which it can be determined where the risk and losses should fall where there has been a unilateral mistake of identity.[1]

[2] Emphasising this distinction will give cohesion to the argument; the rationale of the application of the law to the problem will depend on this point.

[3] The question draws natural comparisons with the facts in *Lewis* v *Averay*. Alternatively, give greater attention to *Phillips* v *Brooks*, then to support the application reinforce the analysis with the case having the same facts.

[4] This picks up on the terminology used and accepted in the area of unilateral mistake.

[5] Marks are gained by clear application of the principles raised; this is reinforced here with a detailed comment from a judge on a case with almost identical facts. Recognising how much of this area is the apportionment of risk demonstrates a depth of understanding.

[6] A good knowledge of *Shogun* is essential in this area of law.

To render a contract void on the grounds of unilateral mistake as to identity, it will have to be demonstrated that the party was truly mistaken as to the individual's identity, genuinely intending to contract with someone else, and not just mistaken as to the individual's attributes, such as being creditworthy.[2] There is a strong presumption that in face-to-face dealings the parties intend to contract with each other. The presumption exists that the person in front of you is the one you intend to contract with, even if the person being dealt with pretends to be someone else, assuming a false name or identity. In **Lewis v Averay** [1972] 1 QB 198 the plaintiff accepted a cheque for the purchase of his car from a man purporting to be the leading actor from the television series *Robin Hood*.[3] The court held that the contract could not be set aside on the grounds of mistake. Two main lines of argument were put forward to support this. First, Mr Lewis intended to contract with the person who turned up at his house to buy the car. There was no evidence that he intended to contract with anyone other than that person. Secondly, the identity of the purchaser was not of fundamental importance to Mr Lewis. In believing him to be a famous actor he had assumed him to be credit-worthy. As in **Phillips v Brooks Ltd** [1919] 2 KB 243 the mistake was as to the rogue's attributes not his actual identity.[4] Justin intended to contract for the sale of the car with the man in front of him. Following the face-to-face principle laid down in **Phillips v Brooks** and **Lewis v Averay**, the contract for the sale of the Zsa Zsa would be valid. As such the rogue took good title to the car, as there is nothing to suggest that Justin did anything to avoid the contract before it was sold to Stella. Stella as a bona fide purchaser would have good title to the car she purchased. Lord Denning in **Lewis v Averay** believed it to be appropriate that the innocent purchaser who had acted perfectly properly should not suffer because of the seller's lack of judgement in allowing the car to be taken.[5]

The situation with regard to Ted is more complex, as in a hire-purchase agreement the creditor becomes the owner of the goods until the final payment is made by the debtor. As such the car was sold by Justin to the finance company who became the owner, with Jack Dockherty having a right to possession only. The right of possession would not allow an individual to transfer title; however, section 27 of the Hire Purchase Act 1964 allows a bona fide purchaser to obtain good title in these circumstances.[6] The finance company can only recover the car by establishing that the contract between them and

Jack Dockherty was void on the grounds of mistaken identity. **Shogun Finance Ltd v Hudson** [2004] 1 AC 919 revisited the decided case law in this area and managed to demonstrate that the finance company only intended to deal with the party named on the contract, on whom they did a credit check, and no other party. They were mistaken as to identity and not attributes.[7] The presence of another party negotiating the contract at the dealership was irrelevant. This was treated as an arm's length transaction.

[7] It would be easy to rely purely on *Shogun* here as the facts of the question precisely mirror the facts of the case, and it would be acceptable to do so; however, by using the authorities relied on in that decision itself, a breadth of knowledge is demonstrated while illustrating the key issues raised in *Shogun*.

[8] This focuses on the question's key issue: the differing judicial attitude towards face-to-face and arm's length transactions.

The courts recognise that where a contract has been concluded at a distance, for example over the phone or in writing, it may be easier to establish that the intention was to contract with someone else.[8] In **Cundy v Lindsay** (1878) 3 App Cas 459 an order for handkerchiefs was accepted and delivered to a Mr Blenkarn who had deliberately made his signature appear to be 'Blenkiron'. The address the goods were dispatched to was in the same street as a respectable firm known to the plaintiff called Blenkiron & Co. Cundy had bought the goods in good faith. If the contract could be set aside for mistake, he could not take good title to the goods and Lindsay would be able to recover them. It was held that the contract between Blenkarn and Lindsay was void as he had only ever intended to deal with Blenkiron & Co. Lindsay could demonstrate that he intended to deal with someone different from whom he did actually deal with and that the identity was fundamental to him. By contrast, in **King's Norton Metal v Edridge Merrett & Co.** (1897) 14 TLR 98 goods were ordered on company notepaper purporting to have various offices and trading under the name of Hallam & Co. This contract was not void on the grounds of mistake as the plaintiffs intended to contract with the company they had been in correspondence with. The distinction was that in **Cundy v Lindsay** they intended to deal with a different customer not a different type of customer, one who paid their bills. Performance Car Finance Ltd intended to deal with the real Jack Dockherty, as it was that client they did the credit check on, and his name they put on the contract.[9] This would render the contract void between the finance company and the rogue and prevent Ted gaining good title to the car.

[9] Relates back to *Shogun*, examiners give credit for a strong logical structure.

[10] Examiners will give marks for incisive commentary as long as it does not slide into personal opinion.

Arising out of the same events, the conclusion can appear harsh in that Stella will gain good title to her car but Ted will not to his. From a blame perspective, perhaps more risk should lie with Justin than the finance company, but it seems rather unfortunate for Ted.[10]

✓ **Make your answer stand out**

■ Consider that perhaps the main difficulty in this area is the all-or-nothing approach rather than an ability to split the losses as suggested by Lord Devlin in *Ingram* v *Little* [1960] 3 All ER 332.

■ However, be careful as the House of Lords in *Shogun Finance* v *Hudson* decided *Ingram* v *Little* was wrongly decided and the idea was rejected by the Law Reform Committee on Transfer of Title of Chattels in 1966 as adding too much uncertainty and complexity to the law.

■ Read MacMillan, C. (2004) Mistake as to identity clarified?, 120 *LQR* 369 and see if you can enhance the depth of your analysis with reference to this.

■ Consider also the views of Hare, C. (2004) Identity mistakes: a lost opportunity, 67 *MLR* 993.

! **Don't be tempted to . . .**

■ Take the easy way and just apply *Shogun*. You can demonstrate a greater breadth of knowledge by showing you understand how the conclusions in that case were reached.

www.pearsoned.co.uk/lawexpressqa

 Go online to access more revision support including additional essay and problem questions with diagram plans, You be the marker questions, and download all diagrams from the book.

7

Duress and undue influence

How this topic may come up in exams

Examiners tend to question these topics separately. Both duress and undue influence are always looking at the limitations of the operation of the doctrine. In both areas a good knowledge of the case law is essential. Ensure you can deal with lawful act economic duress and the tensions at play in the law here. In undue influence an in-depth knowledge of the changes made by the decision in *Royal Bank of Scotland* v *Etridge (No. 2)* [2001] 4 All ER 449 is essential and a knowledge of some of the developments post-*Etridge (No. 2)* will gain higher marks.

Attack the question

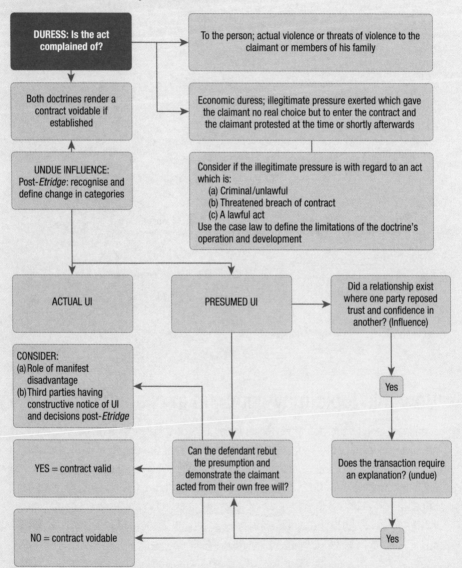

A printable version of this diagram is available from www.pearsoned.co.uk/lawexpressqa

 Question 1

Discuss the current evolutionary state of the doctrine of economic duress and the difficulties inherent in formulating a set of principles to determine the reach of this doctrine.

Answer plan

→ Discuss the development of the doctrine from the limitation of duress to the person to economic duress.

→ Evaluate the problems in determining where legitimate commercial pressure ends and duress begins.

→ Consider the development and distinction between unlawful acts which can amount to economic duress and lawful act duress.

Diagram plan

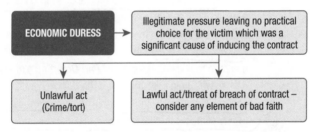

A printable version of this diagram plan is available from www.pearsoned.co.uk/lawexpressqa

Answer

Duress if established renders a contract voidable and gives the innocent party the option to rescind the contract, as their consent to their contract was gained through what the law considers to be illegitimate means. The incremental development of the doctrine of economic duress has meant that hard-and-fast principles defining its presence and parameters have been slow to emerge and a good deal of uncertainty still persists in this area.[1]

[1] This gives context to the focus of the question, which is: what amounts to economic duress?

Prior to 1976 it was only possible to have duress to the person, which involved a party being induced to contract by violence or the threat of violence (***Barton v Armstrong*** [1976] AC 104). The act had to be unlawful and a lawful act would be insufficient (***Williams*** v *Bayley* (1886) LR 1 HL 200). Duress to goods was not possible (*Skeate* v *Beale* (1840) 11 Ad & E 983) until the decision in *Occidental Worldwide Investment Corporation* v *Skibs A/S Avanti,* **The Sibeon** *and* **The Sibotre** [1976] 1 Lloyd's Rep 293, which recognised that one party using their superior economic power in an illegitimate manner could amount to economic duress, rendering a contract voidable.

– The Sibeon
– Sibotre
→ the Sibeon
and the Sibotre

[2] Difficult when dealing with commercial entities as there is usually a choice to lose out financially.

Early attempts at defining what would amount to economic duress focused on the state of mind of the claimant in so far as great emphasis was put on whether or not there had been a 'coercion of the will vitiating consent'.[2] In *North Ocean Shipping Co. Ltd* v *Hyundai Construction Co. Ltd,* **The Atlantic Baron** [1979] QB 705 the increased demand of 10 per cent on the price to complete the construction of an oil tanker was held to be sufficient to amount to economic duress; however, delay in protesting at the pressure was deemed to have affirmed the variation in contractual terms. So it would appear that a threat to breach a contract can amount to economic duress, but to what extent such a threat would 'coerce the will vitiating consent' and what would be legitimate commercial pressure remained uncertain. In *Pao On* v *Lau Yiu Long* [1980] AC 614 it was held that there had been no coercion of will, merely economic commercial pressure in threatening to breach a contract to buy shares if the defendants refused to guarantee the claimants/ plaintiffs against losses.

The Universe Sentinel

[3] Picking up the thread of the last point stressing the problem with the existing test gives the work a logical flow into the next steps taken to develop the doctrine.

The coercion of will test would always be difficult to satisfy as the line of where legitimate commercial pressure ends and duress begins is difficult to define.[3] In *Universe Tankships Inc. of Monrovia* v *International Transport Workers' Federation,* **The Universe Sentinel** [1983] 1 AC 366 the attention of the court shifted from the coercion of the will of the victim to the behaviour of the party exerting the pressure and whether that behaviour was legitimate. In this case the Union insisted on the shipowners paying an amount in back pay and a sum into their welfare fund before they would remove blacklisting from the ship and end the strike action. The money was recovered as, although the shipowners did have a choice – they could have refused and lost money – that choice was only a choice between two evils.[4] The economic pressure applied was illegitimate. In this case, however, the action was unlawful; inducing a breach of contract is a tort. Lord Scarman did point out that such illegitimate

[4] Reflects on the inherent difficulty with the coercion of will test.

[6] Whether the threat of a breach of contract can amount to economic duress is an issue which the law has grappled with and finds various decisions difficult to reconcile; the answer will tackle this complex issue head-on later.

→ breach of contract to amount to econ duress?

[7] This ends up being the theme: in the absence of an unlawful act, economic duress will only be established where the party exerting the pressure has acted in bad faith.

→ absence of an unlawful act, econ duress → only established → where party exerting pressure acted in bad faith

pressure could also apply to lawful acts.[5] This approach was also adopted in **Atlas Express Ltd v Kafco** [1989] 1 All ER 641, whereby the threat to breach a contract[6] for the delivery of goods in the knowledge that this would impact severely on the suppliers' credibility with their buyers was sufficient to amount to illegitimate pressure and economic duress.

In **CTN Cash and Carry Ltd v Gallaher Ltd** [1994] 4 All ER 714 the question arose as to whether a lawful act could ever amount to illegitimate pressure. In this case the defendants mistakenly but genuinely believed that losses incurred in the delivery of supplies lay with the plaintiffs. As such, they refused to give them credit terms until they made good those losses. It was held that there was no economic duress in this case. In this situation there was no threat to breach a contract, just to alter terms, and the defendants did genuinely believe themselves not to be liable for the losses, even though they were wrong in that belief. Refusing to contract with another party is not in itself wrongful. The court did assert that a lawful act could amount to duress but it would be difficult to establish in a commercial context in the absence of bad faith.[7]

In **DSND Subsea Ltd v Petroleum Geo-Services ASA** [2000] BLR 530 Lord Dyson concluded that for actionable duress there must be pressure, the practical effect of which is that there is compulsion on, or a lack of practical choice for the victim: that pressure must be illegitimate and a significant cause inducing the innocent party to enter the contract. Lord Dyson went further and brought together five basic considerations which would assist in determining what would amount to illegitimate pressure beyond the pressures of normal commercial bargaining: first, whether there has been an actual or threatened breach of contract; secondly, has the person exerting the pressure acted in good or bad faith; thirdly, did the victim have any realistic practical alternative but to give in to the pressure; fourthly, did the victim protest at the time; and lastly, could they have been considered to have affirmed the contract.

From the case law, it would appear that if a threat is unlawful, such as a threat to commit a crime or tort, this will generally amount to duress, and the claimant must simply assure that they are not deemed to have affirmed the action by ensuring that they protest effectively and quickly as soon as the pressure is removed.

A threatened breach of contract or the exercise of a lawful choice is less certain to amount to illegitimate pressure unless there is an element of bad faith in those actions. The move away from a concentration on the victim's actual consent being vitiated by the coercion of their will to a focus on the activities of the party exerting the pressure has made it easier for a party to establish economic duress; however, the parameters of its operation are still to some extent uncertain.[8]

[8] The judgment and the conclusion both synthesise the decisions previously discussed into a 'where we are now' test/analysis.

> Move away from the victim's actual consent

✓ Make your answer stand out

- Include the recent decision in *Kolmar Group AG* v *Traxpo Enterprise Pvt Ltd* [2010] ICLC 256, which has very similar facts to *The Atlantic Baron* but was decided according to the principles laid down in *DSND Subsea Ltd* v *Petroleum Geo-Services ASA*, to illustrate the development of the law in this area as analysed above.

- Consider how the doctrine of consideration (*Stilk* v *Myrick* (1809) 2 Camp 317) and promissory estoppel (*D & C Builders Ltd* v *Rees* [1966] 2 QB 617) have had a role to play in situations that today would potentially be covered by economic duress, and whether there is still potential application of those principles with regard particularly to lawful act duress.

! Don't be tempted to . . .

- Be afraid of the topic: students often avoid this area as they find the complexities of the cases off-putting. Lord Hoffmann said in *R* v *Attorney General for England and Wales* [2003] UKPC 22 that you are looking at the legitimacy of the pressure applied from two angles: the nature of the pressure (whether it is unlawful or lawful) and the nature of the demand (whether it is unlawful or has any bad faith).

? Question 2

LN Ltd manufactures nail polish. They have just secured a lucrative contract with a multinational chain of spa hotels.

They contracted with Baltimore & McNulty Ltd to use their new computerised transit system which will ensure that deliveries can be fast-tracked around the world, preceded by electronic paperwork, eradicating delays at customs borders. The Adminstrative Dock Workers' Union have been stopping goods operating on this system and only allowing them on their onward journey when the owner pays the equivalent of an administrator's monthly salary. This has cost LN Ltd £30,000 in the last three months. LN Ltd was aware that this was a wrongful interference with goods and the action unlawful but felt powerless to resist until the strike was over.] —> until the strike was over.

LN Ltd use nitrocellulose which is highly inflammable. It is delivered by DSTR Ltd under a four-year contract, with no price variation clause. Insurance costs have risen over 20 per cent in the last six months. For a hazardous load this is an increase of £1,000 per load. Hearing of LN Ltd's good fortune, DSTR Ltd demand an increase in their haulage rates of 20 per cent with immediate effect otherwise they would cease delivery forthwith. LN Ltd reluctantly agreed and pay £50,000 before they could find an alternative carrier.

Gloop plc provides the pigment for the nail polish. This ingredient now has to be approved by the US Food and Drugs Administration as well as the UK and EU agencies before the point of manufacture. Gloop plc feels that LN Ltd should pay £5,000 per annum to cover the costs of the testing. Unless they agree to do so Gloop plc has said it will cease to offer credit on any orders.

Advise LN Ltd if the monies paid to the Union and DSTR Ltd can be recovered and whether they are bound to Gloop plc to pay for testing.

Answer plan

→ Define economic duress and its effect on a contract.

→ Determine whether the action of the Administrative Dock Workers' Union is unlawful, as commercial pressure exerted is illegitimate where a tort or criminal offence has been committed.

→ Consider the test in *DSND Subsea Ltd* v *Petroleum Geo-Services* as to the situation with DSTR threatening to breach the contract with LN Ltd.

→ Evaluate whether it is possible to have lawful act duress in the context of Gloop plc refusing credit.

Diagram plan

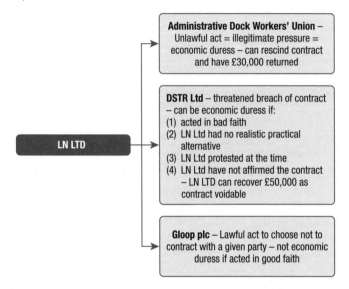

Administrative Dock Workers' Union – Unlawful act = illegitimate pressure = economic duress – can rescind contract and have £30,000 returned

DSTR Ltd – threatened breach of contract – can be economic duress if:
(1) acted in bad faith
(2) LN Ltd had no realistic practical alternative
(3) LN Ltd protested at the time
(4) LN Ltd have not affirmed the contract – LN LTD can recover £50,000 as contract voidable

LN LTD

Gloop plc – Lawful act to choose not to contract with a given party – not economic duress if acted in good faith

A printable version of this diagram plan is available from www.pearsoned.co.uk/lawexpressqa

Answer

The doctrine of economic duress will render a contract voidable and allow the party subjected to the duress to rescind the contract, and where possible to restore the parties to substantially the position they were in before the contract was made. In establishing economic duress LN Ltd will be relying on a still evolving doctrine, the parameters for which can still be unclear.[1]

[1] Clearly identifies that if successful LN Ltd will get their money back, but that is dependent on the reach of the doctrine.

A formal doctrine of economic duress began to emerge following the decision in **Occidental Worldwide Investment Corporation v Skibs A/S Avanti, The Sibeon and The Sibotre** [1976] 1 Lloyd's Rep 293, which began to formulate a test which focused on the victim's ability to make a choice freely to enter the contract or whether there had been some 'coercion of will'. The judgment clearly pointed out that the coercion complained of must be more than commercial pressure and the victim must have protested at the time and not have affirmed the contract. In a commercial context there usually is a choice, probably the lesser of two evils, so the

The Sibeon and The Sibotre
→ *commercial pressure*
→ *victim protested*

coercion of will test perhaps was misdirected, focusing too much on the victim's position rather than the actions of the perpetrator. In **Universe Tankships Inc of Monrovia v International Transport Workers' Federation, The Universe Sentinel** [1983] 1 AC 366 the emphasis changed from the victim's state of mind to the legitimacy of the pressure applied.[2] The choice faced by the owners of *The Universe Sentinel* was similar to LN Ltd and the Administrative Dock Workers' Union: to pay up or have the goods stranded by the industrial action. Where actions are unlawful, involving the commission of a crime or tort, a court would find little difficulty in determining that the commercial pressure was illegitimate. Industrial action does attract some immunity from liability in tort for action taken in furtherance of a trade dispute. It is unlikely to apply in the current situation, as LN Ltd is not party to the dispute.[3] Increasingly emphasis is being put on the nature of the act in determining whether or not there has been economic duress. In **R v Attorney General for England and Wales** [2003] UKPC 22 Lord Hoffmann emphasised that the threat of any form of unlawful act will be regarded as illegitimate.[4] As such, LN Ltd will be able to recover the £30,000, provided they act promptly as soon as the pressure is removed to rescind the contract.[5]

The threat of a breach of contract is not of itself economic duress.[6] In **North Ocean Shipping Company v Hyundai Construction Co., The Atlantic Baron** [1979] QB 705 the defendants secured a modification to the agreement as to price by threatening not to complete the construction of an oil tanker. The court accepted that a threat to breach contract can amount to economic duress, but in this case the delay by the plaintiffs meant that they were deemed to have affirmed the variation in the contract. No consideration was given to whether or not the defendants had acted in bad faith in demanding the extra payment.[7] The more recent case of **Kolmar Group AG v Traxpo Enterprise Pvt Ltd** [2010] ICLC 256 has very similar facts to **The Atlantic Baron** but was decided according to the principles laid down in **DSDN Subsea Ltd v Petroleum Geo-Services ASA** [2000] BLR 530. The courts, while accepting that the threat of a breach of contract may amount to duress, state that normal commercial bargaining must be distinguished from illegitimate commercial pressure. To do this the court would have regard to the following factors: first, whether the person exerting the pressure has

[2] Tracing the development of the doctrine through decided case law with similar facts will give depth of analysis as well as accurate application to the work.

[3] Don't worry too much if you didn't know this; the question itself points out the unlawful act and your presumption would be acceptable.

[4] Use of up-to-date authorities supporting the point being made will impress the examiner.

[5] The right to rescission will be lost if the claimant does not act quickly enough.

[6] Starting from this statement allows you to develop your analysis incrementally to demonstrate what might amount to illegitimate pressure in this context.

[7] This leads neatly into a discussion of the more recent case law and the acceptance of the tests laid down in *DSND Subsea Ltd v Petroleum Geo-Services ASA*.

173

acted in good or bad faith; secondly, whether the victim had any realistic practical alternative; thirdly, whether the victim protested at the time; and finally, whether the victim could be deemed to have affirmed the contract. DSTR Ltd know they have no legal right to pass on the extra costs and are taking advantage of LN Ltd's position in needing to supply their new contractual obligation. It is questionable whether this is bad faith or merely sharp commercial opportunism. LN Ltd had no real practical alternative choice as they would need their raw materials to continue with production. This element of practical choice with the demise of the emphasis on the coercion of will test does tend to be evidential of a causal link between the duress and the contract being entered. LN Ltd communicated their reluctance and secured an alternative haulier as soon as possible. Therefore it is probable that LN Ltd would be able successfully to rescind the contract with DSTR Ltd and recover the £50,000 paid.[8]

[8] The application here is thorough and will gain extra marks, as it takes each element of the test in *DSND Subsea Ltd* v *Petroleum Geo-Services ASA* and applies them one by one to the facts of the question.

> courts have accepted a lawful act

The courts have accepted that a lawful act can amount to economic duress (***CTN Cash and Carry Ltd v Gallaher Ltd*** [1994] 4 All ER 714). In this case the defendants refused to offer credit terms on future orders unless losses following a robbery when goods were delivered to the wrong address were made good. This refusal did not amount to duress as the defendants, although wrong in their assertions as to where the losses should legally fall, did not act in bad faith. Therefore the suggestion would be that, in the absence of bad faith, it will be unlikely that economic duress for a lawful act would be found. Gloop plc are not acting in bad faith; they are not threatening to breach an existing contract or commit an unlawful act and LN Ltd could choose to do the testing themselves. Therefore LN Ltd, using the current tests developed in ***DSND Subsea Ltd* v *Petroleum Geo-Services ASA*** would be bound to the new contractual terms. Using the availability of credit is a legitimate means of securing a better bargain. Gloop plc are entitled to contract with whomsoever they want and to negotiate the best deal they can for themselves.[10]

[9] This is where the extent of the doctrine is still quite equivocal, and the depth of analysis here will take you up the marks.

[10] Again the application is directly structured to match the tests laid down, and spells out exactly why Gloop plc would not in these circumstances be found to have exercised anything other than legitimate commercial pressure.

The doctrine of economic duress has developed to the extent that principles are beginning to emerge. An unlawful act will amount to illegitimate pressure. A higher threshold of bad faith needs to be applied to the threat to breach a contract or a lawful act. What will amount to bad faith remains uncertain. Is it sufficient to take

[11] Conclusion highlights where the law is still in a state of flux, demonstrating an understanding of the law beyond the basic principles.

advantage of a claimant's weakness? The concepts of bad and good faith is not a concept generally recognised in English contract law and will continue to cause difficulty in its definition.[11]

→what is bad faith etc

 Make your answer stand out

- Consider how the recent decision in *Kolmar Group AG* v *Traxpo Enterprises PVT Ltd* puts the test laid down in *DSND Subsea Ltd* v *Petroleum Geo-Services* into practice. Read a case commentary on this: for example, Y. Baatz (2010) International sales: market price – illegitimate seller pressure, 16(2) *JIML* 88–9.

! Don't be tempted to . . .

- Miss the depth of analysis in applying the law supported by cases with similar facts which, although reaching similar conclusions, pre-date current emphasis and tests in this area. For example, *The Atlantic Baron* has very similar facts, but you would miss out on higher marks if you did not apply current developments, as in *DSND Subsea Ltd* v *Petroleum Geo-Services ASA* to the question.

Question 3

Evaluate the decision in *Royal Bank of Scotland* v *Etridge (No. 2)* [2001] 4 All ER 449 from the perspective of a spouse acting as surety for their partner and the effects on a creditor put on notice that the potential for undue influence exists.

Answer plan

→ Define undue influence and its effect on a contract.

→ Consider if a new approach was taken in *Royal Bank of Scotland* v *Etridge (No. 2)*.

→ Evaluate the particular concerns of creditors.

→ Discuss whether *Etridge (No. 2)* potentially has strengthened the creditor's position at the expense of the vulnerable party to whom the doctrine is aimed at affording protection.

Diagram plan

| Royal Bank of Scotland v Etridge (No. 2) |

| Emphasis moved from classification to the transaction being of a type requiring explanation | Manifest disadvantage of evidential value only no longer legal requirement for undue influence | Laid out steps for creditor, put on notice of undue influence, to protect bargain struck with vulnerable party |

A printable version of this diagram plan is available from www.pearsoned.co.uk/lawexpressqa

Answer

The equitable doctrine of undue influence enables a court to set aside or modify the terms of a contract. ***Royal Bank of Scotland v Etridge (No. 2)*** [2001] 4 All ER 449 concerned an application to have a mortgage set aside on the grounds of a husband's undue influence upon his wife. If the contract is set aside the bank would be unable to enforce its security.[1] The case considers the doctrine as a whole and provides clear guidance for creditors as to how their interests can be protected.

[1] This clearly states the potential impact on a creditor.

Before the decision in ***Etridge (No. 2)*** the courts had divided the doctrine into two categories of actual undue influence and presumed undue influence. Actual undue influence has overlaps with duress, as it comprises overt acts of improper pressure which coerce the will, but it is wider than just unlawful threats. Lord Hobhouse in ***Etridge (No. 2)*** described actual undue influence as being a wrong committed by the dominant party against the other which would make it unconscionable for the dominant party to enforce their legal rights against the other.

The category of presumed undue influence has more subtle characteristics and traditionally had two sub-categories of a presumption of undue influence: first, an irrebuttable presumption determined by virtue of the nature of the relationship, for example doctor and patient; and secondly, a rebuttable presumption where a claimant would have to demonstrate that they did actually repose trust and confidence in the dominant party (husbands and wives fell into this category). Having established that influence exists, the claimant has to prove that the transaction requires an explanation. Following ***Etridge (No. 2)*** it was felt that these categories of presumption added little to the analysis of whether the doctrine would operate. Relationships such as doctor and patient evidentially will raise a greater likelihood of a transaction needing to be questioned, but to have one broad category does recognise that relationships vary from individual to individual.[2] Once it is established that one party reposes trust and confidence in the other and the influence is established, it must then be shown that the influence was undue. This raises the question of whether there has to be some element of wrongdoing. It would appear that the approach taken in the older case of *Allcard v Skinner* (1887) 36 Ch D 145 would be favoured post-*Etridge (No. 2)*; the transaction calls for explanation as it cannot be reasonably accounted for on the grounds of friendship, relationship, or other ordinary motive.[3] Inter alia, the case of *Etridge (No. 2)* removed the need to demonstrate manifest disadvantage as a requirement for undue influence, as in *National Westminster Bank plc v Morgan* [1985] AC 686. In this case the claimant lost, as she could demonstrate no manifest disadvantage in having benefitted from remaining in the matrimonial home longer than she would have done without the additional financing. This looks as though the vulnerable spouse in cases such as *Etridge (No. 2)* would benefit from not having manifest disadvantage as a legal requirement for the doctrine to operate, but evidentially the presence of manifest disadvantage as a result of the transaction will usually tip the balance in the finding of undue influence.[4]

Perhaps the balance achieved in *Etridge (No. 2)* between the creditor and the party alleging undue influence is that the creditor will be put on notice that the potential for undue influence exists where the debtor is a non-commercial party.[5] A court will not be too quick to determine a transaction as wrongful, as it would be perfectly natural for a wife to wish to support her husband's business, but the creditor will have to make sure that steps are taken to ensure that a decision is taken freely. This suggests therefore that a wife in this situation will find the doctrine difficult to rely upon unless she can demonstrate that the husband used some unfair means to get her agreement, such as misrepresentation, or a huge disparity exists between the husband's gain and the wife's loss. This would appear to give greater protection to the creditor, but by being put on inquiry there is deemed to be constructive knowledge of any impropriety which they must dispel.[6] This can be done by the party benefitting

[2] Depth is achieved here by recognising in the subsequent analysis that the emphasis is moving to the transaction being questioned rather than the relationship.

[3] This links to a later point of the creditor being automatically put on notice where a wife stands as surety for her husband.

[4] Good application to the question demonstrating the effect in the change in the requirement to demonstrate manifest disadvantage.

[5] Good interpretation of the question looking for the balance the law needs to achieve in protecting a vulnerable party and a creditor.

[6] Excellent point leading into the steps that a creditor must take to protect their investment.

from the transaction demonstrating that the other party acted freely. In an **Etridge (No. 2)** type scenario the best way of doing this is to demonstrate that independent advice was given before entering the transaction. In **First National Bank plc v Achampong** [2003] EWCA Civ 487 it was strongly suggested that the creditor confirm that the independent adviser covered all the essential points as laid out in the decision in **Etridge (No. 2)**. Furthermore in **Pesticcio v Huet** [2004] EWCA Civ 372 the involvement of a solicitor did not assure that a transaction would not be tainted with undue influence.[7]

[7] By using cases decided post-*Etridge (No. 2)* you are demonstrating an up-to-date knowledge of the law and also a recognition that creditors cannot just have a 'tick box' process in place.

Etridge (No. 2) ensured in circumstances where a surety has been provided by a party who potentially has been subjected to undue influence, that, regardless of categorisation of relationship, the creditor is put on notice of the potential threat to the proposed transaction. A creditor would protect their interest best by ensuring that processes are adhered to that would demonstrate that a transaction was freely entered into. Proving undue influence is still burdensome for the claimant where the transaction is not unusual, even though they may have preferred not to assume such a risk. The steps laid down by **Etridge (No. 2)** requiring assurance of having received independent advice did initially appear to let a creditor shift the burden of the accuracy of advice given to another professional. Recent case law has put the emphasis back on to the creditor to ensure that the situation is truly understood. This does perhaps redress the balance to some extent, focusing on the actions of the creditor and not just the claimant.[8]

[8] A strong conclusion directly focused on the question which draws the threads of the analysis effectively together.

✓ Make your answer stand out

- There is plenty of discussion in academic journals of the decision and developments of the law post-*Etridge (No. 2)*: consider incorporating the analysis contained in the following:
  - Developing O'Brien by D.B. O'Sullivan (2002) 118 *LQR* 337;
  - Situation critical by Mike Griffiths (2010) 160 *NLJ* 1251, as this article reinforces the necessity of creditors to ensure that their clients seek independent advice and the consequences of a failure to do so.
- Consider *Annulment Funding Co. Ltd* v *Cowey* [2010] All ER (D) 205 (Jun) and the proposition that the true effect of *Etridge (No. 2)* is to reduce the practical relevance of the presumption of undue influence, concentrating on the fact that there is a transaction before the court which requires an explanation.

> **! Don't be tempted to . . .**
>
> - Miss out on the refinements to the doctrine made in *Etridge (No. 2)*: for instance, the role of manifest disadvantage.
> - Forget that the decision in *Etridge (No. 2)* gives increased protection to the creditor to take steps to protect their interests rather than affording any real additional protection to the vulnerable party.
> - Avoid looking beyond the decision in *Etridge (No. 2)* which is now over 10 years old; examiners will be looking for fresh areas of discussion.

❓ Question 4

Frank is the principal architect in his firm. Jenny has worked in his office for 20 years. Business has slowed down. Frank knows Jenny's mother has just died and left her some money. Frank suggests to Jenny that she could invest in the firm's latest project to redevelop a landfill site and that this would give them all job security. Frank suggests that she purchase £25,000 of shares in CLCU Ltd, contaminated land clean-up specialists, who Frank will use if he gets the development project and in whom he is a major shareholder.

Jenny uses the £25,000 she inherited from her mother's estate to purchase the shares. Frank also says he needs, as a temporary measure, someone to act as surety for the firm's overdraft while his assets are tied up pending divorce proceedings. Jenny goes to the B & C Bank plc, accompanied by Frank to complete the requisite paperwork to secure the overdraft. The B & C Bank plc have dealt with Frank over a number of years and profited greatly from capital projects they have been involved in. Phil, the bank manager, recognises Jenny from Frank's office but does not comment for fear of offending Frank. Phil writes to Jenny suggesting she take independent advice before putting up her home as security against the firm's debts, but he never checks to see if this was done and the transaction proceeds.

Shortly after investing in CLCU Ltd, Jenny is made redundant as Frank did not secure the redevelopment project. Jenny regrets buying the shares and the bank is threatening to repossess her home.

Advise Jenny as she feels she was tricked into purchasing the shares and badly advised in taking out the loan.

Answer plan

→ Introduce the concept of the equitable doctrine of undue influence and its potential effect on a contract.

→ Consider if Frank's actions could amount to actual undue influence.

→ Investigate the presumption of undue influence following the decision in *Etridge (No. 2)* in the context of Jenny and Frank's relationship.

→ Discuss whether the loan from the bank was tainted by any of Frank's influence.

Diagram plan

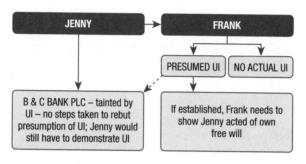

A printable version of this diagram plan is available from www.pearsoned.co.uk/lawexpressqa

Answer

For a contract to be enforceable, agreement to the terms must have been freely given. The equitable doctrine of undue influence will protect a party to a contract where some form of improper pressure has been applied. If Jenny can establish that she entered the contract for the purchase of the shares and took responsibility for the firm's debts acting under Frank's undue influence, the court may have the contracts set aside.[1]

[1] This is an effective opening, going from the general principles concerned to the precise interests of the characters concerned.

There are two ways that a contract can be avoided for undue influence and that is by establishing either actual or presumed undue influence. Actual undue influence was described in *Etridge (No. 2)* [2001] 4 All ER 449 as being an overt act of improper pressure or coercion such as unlawful threats. Suggesting that Jenny's employment was insecure may have induced her to enter the contract; however, Frank did not use an unlawful threat nor were his actions 'overt'.[2] Frank may have gained a personal advantage in securing a capital injection for a company he has an interest in and having Jenny act as surety for the firm's debts, but his actions fall short of cheating, victimisation or being overbearing (***Williams v Bayley*** (1866) LR 1 HL 200).

[2] This point is well made: if too broadly interpreted, it would be difficult to draw the distinction between actual and presumed undue influence.

It is more likely that Jenny will be able to demonstrate presumed undue influence.[3] If she can establish that a relationship of trust and confidence existed with Frank, then she will have established that the influence existed. This type of influence can be open to abuse without overt acts of pressure or persuasion. The relationship of employer and employee never raised an irrebuttable presumption of undue influence, even prior to the decision in *Etridge (No. 2)*.[4] The relationship of employer and employee requires the court to look at the relationship before them to determine if one party reposed sufficient trust and confidence in the other such that the transaction concerned warranted examination, raising a rebuttable presumption of presumed undue influence. Frank and Jenny have worked together for 20 years, she in a subordinate position. As a question of fact, Jenny does appear to have placed trust and confidence in Frank. Not only does she hand over her inheritance money but she also takes Frank with her to secure the bank's overdraft and never appears to question this course of action. Having established that Jenny reposed trust and confidence in Frank, it would be necessary to show that the transaction concerned called for an explanation. Prior to *Etridge (No. 2)* a claimant would have to demonstrate that they had suffered a manifest disadvantage (*National Westminster Bank plc v Morgan* [1985] AC 686). This would not have been a problem for Jenny as she has lost all her savings and potentially will lose her home. Manifest disadvantage is no longer a legal requirement for establishing undue influence but does provide evidence of its presence. The test now to be used in this context would appear to be the one used in *Allcard v Skinner* (1887) 36 Ch D 145, which suggested that the transaction should be capable of explanation on the grounds of friendship, relationship, charity or other ordinary motives on which ordinary men act. Spending all of an inheritance on an employer's business and then providing your home as security for your employer's debts is not the usual type of transaction undertaken between an employer and employee.[5] Frank does appear to have taken advantage of Jenny's trust in him and used her insecurity to gain an advantage for himself. Frank can rebut the presumption of undue influence if he can demonstrate that Jenny acted of her own free will. At no point did he suggest she seek independent advice on the share purchase or the transaction with the bank.[6]

[3] In this topic always demonstrate the influence by explaining why one party would be dominant over the other, and then question the transaction as being undue.

[4] The relationships having previously raised an irrebuttable presumption evidentially may suggest that trust and confidence was present by the very nature of that relationship, but the automatic presumption no longer exists. Alluding to this gives depth to your analysis.

[5] A strong structure to the work allows extra marks to be gained by fully developing your analysis. Here clear application to the question is made while giving depth to the analysis in tracing the current developments surrounding manifest disadvantage.

[6] This analysis emphasises that the claimant must raise the presumption of undue influence which the defendant can then rebut.

With regard to the doctrine of undue influence, it is not unusual for a third party to have their contractual agreement tainted. Phil knew who Jenny and Frank were and, as such, the B & C Bank plc were placed on inquiry that the potential for undue influence existed (**Credit Lyonnais Bank Nederland NV v Burch** [1997] 1 All ER 144).[7] **Etridge (No. 2)** made clear that the true nature of the transaction concerned should have put a lending institution on notice in these circumstances even if Phil had not recognised Jenny and her relationship with Frank. Jenny was putting a domestic property up as security; the person being dealt with was evidently providing a non-commercial service. Following the decision in **Etridge (No. 2)** any creditor in B & C Bank plc's position, once having constructive notice of potential undue influence, will have their transaction impugned by that undue influence unless they can demonstrate that they took reasonable steps to ensure that the other party, in this case Jenny, had given their agreement freely.[8] What amounts to reasonable steps was laid out in **Etridge (No. 2)**. It will be insufficient simply to recommend such action. The bank, to protect its interest, will have to verify that not only did such a meeting take place but also the requisite issues were discussed (**First National Bank plc v Achampong** [2003] EWCA Civ 487). Where the creditor has suspicions of behaviour indicating that the client may not be entering the transaction of their own free will, then those must be communicated to the independent adviser. In **Pesticcio v Huet** [2004] EWCA Civ 372 the involvement of a solicitor did not assure that a transaction would not be tainted with undue influence. Therefore it can be seen that Phil's actions fell short of the requirements in **Etridge (No. 2)** to demonstrate that Jenny entered the transaction of her own free will.[9] Although Phil has not complied with the procedures in **Etridge (No. 2)** Jenny will still have to show that the transaction was wrongful. The emphasis is very much on the behaviour of the wrongdoer, Frank.

The effect of undue influence is to render the contract voidable. The victim must therefore take steps to rescind the contract. Rescission is available provided that restitution must be possible, the contract has not been affirmed or third parties have not acquired title to the property concerned. These bars do not appear to hamper Jenny's remedy should the courts agree that the contract with the bank and for the purchase of the shares should be put aside.

[7] The case concerned the head of a company using a junior employee as a surety – a good knowledge of Etridge (No. 2) would lead you to this conclusion.

[8] Extra marks will be gained for articulating the concept of constructive notice of potential undue influence, even though the bank had actual notice because of Phil's knowledge of the individuals involved.

[9] An adequate answer would have recognised that the bank had notice of the potential undue influence and the steps in Etridge (No. 2) which have not been taken; this analysis builds depth in recognising just how far short the Bank's actions have fallen.

Make your answer stand out

- Consider *Riverpath Properties Ltd* v *Yegres* [2001] All ER (D) 281 (Mar) for an authority as to the requirement of oppressive behaviour to amount to actual undue influence.
- Read P. Birks (2004) Undue influence as wrongful exploitation, 120 *LQR* 34 to help develop depth to your analysis by using the support of academic opinion.

 Don't be tempted to . . .

- Give insufficient depth to your analysis by stopping when you have the instant solution. Phil recognises Jenny: this makes your application obvious and easy; consider if it would have made any difference if he hadn't recognised her. An examiner will be impressed if you stay relevant and fully explore the ramifications of the decision in *Etridge (No. 2)* and beyond in such situations.

www.pearsoned.co.uk/lawexpressqa

Go online to access more revision support including additional essay and problem questions with diagram plans, You be the marker questions, and download all diagrams from the book.

Discharge, performance and breach

8

How this topic may come up in exams

Questions will focus on when the right to terminate a contract arises out of the other party's breach, whether from some defect in performance or an anticipatory breach. Ensure you can deal with deviations from the general rules, such as rendering exact and precise performance of a contractual obligation and any potential limitation to the innocent party's right to affirm a contract following an anticipatory breach.

Attack the question

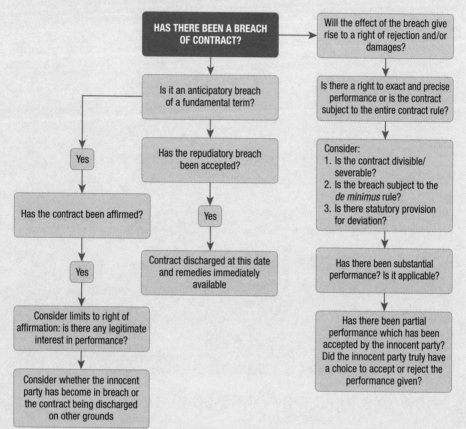

A printable version of this diagram is available from www.pearsoned.co.uk/lawexpressqa

▨ Question 1

Evaluate the extent to which a party to a contract can insist on exact and precise performance of a condition in a contract.

Answer plan

→ Evaluate the entire performance rule and severable contracts.

→ Consider the strict performance rule as outlined in *Arcos* v *Ronaasen* and reflected in the Sale of Goods Act 1979.

→ Evaluate any possible derogation from a strict adherence to these rules.

→ Consider the operation of the doctrines of substantial and partial performance.

Diagram plan

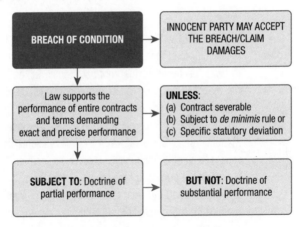

A printable version of this diagram plan is available from www.pearsoned.co.uk/lawexpressqa

Answer

[1] The question is asking about the quality of the performance of a condition that has to be rendered, not the nature of the remedies or terms, therefore to go further than this would detract from the focus of the question asked.

Contracts are formed on the basis of promises made which can be legally enforced. Once a contract is performed the parties' obligations to each other are discharged. If a condition of the contract is not performed, then the contract has been breached and the innocent party may have the right to accept the breach and treat themselves as discharged from the contract and/or claim damages.[1]

In **Cutter v Powell** (1795) 6 Term R 320 the widow of a seaman could not claim for the wages earned by her husband on a *quantum meruit* basis when he died two days before completion of a voyage from Jamaica to Liverpool. The contract had been negotiated at a higher rate, with payment to be made in full on completion of the voyage. Contracts that are drafted so that obligations are conditional on being entirely and completely performed will be subject to the entire contracts rule.[2] This will not apply to a severable contract, whereby the performance rendered raises a contractual obligation to pay as a separate obligation.

The question arises as to what amounts to performance and whether a very minor departure from the terms of a contract can allow a party to treat their obligations as discharged or give rise to a claim in damages, even though their true motivation for doing this is that the contract has proved to be less of a good deal than originally believed.[3]

In **Arcos Ltd v E.A. Ronaasen & Sons Ltd** [1933] AC 470 Lord Atkin reinforced the principle that a party to a contract has the right to have the terms of the contract strictly adhered to: 'A ton does not mean about a ton, or a yard about a yard. Still less when you descend to minute measurements does half an inch mean about half an inch.' Accordingly the purchaser of wooden staves for the manufacture of barrels could reject the whole consignment as they were 1/16th of an inch thicker than contracted for. This deviation did not affect the purpose of the timber or the quality of the end product. However, having the right to terminate the contract if he so wished meant that the purchaser's obligations ceased and he was free to renegotiate the price of the timber or gain supplies elsewhere, profiting from the falling price of timber. Lord Atkin recognised that in order to maintain a good working relationship a party might choose not to enforce strict legal rights. In a falling market a party will be eager to insist on enforcing their legal rights and the courts should support this.[4] A seller can, of course, in negotiating a contract work into the terms some flexibility as to their obligations. Similarly in **Re Moore & Co. and Landauer & Co.'s Arbitration** [1921] 2 KB 519 a contract for the sale of tinned fruit could lawfully be rejected when delivered in cases of 24 instead of 30. The market value was not affected and the correct number of tins was delivered. However, the Sale of Goods Act 1893 provided under section 13 that goods must

[2] This line of argument is a theme throughout the work; the parties themselves decided on the extent of respective obligations.

[3] This short paragraph links neatly from the potential harshness of the entire contracts rule to question whether the law allows any deviation from exact and precise performance of a condition, giving a strong structured flow to the work.

[4] Depth of analysis will achieve a higher grade; here the work follows Lord Atkin's declarations as to precise compliance, on to discussing the commercial reality of why a party might be motivated to take a certain course of action.

correspond to their description and, as such, the purchaser could reject the goods as they did not match their description of being packaged in cases of 30. This was a condition of the contract implied by statute. ***Reardon Smith Line Ltd* v *Yngvar Hansen-Tangen*** [1976] 1 WLR 989 drew a distinction between words identifying goods, in this case 'Yard No. 354 at Osaka', and the actual description of the goods, which would be a condition of the contract. In this case a ship had been built according to the contractual specifications, but when the market in these ships collapsed the purchasers sought to repudiate the contract on the grounds that it did not match its description. Lord Wilberforce considered that the decisions in both ***Arcos* v *Ronaasen*** and ***Moore & Co. and Landauer & Co.*** encouraged the excessive use of the right of repudiation.[5]

[5] Adds balance to the argument (remember if not a condition, no right to repudiation; the question focuses only on breach of conditions).

The strict approach to performance of a condition has statutory support, for example in relation to sections 13, 14, and 15 of the Sale of Goods Act 1979. However, section 15A of the Sale of Goods Act 1979 has provided some relaxation in the harshness of the operation of this rule; in the context of non-consumer transactions, the right to reject goods is limited where the breach is so slight that it would be unreasonable for the buyer to reject the goods, subject to an express or implied term. Additionally, section 4(2) of the Sale and Supply of Goods Act 1994 in non-commercial transactions provides that, where quantities are delivered where the shortfall or excess is so slight that it would be unreasonable for the buyer to reject the goods, they may not do so. In ***Arcos Ltd* v *E.A. Ronaasen & Sons Ltd*** Lord Atkin did accept that 'microscopic' deviations would be ignored by the law under the *de minimis* principle; however, if the contract expressly provided for exact and precise performance, then this would not apply.

The doctrine of substantial performance can be used to mitigate the effects of the entire contracts rule, but not where the breach is a breach of condition as opposed to a breach of a warranty or an innominate term (***Boone* v *Eyre*** (1779) 96 ER 767).[6] The doctrine allows the recovery of the contract price less any amount required to put the defects right (***Hoenig* v *Isaacs*** [1952] 2 All ER 176).

[6] Again, here you demonstrate that you have understood the focus of the question on the performance of conditions.

By contrast the doctrine of partial performance can apply to a breach of a condition. The innocent party may, if they choose to do so, accept partial performance of a contractual obligation and pay on a *quantum meruit* basis for the benefit received, even though the contract was not intended to be severable, and providing the innocent party truly has a choice to accept or reject the work done (**Sumpter v Hedges** [1898] 1 QB 673).[7]

[7] Linking back to the previous issue of severable contracts illustrates a depth of understanding.

Breach of a contractual condition allows an innocent party to accept that repudiatory breach and treat the contract as discharged. The law will not allow for very slight deviations from exact performance in commercial contracts to be tolerated, unless permissible by statute or the *de minimis* rule. The parties can themselves control the requirements of exact or entire performance in the contract they negotiate, and equally the innocent party is at liberty to accept less than perfect performance, but the law will as a general rule not impose an obligation upon them to do so.[8]

[8] A strong conclusion will summarise the main thrust of the analysis, directly focused on the question set.

✓ Make your answer stand out

- Read In defence of *Sumpter* v *Hedges*, by R. Stevens and B. McFarlane (2002) 118 *LQR* 569, which supports the line of argument taken in answer to the above question and will add academic authority to the analysis.

! Don't be tempted to . . .

- Be too general in your analysis. The question asks about performance of a condition, therefore you need to focus on the right to repudiate.
- Lose marks by not having a logical flow to the analysis put forward. The hardest part of this question was determining that structure-planning is key.

? Question 2

Rosa is a builder and she has secured a contract with Nascent Developments Ltd to convert an old public toilet into a three bedroom bungalow. Instead of providing the usual costings for the job, Rosa has negotiated that she will take 10 per cent of the sale price achieved for the property.

Rosa begins work but unfortunately falls ill and cannot continue with the contract. She has already removed the toilets, sinks, doors and tiles. This work has left the surrounding land covered in rubble and the building is now an empty shell with large holes leading to very smelly sewers.

Rosa claims that the work she has done is worth £1,000 on a *quantum meruit* basis.

Nascent Developments Ltd hires Danny to finish the job. This he does, but Nascent Developments refuse to pay him the £10,000 owed as they say the work is shoddy in parts, the back door sticks, the skirting boards do not fit and the outside space still has some rubble on it.

Bertrand had been hired as a freelance property journalist to write and find a publisher for a piece on the refurbishment for £500. The day after the contract was agreed Nascent Developments Ltd said that they no longer wanted him to continue with the project. The reason for this is they have been approached by the BBC to be featured on a magazine programme, which will give them free publicity at no cost whatsoever. Bertrand continues with the work, publishes the article and is claiming his £500.

Advise Nascent Developments Ltd if they have to pay Rosa £1,000, Danny £10,000 and Bertrand £500 in the context of the performance of their contractual duties.

Answer plan

→ Define Rosa's position and the rule in *Cutter* v *Powell*.

→ Explain why the doctrine of partial performance could not operate here.

→ Discuss if Danny has rendered substantial performance.

→ Consider the consequences for Nascent Developments Ltd as a result of their anticipatory breach.

Diagram plan

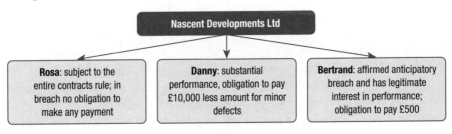

A printable version of this diagram plan is available from www.pearsoned.co.uk/lawexpressqa

Answer

The law of contract looks to enforce agreements and hold parties to the terms they freely agreed to. The extent to which Nascent

Developments Ltd can demand exact and entire performance[1] from Rosa and Danny will depend on the construction of the contract and the intentions of the parties. Nascent Developments Ltd will be discharged from all liabilities as to payment if they are entitled to reject the contract. However, the doctrines of substantial and partial performance can provide some relief for the party in breach. As regards the commissioning of Bertrand, Nascent Developments Ltd may have committed an anticipatory breach of contract in expressly communicating their intention not to perform their contractual obligations.[2]

Rosa and Nascent Developments Ltd have deliberately negotiated their contract in such a way that only on completion of the entire obligation is any payment due. In **Cutter v Powell** (1795) 6 Term R 320 the widow of a sailor, who had negotiated payment at a higher rate than usual, to be paid on completion of the voyage from Jamaica to Liverpool, could not claim for work done when he died two days before completion. Similarly, Rosa cannot claim for any of the work and time she has expended on this project, as Rosa has assumed the risk that she will complete the task. Nascent Developments Ltd will take the benefit of the performance rendered without incurring any legal liability for the benefit they have received. Lord Atkin in **Arcos Ltd v E.A. Ronaasen & Sons Ltd** [1933] AC 470 had little sympathy for those finding themselves in Rosa's position, as had she so wished she could have negotiated a better deal, removing such a risk of completion from herself.[3]

The doctrine of partial performance may provide relief where that partial performance of a contractual obligation is accepted by the innocent party. As the whole of the contract is not rejected on the grounds of the breach, payment has to be made for the benefit received. Rosa, therefore, if the doctrine were to operate, would be able to claim for the work done on a *quantum meruit* basis.[4] In **Sumpter v Hedges** [1898] 1 QB 673 a builder could not claim for work completed before he abandoned work, even though the buildings contracted for were fairly near completion. The defendant had had no option but to accept the performance given. Nascent Developments Ltd is not really choosing to accept Rosa's performance with regard to the work done on the renovation: what they have been left with is a problem which needs a resolution.[5]

Danny is in breach of contract but it could be argued that these are fairly minor breaches. In such circumstances it may be possible for Danny to claim payment on the grounds that he has substantially performed his contractual obligations. This principle was established by Lord Mansfield in the case of **Boone v Eyre** (1779) 96 ER 767. In effect, Danny is claiming the price for the work done and Nascent Developments Ltd is counter-claiming for a breach of warranty, or an innominate term which would be treated as a breach of warranty. Such minor breaches only give rise to an action in damages: they do not allow the innocent party to treat the contract as discharged.[6] In **Hoenig v Isaacs** [1952] 2 All ER 176 the defendants refused to pay the contract price of £750, claiming that the work was defective. The court found that there were defects in the work but these could be rectified at a cost of £55. The plaintiffs could therefore recover the full contract price less the cost of remedial work. Following this principle, Nascent Developments Ltd would have to pay Danny £10,000 less the value of any remedial work.[7]

Bertrand has not started work on the article, however, Nascent Developments Ltd have committed an anticipatory breach in expressly communicating their intention not to perform their contractual obligations. This gives rise to an immediate cause of action (**Hochester v De La Tour** (1853) 2 E & B 678). As the breach by Nascent Developments concerns a fundamental term of the contract, the breach is repudiatory, which means that Bertrand can accept the breach, be discharged from all his obligations under the contract and claim damages (**Afovos Shipping Co. SA v Pagnan & Lli, The Afovos** [1983] 1 All ER 449).[8] In this situation Bertrand would only receive nominal damages as he has not as yet begun any work. It may therefore be to his advantage as the innocent party to affirm the contract, continue with performance and then sue for price. In **White and Carter (Councils) Ltd v McGregor** [1962] AC 413 the appellants successfully sued for price on a contract for advertising the defendant's business, even though they sought to cancel on the same day as the contract was formed. The advertisements ran for the full three years of the contract. An exception to this rule can be found if there is no legitimate interest in performance. Bertrand is a freelance journalist. The more he publishes the more he is likely to gain a reputation as a writer and therefore he does have a legitimate interest in performing the contract with Nascent Developments Ltd.

[6] This really demonstrates a detailed knowledge and understanding of the legal principles involved.

[7] Emphasising the application to the problem will demonstrate the ability to use the knowledge of the legal principles discussed effectively.

[8] This paragraph has a strong build of the principles under discussion with accurate application threaded all the way through.

From the above application of the law, it can be seen that insistence on exact and precise performance of a contract can have quite harsh repercussions on the party in breach where the contract can be terminated by reason of the breach. Rosa will not be able to recover any monies for her endeavours; however, she did assume this risk. Rosa will not be able to rely on the doctrine of partial performance as Nascent Developments Ltd had no real option but to accept the work done, receiving a problem rather than a benefit. The doctrine of substantial performance also prevents unjust enrichment whereby the innocent party to a breach could escape any liability whatsoever for very minor defects in performance. This will allow Danny to recover for work done but not allow him to profit from his skimped performance. The doctrine of anticipatory breach leaves Bertrand, as the innocent party, the choice of accepting that breach and continuing with performance. As he has done this he is entitled to recover the £500.[9]

[9] The conclusion directly answers all the factual issues raised by the question.

✓ Make your answer stand out

- Consider the interpretation and commentary given by M. Dockray in *Cutter* v *Powell*: a trip outside the text (2001) 117 *LQR* 664.
- Read J. Fisher's (1981) Contract – repudiation of substantially performed contract for defective workmanship, 84 *LS Gazette* 30; academic and practitioner's opinions like this will help you follow the legal thinking behind the way the principles you have learnt are being applied in practice.
- Consider developing the analysis around anticipatory breach and a legitimate interest in performance, try to use some cases decided after *White & Carter* v *McGregor*, such as *Ocean Marine Navigation Ltd* v *Koch Carbon Inc.*, The Dynamic [2003] EWHC 1936 (Comm).

! Don't be tempted to . . .

- Lose depth of analysis in not fully exploring issues raised by very straightforward facts which have provided a simple structure for you.

 **Question 3**

Discuss the proposition that the law surrounding anticipatory breach of contract overly favours the innocent party.

Answer plan

→ Define anticipatory breach and the choice of response the innocent party has.

→ Evaluate any risks on the part of the innocent party in not accepting the anticipatory breach when communicated.

→ Consider the decision in *White & Carter (Councils) Ltd* v *McGregor*.

→ Discuss whether Lord Reid's assertions as to a 'legitimate interest' requirement have been followed.

Diagram plan

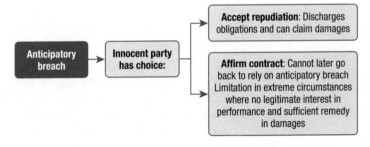

A printable version of this diagram plan is available from www.pearsoned.co.uk/lawexpressqa

Answer

A breach of a condition in a contract will give the innocent party the option to accept that breach and treat the contract as discharged, or to affirm the contract and claim damages. A breach of warranty or innominate term where the consequences of breach are less serious will only give rise to a claim of damages. An anticipatory breach will usually be a repudiatory breach signalling that no performance, or performance inconsistent with the contractual agreement, will be tendered.[1] The innocent party has the same rights as an innocent party dealing with a breach of a fundamental term to affirm

[1] This topic requires the accurate use of technical language.

or accept the repudiation and treat the contract as discharged (*Afovos Shipping Co. SA* v *Pagnan & Lli,* **The Afovos** [1983] 1 All ER 449).

Communication of the anticipatory breach can be expressly or impliedly made. Communicating that the contractual obligations will not be met provides the innocent party with an opportunity to seek performance elsewhere and could well reduce the liability of the party in breach. This can reduce hardship and loss on both sides.[2]

[2] Focusing directly on the question demonstrates the ability to address knowledge to pertinment issues, showing understanding rather than rote learning.

The innocent party, having received communication of an anticipatory breach, can treat the contract as discharged even though no actual breach has occurred, provided that they communicate their intention to accept the breach and to terminate the contract (*Hochester* v *De La Tour* (1853) 2 E & B 678). This does appear to favour the innocent party as the options all remain with them.

Greater care has to be taken with implied communications of anticipatory breaches or, indeed, express communications which are not in actual fact a repudiation of the contract but a disagreement as to the true construction of the contract (*Woodar Investments Development UK Ltd* v *Wimpey Construction Ltd* [1980] 1 WLR 277). In *Vitol SA* v *Norlef Ltd,* **The Santa Clara** [1996] 3 All ER 193 it fell to be decided whether simply not performing an obligation could amount to communication of acceptance of a repudiatory breach. It was held that it depended on the circumstances and the construction of the contract.[3]

[3] Depth of analysis gains higher marks here: recognising how careful the 'innocent party' has to be in reacting to an anticipatory breach in not putting themselves in breach or being liable for a wrongful repudiation of the contract.

A party that has been made aware of an anticipatory breach can choose to accept the breach and continue with performance of the contract. This contains certain risks. The innocent party will be liable to perform their obligations and, should they subsequently be in breach of contract themselves, they cannot go back and rely on the earlier anticipatory breach (*Fercometal SARL* v *Mediterranean Shipping Co. SA,* **The Simona** [1989] AC 788). Even a frustrating event which occurs after affirmation will mean that both parties are excused from further performance, and again the innocent party cannot look back to an earlier anticipatory breach (*Avery* v *Bowden* (1855) 5 E & B 714). The choice as to accepting the repudiation or affirming the contract lies with the innocent party, who is then bound by that choice and runs the risk in affirmation that the other party will

[4] This analysis demonstrates that the innocent party does not completely have it their own way; once they have made a decision, they must abide by that choice and any resulting consequences.

escape any future liability on account of that anticipatory breach.[4] Of course, if the party in breach remains in breach at the date fixed for performance, even having affirmed the contract the innocent party may accept the repudiatory breach, treat the contract as discharged and claim damages.

In affirming the contract the innocent party is obliged to continue with the performance of their obligations. This can cause injustice where the other party does not want the performance. In *White & Carter (Councils) Ltd* v *McGregor* [1962] AC 413 the defendants entered a three-year contract for advertisements on the plaintiff's litterbins. They sought to cancel their order the same day. The contract had been formed. The act of cancellation was an anticipatory breach communicating that they did not wish to continue with the performance of the contract. As the innocent party, the plaintiffs had the option to accept the repudiation and claim damages. At this point, there would not have been any losses other than the actual breach of contract, which gives nominal damages as of right. Alternatively, the plaintiffs could affirm the breach, continue with the contract and then at the end of the three years sue for the contract price.[5]

[5] A coherent flow to the argument will demonstrate a depth of understanding; here the issue is described, illustrated with the facts of the case, which are then transformed into a technical legal analysis of the emergent principle.

There is no obligation to mitigate losses with anticipatory breach, nor can a claimant be forced to accept the repudiation. The House of Lords held that the plaintiffs were entitled to recover the contract price, even though all they had received was a contract which turned out to be an apparent waste of time and money. Lord Reid did, however, put a limitation on this principle in that the innocent party will not be able to affirm a contract in such circumstances where they have no legitimate interest in its performance. In *Clea Shipping Corp.* v *Bulk Oil International Ltd,* **The Alaskan Trader** [1984] 1 All ER 129 it was found that the claimants had acted 'wholly' unreasonably in refusing to accept the defendants' repudiatory breach when the ship which they had hired for 24 months was put in for repairs after 12 months and they said they had no further use for it. As such, the claimants could recover only for damages and not the contract hire. The case law began to distinguish between 'unreasonable' and 'wholly unreasonable behaviour', as the limitation to the decision in *White & Carter (Councils) Ltd* v *McGregor* should only apply in extreme cases. In *Ocean Marine Navigation Ltd* v *Koch Carbon Inc.,* **The Dynamic** [2003] EWHC 1936 (Comm) it was held that the word 'wholly' added nothing to the test and that the exception to the rule would only apply in extreme cases where keeping the contract alive was unreasonable and damages would provide an adequate remedy.[6] This exception will not be applied if the contract needs the cooperation of the other party to be completed (**Hounslow London Borough Council v Twickenham Garden Developments Ltd** [1971] Ch 233). The balance here is achieved between the innocent party having the choice of how to react to an anticipatory breach and being put in a position of taking advantage of the situation to an unconscionable degree.[7]

[6] This analysis goes beyond the norm of recognising potential limitations to the rule in *White* v *McGregor* to considering the developments in subsequent case law. Depth and evidence of wider research and understanding achieves higher grades.

[7] However good the analysis, always remember to apply that reasoning to the question set; without the application, you will lose marks.

The innocent party to an anticipatory breach is initially in a position of power, determining whether the contract will continue or not. Once that decision is made, however, they will be bound by it and cannot attempt to turn back the clock and revive an alternative course of action based on the anticipatory breach. The courts will limit the innocent party's choice of action in very limited and extreme circumstances.

✓ Make your answer stand out

- Michael Whincup's (1996) two articles, Reacting to repudiation, 146 *NLJ* 674 and 729, will assist you in dealing with some of the issues raised as to potential misinterpretations and the consequences for a party believing themselves to be reacting to a repudiatory breach.

! Don't be tempted to . . .

- Forget to apply your analysis to the question set. Easy to do when dealing with the technical details of a complex topic.
- Miss out on marks by not discussing the potential disadvantage to the innocent party in not accepting an anticipatory breach.
- Stop too soon your analysis of the potential for an innocent party to affirm an anticipatory breach in a *White & Carter* v *McGregor* situation, and not consider the limitations to this in more recent decisions.

❓ Question 4

The Shotgun Trifles are musicians specialising in protest songs. They are planning a concert on a floating stage which will sail up and down the Thames past the Houses of Parliament on 5 November. The London Docks Boatyard Ltd had contracted with the Shotgun Trifles for the hire of the *Maggie May* for that night. On 2 October the London Docks Boatyard Ltd received a better offer from Westminster Borough Council to host a floating firework display and inform the Shotgun Trifles that the barge is not available. The Shotgun Trifles express their disappointment but still want to hire the *Maggie May*.

On the morning of 1 October, the Shotgun Trifles had agreed with Fly Promotions Ltd to run a series of advertisements on 31 October, 2 and 3 November, using sky-writing at a cost of £5,000. They ring Fly Promotions Ltd on the afternoon of 1 October to cancel their deal, as they decide that sky-writing is contrary to their ecological credentials and might offend some of their fans. Fly Promotions Ltd say it is too late and they will run the promotion regardless.

On 4 November the *Maggie May* was struck by lightning and sank.

Advise the Shotgun Trifles as to whether they have any cause of action against the London Docks Boatyard Ltd for breach of contract, and whether they have to pay Fly Promotions Ltd who ran the sky-writing and are now threatening to sue for price.

Answer plan

→ Define anticipatory breach.

→ Identify that the innocent party has the choice to affirm or accept the repudiatory breach.

→ Discuss the effect of frustration on the Shotgun Trifles following their affirmation of the contract for hire.

→ Consider that Fly Promotions Ltd affirmed and can sue for price unless there was no legitimate interest in performing the contract.

Diagram plan

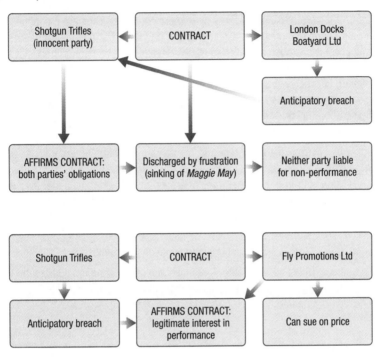

A printable version of this diagram plan is available from www.pearsoned.co.uk/lawexpressqa

Answer

An anticipatory breach occurs where a party to a contract communicates expressly or impliedly that they will be unable to fulfil their contractual obligations. Although the time for performance has not yet arrived, the innocent party has an immediate cause of action (***Hochester v De La Tour*** (1853) 2 E & B 678). If the anticipatory breach concerns a fundamental term of the contract, then the innocent party may accept that breach as repudiatory, be discharged from all existing obligations under the contract and claim damages (***Afovos Shipping Co. SA v Pagnan and Lli, The Afovos*** [1983] 1 All ER 449). Alternatively, the innocent party can choose to affirm the contract and continue with the performance of the contract or wait for performance of the other party to fall due.[1]

[1] The introduction has defined the key concepts of anticipatory breach and the potential responses to such a breach.

The London Docks Boatyard Ltd has committed an anticipatory breach in hiring out the *Maggie May* elsewhere. The anticipatory breach is a fundamental term and therefore the Shotgun Trifles have the option to accept the repudiatory breach and treat the contract as discharged. In such circumstances the innocent party must inform the other party of their decision to terminate the contract. At that point all obligations under the contract cease and the innocent party can seek an immediate remedy in damages. In this situation the Shotgun Trifles would have been able to recover any losses which were naturally flowing from the breach, provided that they were not too remote (**Hadley v Baxendale** (1854) 9 Exch 341).[2]

[2] The choice outlined in the introduction is to accept the repudiatory breach or affirm the contract. A depth of knowledge is shown here by outlining the results of the alternative course of action in accepting the breach.

In affirming the contract, however, the contract remains in force on both sides. The innocent party must continue with the performance of their own obligations under the contract, running the risk that they may end up in breach themselves and the other party may escape liability (**Fercometal SARL v Mediterranean Shipping Co. SA, The Simona** [1989] AC 788). Equally, in the event of the contract being discharged on the grounds of the operation of the doctrine of frustration, this would mean that the liabilities of both parties are also discharged at the date of the terminating event.[3] In **Avery v Bowden** (1885) 5 E & B 714 the defendants had promised a cargo within 45 days of arrival in port. The plaintiffs were repeatedly told that no cargo would be forthcoming. The plaintiffs remained in the port in the hope that the promise would be fulfilled. Before the 45 days had expired the Crimean War broke out, which was a frustrating event which discharged the obligations of both parties from that date. The plaintiffs could not then look to the anticipatory breach as a cause of action to recover their losses, even though the repudiating party would not have been able to perform their obligations in any event. In not accepting the repudiation, the Shotgun Trifles ran the risk of the contract being discharged on other grounds. The sinking of the *Maggie May* is a frustrating event. Both the Shotgun Trifles and the London Docks Boatyard Ltd are discharged from their obligations from 4 November. The Shotgun Trifles cannot rely on the anticipatory breach, even though the London Docks Boatyard Ltd had no intention of performing the contract. The London Docks Boatyard will escape all liability to the Shotgun Trifles for failing to make the *Maggie May* available for hire as agreed on 5 November.[4]

[3] These are the potential risks of affirmation; providing a link between the general point of law and the requisite application to the problem.

[4] This is the specific application to the question asked. Marks are gained by having a logical flow and build to an answer.

[5] Basic statements of the legal choices open to the parties leading in to an investigation of the consequences of one course of action over the other.

[6] This would provide an accurate analysis and application of *White & Carter (Councils) Ltd* v *McGregor*, but what follows will give depth and illustrate an up-to-date knowledge of the topic area.

[7] This recognition of the principle as still being developed will gain extra marks, as it evidences wider reading, research and understanding.

As regards the contract for the sky-writing, it is the Shotgun Trifles who have committed an anticipatory breach. Fly Promotions Ltd as the innocent party are free to accept this repudiation of the contract or to affirm the contract and continue with performance.[5] In *White & Carter (Councils) Ltd* v *McGregor* [1962] AC 413 the appellants had continued to supply advertisements on litter bins for the defendants' garage business, even though on the same day as concluding the contract they had sought to cancel the order. The contract continued for three years and at the end of this time the appellants sued for price. The appellants were successful in their claim. It would appear that Fly Promotions Ltd would therefore be entitled to continue with performance and then sue for the price of £5,000.[6] This can appear rather harsh on the party committing the original breach, as until there is an actual breach of contract there is no obligation on the innocent party to mitigate their loss. Lord Reid suggested that the decision has a limitation in that a plaintiff should not be allowed to affirm the contract and continue with it unless they have a legitimate interest, financial or otherwise, in performing the contract. This deviation from allowing the innocent party to enforce their strict legal rights has been applied in subsequent judicial decisions. There is no requirement for the innocent party to act reasonably in choosing to affirm a contract, and therefore the other party must show that there was no legitimate interest in performance. Tests began to develop requiring an examination of whether or not in refusing to accept a repudiatory breach the innocent party had acted wholly unreasonably (*Clea Shipping Corp.* v *Bulk Oil International Ltd, The Alskan Trader* [1984] 1 All ER 129). In *Ocean Marine Navigation Ltd* v *Koch Carbon Inc., The Dynamic* [2003] EWHC 1936 (Comm) it was held that the word 'wholly' added nothing to the test as to whether or not a legitimate interest existed in performance. Furthermore, the exception to the rule that an innocent party has a right to affirmation will only apply in extreme cases where damages would provide an adequate remedy and to keep the contract alive would be unreasonable.[7] *White & Carter (Councils) Ltd* v *McGregor* never raised the issue of whether there was a legitimate interest in the performance of the contract. Therefore the Shotgun Trifles could raise this as a line of argument. On the one hand, Fly Promotions had not as yet incurred any costs, but on the other that type of advertising is unusual and could encourage others to use this as a means of promoting goods, services or events. There

[8] This application of the principle demonstrates that not all legitimate interests are purely financial.

could indeed be some legitimate interest in performance, even though not wanted on the part of the band.[8]

The Shotgun Trifles will have no cause of action against the London Docks Boatyard Ltd as the contract has been discharged on the grounds of frustration. In all probability they will also be liable to Fly Promotions Ltd for the advertising undertaken, as the contract still had some legitimate interest in performance from the perspective of the innocent party.

✓ Make your answer stand out

- Consider giving depth to your analysis by including some academic authority. This problem is very focused on affirmation of a repudiatory breach, as is G. Treitel's (1998) article: Affirmation after a repudiatory breach, 114 *LQR* 22.

! Don't be tempted to . . .

- Forget to consider the alternatives to accepting the repudiatory breach, and the potential consequences of affirming the contract.
- Recognise the facts as being similar to *White & Carter (Councils) Ltd* v *McGregor* and stop your analysis there. This judgment has been the subject of severe criticism and some development.

www.pearsoned.co.uk/lawexpressqa

 Go online to access more revision support including additional essay and problem questions with diagram plans, You be the marker questions, and download all diagrams from the book.

Frustration

How this topic may come up in exams

Remember the doctrine has narrow application and examiners will require you to demonstrate that you understand the nature of the doctrine, the consequences of its operation, and the limitations to its operation. The doctrine of frustration operates to discharge a contract where the effect of an unforeseen event renders the contract impossible, illegal or radically different in performance from that originally agreed upon. The common law defines a frustrating event. The legislation determines the effects of the operation of the doctrine. This will provide the structure for any answer on this topic.

■ Attack the question

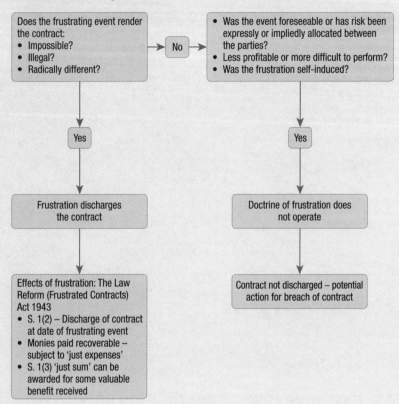

A printable version of this diagram is available from www.pearsoned.co.uk/lawexpressqa

Question 1

'The essence of frustration is that it is caused by some unforeseen supervening event over which the parties to the contract have no control and for which they are therefore not responsible' Lord Justice Griffiths: *The Hannah Blumenthal* [1983] 1 AC 854: 882.

Discuss this definition of frustration in the context of the narrow application of the doctrine and the limited recovery of losses incurred in the performance of a contract which is later frustrated.

Answer plan

→ Define a 'supervening event' and the concept of being 'radically different'.

→ Consider frustration in terms of its limitations.

→ The supervening event must not be foreseeable. Discuss express and implied allocation of risk.

→ Analyse whether any control over the events will lead to a finding of self-induced frustration.

→ Outline the limitations of sums that can be recovered under section 1(2) and section 1(3) of the Law Reform (Frustrated Contracts) Act 1943.

Diagram plan

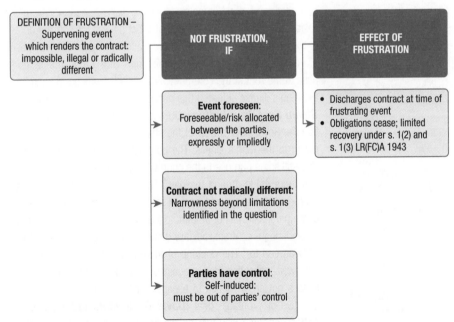

A printable version of this diagram plan is available from www.pearsoned.co.uk/lawexpressqa

Answer

[1] This point demonstrates that you have understood the context in which the doctrine operates and its origins.

The effects of the absolute contracts rule as in **_Paradine_ v _Jane_** (1647) Aleyn 26 have been mitigated to a large extent by the development of the doctrine of frustration, which allows a change of circumstance to discharge the contractual obligations from the date of the frustrating event (**_Taylor_ v _Caldwell_** (1863) 3 B & S 826).[1] **_Davis Contractors Ltd_ v _Fareham UDC_** [1956] AC 696 reflects this decision and articulates the modern test for frustration as being an event which has made the contract impossible to perform, illegal or radically different from that originally agreed to.[2] Lord Griffiths's definition articulates the doctrine's further limitations: there must be a supervening event which is unforeseen and beyond the control of either party.[3]

[2] Here you are already introducing a further limitation to the doctrine of frustration not included in the quote but crucial to the understanding of the narrow application of the doctrine. _Davis_ provides good authority as it articulates the modern definition of frustration.

[3] Remember a good introduction will put your marker on side. This paragraph clearly demonstrates that the question asked is specifically addressed and the pertinent issues identified.

The categories of frustration are not closed. Of importance is the effect the 'supervening event' has on the contract rather than the nature of the event itself. The 1903 Coronation cases illustrate how the same supervening event may be frustrating in one set of circumstances but not in another. In **_Krell_ v _Henry_** [1903] 2 KB 740 the cancellation of the Coronation operated as a frustrating event in relation to a contract for the hire of a flat on Pall Mall on the dates of the Coronation procession.[4] There was no mention of the purpose of the rental in the contract. It was found that the fundamental purpose at the root of the contract was to view the procession and that the King's illness defeated this purpose. By contrast, in **_Herne Bay Steam Boat Co._ v _Hutton_** [1903] 2 KB 683 the contract did mention the Royal Navy review of the ships, which again was cancelled owing to the King's illness. The contract was not frustrated. There was still some purpose to the contract, the fleet could still be viewed and tours made around the bay.[5] Therefore even if a supervening event is unforeseen, and beyond the control or even contemplation of the parties, it will not amount to frustration unless it has the effect of rendering a contract radically different from that which was originally agreed to.[6] The doctrine of frustration therefore has an even narrower application than suggested in the quotation.[7] Furthermore, it does not allow parties to escape from what has become a less lucrative or profitable deal (**_Davis Contractors Ltd_ v _Fareham UDC_**.[8] Contracts will only be discharged in the most exceptional circumstances.

[4] A discussion of the facts of the case has been included here as they add clarity to the understanding of the legal point being made.

[5] _Krell_ v _Henry_ and _Herne Bay Steam Boat Co._ v _Hutton_ help you define the extent to which an event must render a contract radically different; learn them together.

[6] Recognising this will increase your grade.

[7] Reinforces the previous point but emphasises your application to the question set.

[8] Using _Davis_ provides you with both a good authority for demonstrating narrowness of application of the doctrine as well as a modern definition of frustration.

Lord Griffiths recognises that in order for the doctrine of frustration to operate the supervening event must be unforeseen. If the parties have made express provision for the event which it is alleged frustrated the contract, the doctrine will not apply as the parties have allocated the risk between themselves. This is frequently done through the use of hardship or *force majeure* clauses. Risk can also be implied to lie with one party rather than the other. In ***Amalgamated Investment and Property Co. Ltd v John Walker & Sons Ltd*** [1977] 1 WLR 164 the risk of an older building being listed would be with the buyer.[9]

Lord Griffiths's definition requires that the parties have no control over the supervening event. This goes beyond a blatantly culpable or negligent act to a situation where a party having any control or choice will be prevented from relying on the doctrine as the frustration will be deemed to be self-induced.[10] In ***Maritime National Fish Ltd v Ocean Trawlers Ltd*** [1935] AC 524 the choice of to which boats to allocate a finite number of licences meant that the remaining boats could not be hired to fish lawfully. This decision sits comfortably with Lord Griffiths's assertions as to control. In the case of the ***Super Servant II*** [1990] 1 Lloyd's Rep. 1 the sinking of one of two vessels capable of carrying drill rigs amounted to self-induced frustration as there was a choice as to which vessel could have carried the rig, even though in reality the only control or choice open was which contract to break. To avoid a finding of self-induced frustration in this case, the contract must have specifically allocated the services of the ***Super Servant II*** or both ships must have been destroyed.[11] The decision can appear harsh: however, it does encourage the parties to allocate risk between them and prevents preferences. Perhaps it is worth noting that the ***Super Servant I*** was allocated to the claimants, demonstrating a preference by the defendants towards honouring contractual obligations to hirers with whom a contract was formed at a later date but at a higher price.[12]

The Law Reform (Frustrated Contracts) Act 1943 allows for limited recovery of monies paid, expenses incurred, or valuable benefit gained; it does not apportion losses. Prior to the Act, losses fell where they lay at the date of the frustrating event, discharging all contractual obligations at that date. As such any deposit paid or money due before the date of frustration remained due or could not be recovered, whereas money payable after the supervening event

[9] Identifying the link of an event being foreseeable with allocation of risk will demonstrate your greater depth of knowledge and will achieve the higher marks.

[10] The use of the word 'control' should immediately raise the issue of self-induced frustration.

[11] This sophisticated point aims at gaining you those top marks.

[12] Developing your analysis in this way demonstrates a depth and knowledge of the issues surrounding both the case and the underlying policy behind the narrow application of the doctrine, and moves the answer on to a higher level of achievement.

ceased to be payable. Following the decision in ***Fibrosa Spolka Akcyina v Fairburn Lawson Combe Barbour Ltd*** [1943] AC 32 money paid could be recovered if there was a total failure of consideration. The 1943 Act also discharges all obligations on the date of the frustrating event. However, the Act also provides that monies paid prior to the frustrating event are recoverable without the requirement of a total failure of consideration, but subject to the retention of monies by the other party who has incurred expenses in the performance of the contract section 1(2).[13] Just expenses cannot exceed amounts paid or due before the date of the frustrating event. Just expenses awarded are at the court's discretion (***Gamerco SA v ICM/Fair Warning (Agency) Ltd*** [1995] 1 WLR 1226).

The court can award a just sum for a valuable benefit that survives the frustrating event (s. 1(3)). ***BP Exploration Co. (Libya) Ltd v Hunt*** [1979] 1 WLR 783 provides the only authority on these awards. The effect of this decision has been that the decision in ***Appleby v Myers*** (1867) LR 2CP 651 would remain the same, as none of the machinery survived the fire and as such no valuable benefit would survive to benefit the other party, and therefore no just sum awarded. The definition given by Lord Griffiths of frustration encapsulates the narrow parameters within which the doctrine operates. Frustration will not easily be established to allow a party to escape what has become a bad bargain and any remedies do not allow for loss apportionment. The doctrine will have limited applicability, and more often than not will be a last ditch attempt to defend a claim for breach of contract.[14]

[13] By comparing the situation before the 1943 Act, you can demonstrate that although the recovery allowed is less based on chance it is still limited.

[14] The conclusion draws the threads of the analysis back to the question; all issues raised are covered in those five lines, with a punchline as to why frustration is often an argument of last resort.

 Make your answer stand out

- The best answers recognise the quotation as identifying limitations to, rather than a definition of the doctrine.

- Stronger analysis will recognise that frustration is fundamentally about the allocation of risk. Risk, however, in UK law is not simply a measure of continued commercial viability; compare cases such as *Davis Contractors* v *Fareham UDC* and *FA Tamplin Steamship Co. Ltd* v *Anglo Mexican Petroleum Products Co. Ltd* [1916] 2 AC 397.

- An excellent answer would consider the extent to which the decision in *Super Servant II* is consistent with the limited operation of the doctrine of frustration, or its potential application too harsh.

- Run through the definition of frustration but fail to relate your answer specifically to the question set.

- Give insufficient depth to the analysis: for instance, recognising that control referred to in the quotation relates to self-induced frustration will get you some marks; fully exploring the limitation and the rationale for such an approach will gain a much higher grade.

? Question 2

Lucia has contracted with Find Us Ltd to provide an expedition around Fosbeck Bay in a glass-bottomed boat, for herself and 20 friends.

Two days before Lucia's trip the cargo ship, *The Fundamental*, spilt her load. As a result the bay has been inundated with people looking for 'treasure'. Coastguard patrols are checking the purpose of boats on the water. This increased activity will potentially drive away much of the marine wildlife or cause it to remain well hidden. Lucia has paid £500 for the hire of the boat; this is advance payment of the total amount due.

Lucia intended to have a beach party. The beach has been closed and all access denied. BBQ Delights Ltd was to have provided the food and drink at a total cost of £700; £150 has been paid as a deposit.

Lucia booked overnight accommodation in the Rascal's Rest Hotel. One of the floors of the hotel has been closed during the investigation of a suspicious death. Lucia is told there is no available room for her. She has paid £200 deposit, with £200 payable on checking out. The only alternative accommodation Lucia found was a suite at the Quatre Gatts Country Manor at the cost of £800.

Advise Lucia whether or not the contracts with Find Us Ltd, BBQ Delights and the Rascal's Rest are frustrated and whether or not any monies paid are recoverable.

Answer plan

→ Deal with each contract in turn.

→ Consider whether more visitors to the area and the presence of the coastguard makes the contract radically different from that originally agreed to.

→ Discuss whether the closing of the beach is frustration on the grounds of government intervention or supervening illegality.

→ If the contract is frustrated, is Lucia entitled to all her deposit back?

→ Explain how the cancellation of the hotel room could amount to self-induced frustration.

→ If the contract for the hotel room is not terminated, what remedy can Lucia seek against the Rascal's Rest?

Diagram plan

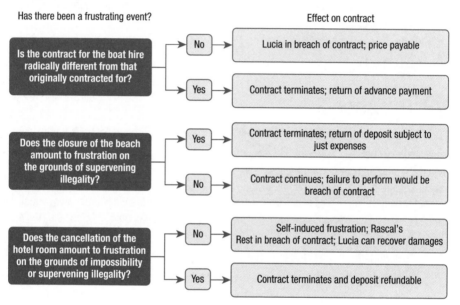

Has there been a frustrating event?   Effect on contract

Is the contract for the boat hire radically different from that originally contracted for?
— No → Lucia in breach of contract; price payable
— Yes → Contract terminates; return of advance payment

Does the closure of the beach amount to frustration on the grounds of supervening illegality?
— Yes → Contract terminates; return of deposit subject to just expenses
— No → Contract continues; failure to perform would be breach of contract

Does the cancellation of the hotel room amount to frustration on the grounds of impossibility or supervening illegality?
— No → Self-induced frustration; Rascal's Rest in breach of contract; Lucia can recover damages
— Yes → Contract terminates and deposit refundable

A printable version of this diagram plan is available from www.pearsoned.co.uk/lawexpressqa

Answer

The doctrine of frustration will operate where unforeseen events render a contract impossible to perform, illegal or radically different from that originally agreed to. Frustration is determined by the effect that an event has on the contract not the nature of the event itself. In the event of a contract being frustrated the contract is discharged at that date. The Law Reform (Frustrated Contracts) Act 1943 determines where losses will lie.[1]

[1] You have clearly identified the issues here and defined your approach to the question set.

To discharge the contract with Find Us Ltd on the grounds of frustration, Lucia will have to establish that the increased traffic in the bay and the activities of the coastguard have rendered the tour round the

[2] Using the relevant part of the definition given in the introduction has focused your application of the law to the problem.

[3] This is emphasising the legal point, which the following application to the problem will build on.

[4] Introducing the concept of risk here demonstrates a depth of understanding of the topic area, which will gain much higher marks.

[5] This application draws parallels with *Herne Bay* in that there is still purpose to the contract.

[6] The question of who should bear the risk is again raised, and the application further persuades us that the contract for the boat hire will not be discharged on the grounds of frustration.

[7] Recognising that the doctrine of frustration will not operate is accurate application; knowing the financial consequence of this for the parties involved is excellent application.

bay radically different from that originally contracted for.[2] The cancellation of the King's Coronation in **Krell v Henry** [1903] 2 KB 740 was held to be a frustrating event as the hiring of the flat had no other purpose than to view the procession. By contrast, in **Herne Bay Steam Boat Co. v Hutton** [1903] 2 KB 683 the cancellation of the Royal Navy review was not frustration as there was still some purpose to the contract. It is, therefore, the effect that the event has on the contract that is important, not the nature of the event itself that will determine whether or not the doctrine will operate.[3] It should also be noted that in **Herne Bay Steam Boat Co. Ltd v Hutton** the hirer of the boat had intended to take parties of tourists round the bay; potentially there is an argument that the risk of profitability of the venture was his,[4] and that in actual fact what had happened in the cancellation of the review was that the contract had simply become less profitable, as in **Davis Contractors Ltd v Fareham Urban District Council** [1956] AC 696. Find Us Ltd can still provide a tour round the bay, although with a greater number of other visitors and potential interference from the coastguard perhaps detracting from the enjoyment, but not the ability to perform the contract nor Lucia's ability to gain some benefit from it.[5]

The doctrine of frustration will not operate if an event is foreseeable. Foreseeability has a strong relationship to who should bear the risk of a particular eventuality. In **Amalgamated Investment and Property Co. Ltd v John Walker & Sons Ltd** [1977] 1 WLR 164 it was an inherent risk on the purchaser of an older property that it might at some point be listed and subject to greater planning and development regulations. The presence or non-presence of marine life in a given location is to a large extent fortuitous, and therefore it could be suggested Lucia bears the risk of how much marine life is visible.[6]

The contract between Lucia and Find Us Ltd is not frustrated; there is still a purpose to the contract; it is not radically different from that originally agreed to and the risk of how much marine life is present is inherent in the nature of the expedition. The money paid in advance is the total price of the boat hire, and as the contractual obligations have not been discharged on the grounds of frustration the £500 is not recoverable from Find Us Ltd.[7]

The closing of the bay and the consequential inability to hold the beach party would appear to be a frustrating event on the grounds of supervening illegality, which would include an event which triggers the operation of law. In *Fibrosa Spolka Akcyina* v *Fairburn Lawson Combe Barbour Ltd* [1943] AC 32 the outbreak of war rendered the performance of the contract unlawful as it would have constituted trading with the enemy. Similarly, in *Gamerco SA* v *ICM/Fair Warning (Agency) Ltd* [1995] 1 WLR 1226 the permit to hold a rock concert in a sports stadium was withdrawn as a result of safety concerns. The closing of the beach is unforeseen; neither party is responsible for its closure and the parties do not appear to have allocated risk between them for such an occurrence.[8] The contract could therefore be discharged on the grounds of frustration. The Law Reform (Frustrated Contracts) Act 1943 provides that the contract is terminated automatically at the date of the frustrating event. Section 1(2) allows money paid prior to the frustrating event to be returned, whether or not there is a total failure of consideration, and monies due prior to the date of frustration cease to be payable. Section 1(2) also allows for the recovery or retention of money to cover expenses incurred in relation to the contract. The extent of such an award is at the discretion of the court and is limited to the amount paid or due to be paid before the frustrating event. Therefore, Lucia will be able to recover the £150 deposit, less any just expenses incurred by BBQ Delights Ltd. Even if expenses have been incurred, it is possible for the judge to make no award and order the full amount to be returned, as in *Gamerco*.[9]

The police investigation into the suspicious death would suggest that the contract has been rendered impossible to perform as a result of an unforeseen event[10] (*Taylor* v *Caldwell* (1863) 3 B & S 826). However, the doctrine of frustration will not operate if the frustrating event was self-induced (*Maritime National Fish Ltd* v *Ocean Trawlers Ltd* [1935] AC 524). This limitation to the doctrine will apply even where the choice is simply as to which contract to breach, as in the *Super Servant II* [1990] 1 Lloyd's Rep 1. In allocating rooms to other guests rather than Lucia, the Rascal's Rest exercised choice.[11] Therefore the contract is not frustrated. The Rascal's Rest has breached their contract with Lucia. As such Lucia will be able to recover at least the difference in price between what she had to spend on the more expensive room and what she would have paid at the Rascal's Rest, a total of £400. Any other losses would be recoverable, subject to the usual rules on remoteness and causation.[12]

[8] Here you have the artful inclusion of the potential limitations to the operation of the doctrine, which do not apply but are introduced in such a way as to be relevant and give you credit for your depth of knowledge.

[9] Including some analysis surrounding an award of just expenses demonstrates your ability to deal with the more complex issues.

[10] A trap for the unwary!

[11] Neat application demonstrating the potential harshness of the law surrounding self-induced frustration.

[12] You have the opportunity here to show that you understand fully the consequences of a finding that the contract has been breached rather than terminated on the grounds of frustration.

The doctrine of frustration has a narrow application and will not allow parties to escape what has turned out to be a bad bargain. Only the cancellation of the beach party would amount to frustration. The Law Reform (Frustrated Contracts) Act 1943, section 1(2) provides for the deposit to be returned to Lucia, subject to any just expenses. The cancelled boat trip and hotel room do not discharge the contracts on the grounds of frustration. Therefore, Find Us Ltd is entitled to keep the price of the boat hire and Lucia can recover damages for the breach of contract by the Rascal's Rest.[13]

[13] Notice how the conclusion pulls together all the key points from each part of the preceding analysis, answering every part of the question set.

✓ Make your answer stand out

- Better answers will have identified the more complex issues of self-induced frustration; if all the rooms in the hotel were unavailable, or if the hotel had specifically allocated a particular room at the time the contract was made, would a finding of self-induced frustration be avoided?
- An excellent answer would perhaps have tried to distinguish the decisions in the *Super Servant II* [1990] 1 Lloyd's Rep. 1, where a preference over one contracting party was made, to the present scenario where there was no such suggestion.

! Don't be tempted to . . .

- Thwart the logical flow of your answer by dealing with the entire scenario in terms of whether or not it is discharged by frustration and then deal with remedies at the end.
- Avoid exploring the issues fully: for example, remembering the potential claim for just expenses by BBQ Delights Ltd, and the court's discretion to award such an amount out of monies paid as a deposit.
- Presume that an event is automatically frustrating – tempting in this scenario, with the police presence and investigation into a suspicious death.

📝 Question 3

Evaluate whether good contractual drafting can provide a better remedy for contracting parties than the operation of the doctrine of frustration and the meagre remedies provided by the Law Reform (Frustrated Contracts) Act 1943.

Answer plan

→ Consider when the doctrine of frustration operates, and the effect of *force majeure* and hardship clauses.

→ Examine whether the use of such clauses always eradicates the need for reliance on the doctrine of frustration.

→ Discuss the effect of frustration on the contract and the lottery of the recovery of a 'just sum' under the Act.

Diagram plan

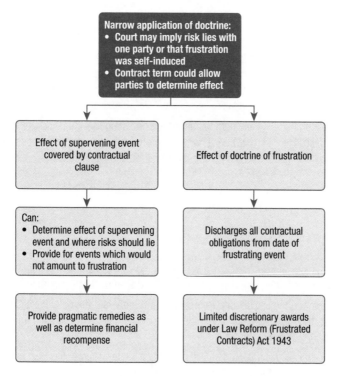

Narrow application of doctrine:
- Court may imply risk lies with one party or that frustration was self-induced
- Contract term could allow parties to determine effect

Effect of supervening event covered by contractual clause

Effect of doctrine of frustration

Can:
- Determine effect of supervening event and where risks should lie
- Provide for events which would not amount to frustration

Discharges all contractual obligations from date of frustrating event

Provide pragmatic remedies as well as determine financial recompense

Limited discretionary awards under Law Reform (Frustrated Contracts) Act 1943

A printable version of this diagram plan is available from www.pearsoned.co.uk/lawexpressqa

Answer

The doctrine of frustration was developed to provide relief to the common law's expectation that contracting parties must perform their contractual obligations fully, even where there has been a significant change in circumstances (**Paradine v Jane** (1647) Aleyn 26). The doctrine developed incrementally but has always operated within narrow parameters, as its effects are to discharge all contractual obligations from the date of the frustrating event and before the Law Reform (Frustrated Contracts) Act 1943 to let the losses fall where they were at that date. The parties can of course agree contractually what the consequences of certain specified eventualities will be, which may be wider than the doctrine of frustration and provide a more suitable remedy as well as fulfilling the intentions of the parties.[1]

[1] A strong introduction immediately taking a line of argument puts your marker 'on side'.

Taylor v Caldwell (1863) 3 B & S 826 defines the turning away from the absolute contracts rule to the ability to have a contract discharged on the grounds of unforeseen supervening events. In this case a fire rendered the contract for the hire of a music hall impossible to perform. Therefore, all obligations were discharged at the date of the frustrating event.[2] The nature of the event is not important: it is the effect that the event has on the contract. In **Krell v Henry** [1903] 2 KB 740 and **Herne Bay Steam Boat Co. v Hutton** [1903] 2 KB 683, the event concerned was the cancellation of Edward VII's Coronation. In **Krell v Henry** the contract was discharged on the grounds of frustration as the fundamental purpose of the contract had ceased to exist, even though the contract could still be performed. By contrast, in **Herne Bay Steam Boat Company v Hutton** there was still some purpose to the contract. The trips round the bay could still be made. Fewer visitors were likely to avail themselves of the opportunity, and therefore the contract to hire the boat for prospective tours was likely to be less lucrative but not impossible nor fundamentally different from the performance agreed to.[3] The courts have, therefore, never been willing to allow the doctrine of frustration to develop in such a way as to allow a party to discharge themselves from a bad bargain. In **Davis Contractors Ltd v Fareham Urban District Council** [1956] AC 696 the claimants sought to have the contract discharged on the grounds of frustration, as shortages in labour had made the contract far more expensive to perform than they had originally bargained for. Lord Radcliffe was clear that frustration was not to be 'lightly invoked as the dissolvent of a contract'. As such, hardship of itself will not amount to a frustrating event. The frustrating event must render the contract impossible, illegal, or radically different from that which was originally agreed to. With regard to a change in circumstance making a contract less

[2] This point will be a recurring theme; frustration has little to mitigate its effects. The contract ends.

[3] The facts of the case have been effectively used here illustrating the definition of 'fundamentally different', but also leading into the next paragraph which demonstrates that the doctrine does not relieve what turns out to be a bad bargain.

lucrative, the parties can between themselves agree what will happen to provide a contractual solution for eventualities such as a market collapsing, supplies becoming scarce, or price fluctuations. So-called hardship clauses can provide a pragmatic solution to such commercial uncertainties.[4] The risk can be shared and the legal relationship preserved: for example, a contract could be suspended or more time for performance negotiated. *Force majeure* clauses can be used to plan for the 'unexpected', such as an Act of God, strikes, fire, accidents or incidents outside of the control of the relevant party. Care has to be taken to ensure that such terms of the contract cover the event contemplated.[5] An agreement to negotiate if certain conditions arise could be invalid as being too vague (***Walford v Miles*** [1992] 1 All ER 453). A less rigid approach to such agreements to negotiate has been noted in more recent cases, such as ***Petromec Inc. v Petreleo Basileiro SA Petrobas (No. 3)*** [2006] 1 Lloyd's Rep 121. The courts here are reflecting the wish to give effect to the intentions of the parties; this sits comfortably with the attitude towards the doctrine of frustration that the doctrine will not operate where the event was foreseeable or risk has been allocated between the parties.[6]

The use of the contract to deal with supervening events allows for the parties to determine the consequences of an event. It will also avoid the consequences of the courts deciding that risk would lie wholly with one party rather than the other (***Amalgamated Investment and Property Co. Ltd v John Walker & Sons Ltd*** [1977] 1 WLR 164), or that the frustration was self-induced (***J Lauritzen AS v Wijsmuller BV, The Super Servant II*** [1990] 1 Lloyd's Rep 1).[7]

Frustration terminates a contract regardless of the party's wishes. A contract can provide a remedy whereby a term can be renegotiated, suspended or ignored, preserving the relationship and achieving a commercially pragmatic solution as well as quantifying financial recompense. Parties between themselves can decide who should insure against certain risks; such an allocation of risk would again displace the operation of the doctrine of frustration and provide compensation for losses.[8] The recovery of financial loss where the doctrine of frustration operates is governed by the Law Reform (Frustrated Contracts) Act 1943. Section 1(2) provides that money paid prior to the frustrating event is recoverable, subject to a just sum, awarded at the discretion of the court, being deducted to cover any reliance expenditure incurred by the other party (***Gamerco SA***

[4] This argument has been well developed, demonstrating how the parties themselves can provide their own pragmatic solution, avoiding hardship, potentially maintaining a commercial relationship and giving a contract viability when something has gone wrong.

[5] The more liberal interpretation of contractual terms will facilitate reliance upon them rather than the doctrine of frustration.

[6] Identifying current developments and the rationale for these developments demonstrates wider reading and up-to-date research which gives depth to the analysis and will gain higher marks.

[7] This recognises that even where the courts would find that the doctrine would not operate the parties could allocate the risk between themselves to avoid liability falling completely on one party.

[8] This point is well directed to the question; by articulating the contractual remedies first, emphasis is put on their advantages over the statutory remedies provided for by the LR(FC)A 1943.

v **ICM/Fairwarning (Agency) Ltd** [1995] 1 WLR 1226). Section 1(3) provides that a just sum can be awarded for any valuable benefit that survives the frustrating event (**BP Exploration Co. (Libya) Ltd v Hunt** [1979] 1 WLR 783). Again, any financial award is discretionary and to some extent reliant on good or bad fortune. Such uncertainty is removed by good contractual planning.[9]

[9] Emphasising that the award is discretionary and based on fate reinforces the thrust of your argument in so far that a well-drafted contract will provide a superior remedy to relying on the default position of frustration.

The doctrine of frustration has a narrow application. Contracting parties can plan for uncertainty, ousting the effects of the doctrine, determining the outcomes, salvaging some commercial viability from an agreement by allocating risk and loss between them as they deem appropriate at the time the contract was formed.

✓ Make your answer stand out

- Consider the attitude towards the interpretation of a clause purporting to exclude or limit liability by comparison to a clause that attempts to plan to deal with the risks that could amount to frustrating events.

- Expand on the potential harsh repercussions which emanate from the courts implying risk on one party or finding that the frustration was self-induced.

! Don't be tempted to . . .

- Forget to focus on the question. This question is phrased from the perspective of preventing the doctrine's operation and why this may have advantages to the contracting parties.

? Question 4

Motivent Ltd has been commissioned by C21st Ball Ltd to create a simulation of the inside of a spacecraft used in a cult science fiction television series in the Chrystal Jubilee Conference Centre, which is to be the centrepiece of their week-long SciFi UK event. The spacecraft simulation was to be housed in the top floor of the venue and the remaining two floors were to be used to host talks and exhibition stands. The work is three days from completion when a freak storm causes part of the roof of the Conference Centre to collapse. All the work done on the simulated spacecraft is destroyed. All monies for the work done were payable on completion of the project.

Trulitious Ltd had contracted with C21st Ball Ltd to provide food, drink and entertainment for the opening night. Following the damage, C21st Ball Ltd wish to cancel the event as they feel fewer people will attend if there is to be no special effects provided by the spacecraft simulation. Trulitious Ltd refuse to accept the cancellation.

The day before the opening event Trulitious Ltd is the subject of an emergency prohibition order preventing them from the provision of food, following a health inspection.

Advise C21st Ball Ltd as to the potential effects the doctrine of frustration may have with regard to the contracts with Motivent Ltd and Trulitious Ltd.

Answer plan

→ Define the doctrine of frustration and its effects on a contract.

→ Explain why, under the Law Reform (Frustrated Contracts) Act 1943, in the absence of agreement or allocation of the risk, there will be no monies recoverable for Motivent Ltd.

→ Consider the effect of the non-acceptance of the anticipatory breach by Trulitious Ltd.

→ Discuss whether the emergency prohibition order is a frustrating event or would amount to self-induced frustration on the part of Trulitious Ltd.

Diagram plan

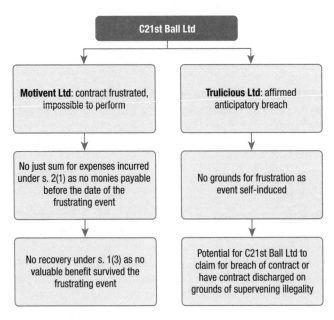

A printable version of this diagram plan is available from www.pearsoned.co.uk/lawexpressqa

Answer

A contract being rendered impossible to perform, illegal, or radically different from that originally contracted for by a supervening event may be discharged on the grounds of frustration. This doctrine is narrowly applied and its operation will be ousted if the risk was foreseeable, can be or was allocated between the parties, or was self-induced. The contractual obligations are discharged at the date of the frustrating event, and the statutory provision for the recovery of losses under the Law Reform (Frustrated Contracts) Act 1943 are very limited and at the discretion of the court.[1]

Taylor **v** *Caldwell* (1863) 3 B & S 826 concerned the destruction of the subject matter of the contract. This frustrating event discharged all contractual obligations at the date of the frustrating event. The work done by Motivent Ltd has been destroyed before the work was completed. No fault can be attributed to either side. The event was not foreseeable or self-induced. In the absence of one party having assumed responsibility for the risk through insurance or a term, such as a *force majeure* clause, in the contract providing for such eventualities, there is nothing to oust the operation of the doctrine of frustration.[2] The contract between Motivent Ltd and C21st Ball Ltd will be discharged on the date of the unforeseen event. All obligations on both parties cease on that date, including the obligation to pay for the work done. *Appleby* **v** *Myers* [1867] LR 2 CP 651 concerned the installation of machinery, which was close to completion when a fire destroyed it and the premises in which it was housed. In this case no money was recoverable, as all monies payable were due on completion and nothing survived the fire. Prior to the Law Reform (Frustrated Contracts) Act 1943, losses fell where they lay at the date of the frustrating event and as such nothing was payable or forfeited.[3]

The Law Reform (Frustrated Contracts) Act 1943 provides under section 1(2) that a just sum can be awarded up to the amount of any monies payable prior to the frustrating event to recover expenses incurred for the purpose of the performance of the contract prior to the frustrating event. As no monies were paid in advance, or were due, before the date of the frustrating event, Motivent Ltd have no possibility of recovering any losses under section 1(2).[4] Under section 1(3) a just sum can be awarded by the court for any valuable

[1] The introduction identifies the legal issues raised by the facts of the problem initiating a consideration of more complex matters requiring consideration.

[2] In reality the doctrine rarely operates as a contract would usually allocate risk between one party or the other.

[3] Good lead into a discussion of the limited remedial effects of the LR(FC)A 1943.

[4] Depth of knowledge demonstrated in the application here as any just sum is limited to a maximum of monies paid or payable prior to the frustrating event.

221

benefit conferred which survives the frustrating event. As all Motivent Ltd's work was destroyed, no amount is recoverable under this section. The restrictive interpretation of section 1(3) in **BP Exploration Co. (Libya) Ltd v Hunt** [1979] 1 WLR 783 has not improved the situation for parties such as Motivent Ltd, and the decision in **Appleby v Myers** would still operate in the same way.[5]

[5] Drawing the threads of an argument together in this way demonstrates a strong logical flow to the analysis which will add depth and gain higher marks.

In notifying Trulitious Ltd of their wish to cancel the contract, C21st Ball Ltd is committing an anticipatory breach of contract in declaring their intention not to perform their obligations.[6] The case of **Herne Bay Steam Boat Co. v Hutton** [1903] 2 KB 683 illustrates the point that having fewer people interested in the event will be insufficient to render the contract radically different from that originally agreed to. Simply being less lucrative or harder to perform will not allow C21st Ball Ltd to be discharged from performance of their contractual obligations on the grounds of frustration (**Davis Contractors Ltd v Fareham Urban District Council** [1956] AC 696). Trulitious Ltd had the option to elect to accept the breach and treat the contract as discharged and claim damages or affirm the contract and wait for the actual breach to occur. In affirming the contract, they are under an obligation to perform their own part of the bargain and run the risk of being in breach of contract themselves (**Fercometal SARL v Mediterranean Shipping Co. SA, The Simona** [1989] AC 788), or the contract being discharged on other grounds (**Avery v Bowden** (1855) 5 E & B 714).[7]

[6] This statement clearly opens up the complex discussion surrounding the anticipatory breach.

[7] This leads neatly on to the discussion surrounding their own self-induced frustration. A strong structure to an answer will be rewarded by an examiner.

In **Avery v Bowden** the plaintiffs were told there was no cargo for them. The plaintiffs refused to accept the anticipatory breach and decided to wait to see if the situation changed. During this period the Crimean War broke out. The outbreak of the war was a frustrating event and as such the contract was discharged from that date. The plaintiffs could not then elect to rely on the anticipatory breach. The doctrine of frustration operated to destroy the contract they had affirmed. Similarly, in not accepting C21st Ball Ltd's anticipatory breach Trulitious Ltd cannot later attempt to rely on it when other events make them liable for their own breach or indeed the contract is frustrated on other grounds.[8]

[8] Clear application of the initial point relating to the anticipatory breach which is then developed upon.

Denny, Mott and Dickson Ltd v James B. Fraser & Co. Ltd [1944] 1 All ER 678) provides authority for the proposition that supervening illegality is capable of being a frustrating event. C21st Ball Ltd could, if they chose to, rely on this as grounds for the contract for the opening night entertainment to be frustrated. The contract would be discharged at that date and all obligations would cease; any deposit paid would be returned subject to a just sum awarded at the discretion of the court for expenses incurred in performance of the contract by Trulitious Ltd (s. 1(2) Law Reform (Frustrated Contracts) Act 1943).[9] C21st Ball Ltd would, as an alternative, have an action in breach of contract against Trulitious Ltd as the latter will not be able to rely on the doctrine of frustration. If they failed to meet hygiene standards the emergency prohibition notice being put on them would be foreseeable. The risk of non-compliance lay with them. In effect they had a choice of whether or not standards were met. The prohibition on them from providing food would amount to self-induced frustration rather than supervening illegality or government intervention preventing the performance of their obligations (*F.C. Shepherd & Co. Ltd v Jerrom* [1987] 1 QB 301). Frustration does not have to be available to both parties.[10]

The contract between C21st Ball Ltd and Motivent Ltd is frustrated on the grounds of impossibility of performance. No monies are therefore payable to Motivent Ltd. From C21st Ball Ltd's perspective, the contract with Trulitious Ltd can be discharged on the grounds of frustration; however, the award of damages would be higher if they were to sue for breach of contract. In either instance all liabilities under the contract with Trulitious Ltd are discharged, including the right to discharge the contract on the grounds of C21st Ball's earlier anticipatory breach.[11]

[9] The application is very strong here as the facts do not give the details as to whether any deposit or monies were payable, but that eventuality has been covered.

[10] Succinctly put, but accurately covers several complex issues.

[11] The application is clearly and practically focused on the question set.

 Make your answer stand out

- Demonstrate up-to-date knowledge by using the case of *Gold Group Properties Ltd* v *BDW Trading Ltd* [2010] BLR 235, which reinforces the narrowness of the application of the doctrine where performance has become more onerous to perform rather than radically different.

- Expand your analysis of self-induced frustration and 'choice' with some discussion of *Lauritzen (J) AS* v *Wijsmuller BV*, The Super Servant II [1990] 1 Lloyd's Rep 1.

- Consider reading P. Davis's article Wynn or lose, (2007) 157 *NLJ* 535 to help you understand and explain the concept of when the doctrine might be available to one party but not the other, and the alternative of bringing an action for breach of contract.

! Don't be tempted to . . .

- Forget to plan. The key to success with this question is a strong coherent structure.
- Miss the point of the problem, which is application when dealing with some of the more complex legal issues raised.
- Be too quick to recognise an event or similarities to a well-known case in frustration and presume that the result will be the same in the problem given. Remember you are looking at the effect the event has on the contract, not the nature of the event itself, and you need to consider all the other limiting factors which would exclude the operation of the doctrine such as allocation of risk or self-induced frustration.

www.pearsoned.co.uk/lawexpressqa

 Go online to access more revision support including additional essay and problem questions with diagram plans, You be the marker questions, and download all diagrams from the book.

10

Remedies for breach of contract

How this topic may come up in exams

Questions on remedies for breach of contract will focus on the measure of damages and the limitations of any award on the grounds that the consequences of the breach did not cause the loss claimed for, or that the loss is too remote a consequence of the breach. Ensure you can deal with the current issues surrounding the extent and reach of expectation interest and the rationale behind making a party account for some or all of the profit made from a breach of contract. Examiners will occasionally throw in potential alternative remedies such as liquidated damages clauses, injunctions, or orders of specific performance.

Attack the question

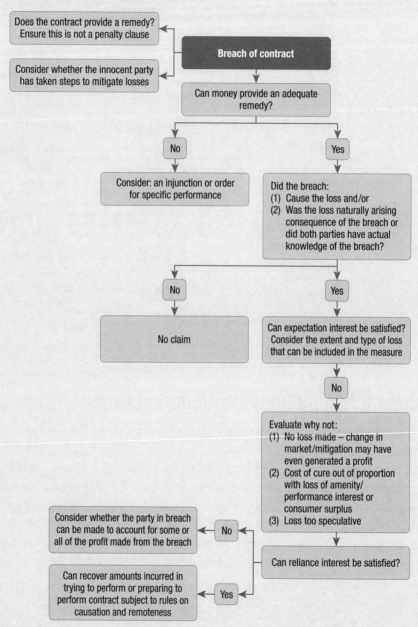

Does the contract provide a remedy?
Ensure this is not a penalty clause

Consider whether the innocent party
has taken steps to mitigate losses

Breach of contract

Can money provide an adequate
remedy?

No

Yes

Consider: an injunction or order
for specific performance

Did the breach:
(1) Cause the loss and/or
(2) Was the loss naturally arising
consequence of the breach or
did both parties have actual
knowledge of the breach?

No

Yes

No claim

Can expectation interest be satisfied?
Consider the extent and type of loss
that can be included in the measure

No

Evaluate why not:
(1) No loss made – change in
market/mitigation may have
even generated a profit
(2) Cost of cure out of proportion
with loss of amenity/
performance interest or
consumer surplus
(3) Loss too speculative

Consider whether the party in breach
can be made to account for some or
all of the profit made from the breach

No

Can recover amounts incurred in
trying to perform or preparing to
perform contract subject to rules on
causation and remoteness

Yes

Can reliance interest be satisfied?

A printable version of this diagram is available from www.pearsoned.co.uk/lawexpressqa

 Question 1

Evaluate the extent to which the aim of an award of damages for breach of contract is to satisfy the innocent party's expectation interest.

Answer plan

→ Define expectation interest, the market rule.

→ Consider the potential expansion of the concept of expectation and the impact of the decision in *Farley* v *Skinner* as regards awards for non-pecuniary losses such as disappointment.

→ Evaluate when such an award satisfying expectation interest is not appropriate.

→ Discuss when only a reliance measure will be available and the circumstance where a defendant might be made to account for profit made in breaching a contract.

Diagram plan

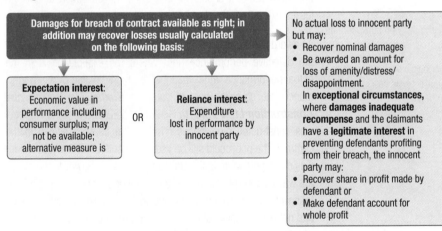

A printable version of this diagram plan is available from www.pearsoned.co.uk/lawexpressqa

Answer

[1] A punchy opening line has the marker's attention; it is of course the loss of this expectation that the law tries to redress.

Parties to a contract agree to terms in the expectation that the other party's obligations will be performed.[1] Any breach of contract gives rise to a right of action for nominal damages. The law seeks to compensate beyond such an amount by compensating for the losses which are incurred by contractual obligations not being satisfied. The courts, therefore, attempt to put the claimant in the position they would have been in had the contract been performed satisfying the so-called expectation or performance interest.

In **Robinson v Harman** (1848) 1 Ex Rep 850 expectation interest was defined as being that money would, as far as possible, put the innocent party in the position they would have been in had they received performance.[2] This is easy to measure if goods were bought to be sold on at a profit. Satisfying expectation interest is usually calculated using the difference in value between the goods received and the market value of those goods. Sections 50 and 51 of the Sale of Goods Act 1979 provide for the calculation of loss according to the market rule, whereby the amount is calculated by subtracting the contract price from the market price at the time of the sale. It is therefore possible that no actual loss is made as the market has risen or the goods in question are easily resold. In such a situation only nominal damages are recoverable. It should be noted that an obligation to mitigate losses exists from the date of an actual breach of contract.[3]

An award can be alternatively calculated based on the cost of putting the defective performance right where the expectation is in the actual performance rather than just the market value of that performance, the so-called cost of cure.[4] In **Ruxley Electronics and Construction Ltd v Forsyth** [1995] 3 All ER 268 a swimming pool was constructed nine inches short of the depth specified in the contract. The pool could still be used as intended but the cost of cure was disproportionate to the claimant's real loss. However, the claimant was disappointed in the performance of the contract. His expectation of the swimming pool being to the contractual specification had not been satisfied and, as such, an award was made for his loss of amenity and disappointment in this regard.[5]

Contracts are often entered into for motives beyond profit. Can this element of loss also amount to part of the expectation interest? Damages for non-pecuniary loss can be recovered where the 'very' object of the contract[6] is to provide, pleasure, relaxation, peace of mind, or freedom from molestation or where physical inconvenience flowed from the breach of contract (**Watt v Morrow** [1991] 1 WLR 1421). In cases such as **Jarvis v Swan Tours Ltd** [1973] 1 QB 233 and **Jackson v Horizon Holidays Ltd** [1975] 1 WLR 1468, the

[2] This point is well made; note the emphasis on financial recompense, not specific performance.

[3] As opposed to an anticipatory breach where no such obligation exists.

[4] A logical structure; ensure your analysis flows and builds in depth.

[5] This point moves neatly from a limitation to the cost of cure award to some recompense for disappointment beyond economic loss in the next paragraph.

[6] This point will be picked to add depth to the analysis.

main object of the holiday would be enjoyment, not just travel and board. The words 'very object' of the contract used in **Watt v Morrow** suggests a limitation to this principle. In **Farley v Skinner** [2001] 4 All ER 801 it fell to be decided if this term would be flexible enough to cover a situation where the pleasure or peace of mind was just an important feature of the contract, not the primary or fundamental purpose. The purchaser of a property in **Farley v Skinner** successfully recovered £10,000 from the surveyor of a property he had bought, as he had specifically asked him to investigate the aircraft noise and he had failed to do so. From this case it can be deduced that consumer contracts are much more likely to have an element of 'consumer interest' in their performance forming part of the expectation interest moving beyond pecuniary losses only, and that the loss has to arise out of a major or important object of the contract.[7] Such considerations and compensation for distress arising out of a breach of contract will not apply to commercial contracts (**Hayes v James & Charles Dodd (a firm)** [1990] 2 All ER 815).

[7] Using case law effectively will enhance marks; detailing the facts of the case here helps articulate the point of law you are making.

Expectation interest cannot be the basis of calculating an award of damages if the losses are too speculative. In **McRae v Commonwealth Disposals Commission** (1951) 84 CLR 377 the compensation in terms of the expectation of the profit to be made from the salvage for a non-existent tanker on a non-existent reef was held to be too speculative. How could a value be put on a non-existent ship? The claimants could, however, recover an amount based on wasted expenditure incurred in reliance that the contract would be performed. This measure of damages puts the party in the position they were in before the unfilled promises were made.[8]

[8] A structured approach ensures that the law is communicated effectively and clearly: here by stating the principle involved, using supporting authority and providing the solution in the award that would be available in these circumstances.

The law of contract primarily aims to compensate the innocent party to a breach of contract. In the event that no loss has been actually suffered, then only nominal damages are available. The law of contract does not seek to punish, and only in very limited circumstances can a claimant recover a profit made by the defendant from their breach of contract where the claimant had suffered no actual pecuniary losses.[9] In **Attorney General v Blake** [2001] 1 AC 268 the defendant revealed information and events he was contractually bound not to divulge in his autobiography. The Crown suffered no financial loss but could recover the whole of Blake's profits. The House of Lords in this case believed that the decision would apply only in very limited and exceptional circumstances, only where other contractual remedies

[9] Picking up on the issue raised earlier that only nominal damages available where no actual loss has been suffered.

[10] Succinctly put, allowing the application of these limited circumstances to be tested against subsequent cases, demonstrating an up-to-date knowledge dealing with subtleties and uncertainties in this area.

were inadequate, and where the claimant had a legitimate interest in preventing the defendant retaining his profit.[10] In subsequent cases the courts appear to be more willing to make a defendant in such circumstances account for a share in the profits made (**Experience Hendrix LLC v PPX Enterprises** [2003] 1 All ER (Comm) 830). Judicial and academic arguments surround whether or not these are two different remedies: a whole account of profits as in **Blake** being restitutionary, and a partial account or share of profits being compensatory. **Devenish Nutrition Ltd v Sanofi-Aventis SA** [2009] 3 WLR 198 suggests that perhaps the concepts do not have to be regarded as completely distinct. It can be argued perhaps in the light of these cases that the compensatory element of these awards has further expanded what amounts to expectation interest.[11]

[11] The law is in a state of flux on this point; here the issue has been neatly drawn into the application to the question.

[12] Simply put, but neatly concludes the answer.

The satisfaction of expectation interest as the primary aim of compensation for breach of contract encourages the performance of obligations: the innocent party being truly compensated for what they should have had in the first place.[12]

✓ Make your answer stand out

- Perhaps with regard to damages for the loss of an opportunity, consider the developments in cases such as *Allied Maples Group Ltd* v *Simmons & Simmons* [1995] 1 WLR 1602 decided after the case of *Chaplin* v *Hicks* [1911] 2 KB 786, which try to draw a dividing line between where a chance is purely speculative and where the chance of success is substantial.

- Consider reading and including some of the analysis put forward by C. Webb (2006) in Performance and compensation: an analysis of contract damages and contractual obligation, 26 *OJLS* 41 concerning the development of expectation interest and why specific performance still will be rarely used.

! Don't be tempted to . . .

- Treat this superficially: this question required an analysis of the potential expansion of what can fall within expectation interest.

- Avoid some discussion of the uncertainties surrounding the decision in *Attorney General* v *Blake*.

❓ Question 2

Sally is the proprietor of the Zen Garden Centre.

She has placed an order for 1,000 plaster meercat garden ornaments from Paul's Pots and Plants Ltd at a cost of £2,000. She has been selling these ornaments for £4 each. Paul's Pots and Plants Ltd are unable to fulfil the latest order. Sally immediately contacts Bernard who says that in return for a 10 per cent commission he will try to find an alternative supply. He does this within a day at a price of £1 per unit. Sally pays the new supplier £1,000 for the meercats and Bernard £100 in commission.

Sally has commissioned Nicky to landscape her private water garden at a total cost of £12,000. The height of the waterfall features was specified to obtain the maximum 'splash and burble effect'. The drop is six inches less than in the contractual specification. Only with scientific measuring equipment can the difference in 'splash and burble' be detected. The cost of putting the waterfall features right would be £20,000.

Sally's son Owen is to marry a famous actress. At the wedding a local photographer, Peter, has been hired. In his contract it specifies that all rights to the photographs remain with Sally. Peter made copies of the photographs and sold them for £10,000 to a national newspaper. Sally had lined up negotiations with a glossy magazine for an exclusive run with the photographs for around £20,000. They are no longer interested as the photographs are now old news.

Advise Sally as to the principles applied in assessing the amount of damages which may be awarded to her as the innocent party to the breaches of contract committed by Paul's Pots Ltd, Nicky and Peter.

Answer plan

→ Consider that the usual measure of damages is to satisfy expectation interest.

→ Discuss the calculation of expectation interest by reference to the market rule. Sally has actually made a profit from the breach and therefore is entitled to nominal damages only.

→ Expectation interest can be satisfied by curing the defect. It is possible that the cost is disproportionate with regard to the waterfall features and therefore perhaps only an amount for the loss of amenity or disappointment can be awarded.

→ Sally has not suffered any economic loss by the fact that Peter has sold the pictures, but potentially as she had also intended to profit from the sale she may have a restitutionary remedy against Peter.

Diagram plan

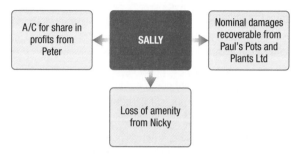

A printable version of this diagram plan is available from www.pearsoned.co.uk/lawexpressqa

Answer

An award of contractual damages attempts, as far as a monetary award can do so, to put the innocent party to a breach in the position they would have been in had the contract been performed, satisfying expectation interest. Contractual damages are, however, not punitive and therefore as Sally has not actually suffered any economic loss as a result of any of the breaches of contract, the measure of damages will be quantified on a potentially less generous measure.[1]

[1] The introduction recognises that an understanding of the principles is involved in determining in a *quantum meruit* of damages where no actual pecuniary loss has been sustained.

The expectation measure of damages seeks to put the innocent party to a breach of contract in the financial position they would have been in had the enforceable promise made to them been performed. This measure of damages therefore goes beyond just putting the parties back in the position they were in before the contract was made: it will aim to recompense for potential loss of profit.[2]

[2] Stating the general rule here allows you to articulate the potential problem arising where there has been no loss of profit.

In the problem, there is an available market in meercats and therefore the losses are easily calculable as being the difference in the price quoted by Paul's Pots and Plants Ltd and the replacement price paid (s. 51(3) Sale of Goods Act 1979). Compensation will not be paid for amounts that could have been mitigated by the claimant taking reasonable steps to avoid those losses (**British Westinghouse Electric and Manufacturing Co. Ltd v Underground Electric Rly Co. of London Ltd** [1912] AC 673). Sally has acted swiftly to avoid compounding potential losses. She has been so successful in doing this she has actually suffered no loss and made a profit.[3] The law of contract aims to compensate for losses, not allow for a claimant to profit further from the breach; as such, only nominal damages would be awarded. Neither the amount she would have received had the meercats been delivered nor the amount paid to Bernard to find an alternative source of the goods are recoverable, as only benefit was derived and no loss incurred.

[4] Picks up the point of law from the previous paragraph and develops the analysis by reference to that, giving a logical structured flow to the answer.

There will be no available market as regards the commissioned water garden, therefore the expectation interest can only be quantified in terms of the cost of cure of the defective work.[4] In *Ruxley Electronics and Construction Ltd* v *Forsyth* [1995] 3 All ER 268 a swimming pool was nine inches shallower than contracted for. The cost of curing the defective work was £21,560, an amount thought to be disproportionate to the benefit to be derived from the remedial work. On the other hand, performance had not been rendered in accordance with the contract. Accordingly, an amount of £2,500 was awarded for loss of amenity. *Ruxley Electronics and Construction Ltd* v *Forsyth* does recognise that there is value in performance. *McAlpine* v *Panatown* [2001] 1 AC 518 recognised the principle of performance interest in commercial contracts, and the idea of consumer surplus forming part of the expectation interest in consumer contracts was further discussed and expanded in *Farley* v *Skinner* [2001] All ER 801. It can be argued that *Ruxley Electronics and Construction Ltd* v *Forsyth* recognises the economic value of exact performance and made an award only for this element of disappointment. The courts in *McLaren Murdoch & Hamilton Ltd* v *The Abercromby Motor Group Ltd* (2003) SCLR 323 held that the decision not to award cost of cure damages means that the cost

[5] Reinforcing the principle with a more recent authority demonstrates currency of knowledge.

must be manifestly disproportionate to the benefit to be received.[5] No real benefit would be gained by the very expensive work required to render exact and precise performance with regard to the waterfall features. A claimant cannot be forced to spend an award in a particular way and the decision in *Ruxley Electronics and Construction Ltd* v *Forsyth* prevents a claimant being overcompensated for repairs they would have no intention of carrying out (*Birse Construction Ltd* v *Eastern Telegraph Co. Ltd* [2004] EWHC 2512 (TCC)). As in *Ruxley Electronics and Construction Ltd* v *Forsyth* Sally has not received exact and precise performance in accordance with the contractual specifications, but she has suffered no economic loss and there is nothing to suggest that Nicky has profited from her 'skimped performance'. If she had, following the decision in **Attorney General v Blake** [2001] 1 AC 268, she might well have to account for those profits.[6] As such, Sally would receive some award for the loss of her consumer interest in the performance of her contract.

[6] Adding this level of depth to the analysis will gain higher marks.

Peter is in breach of his contract with Sally as regards the photographs taken at the wedding. Sally has suffered no pecuniary loss and it would be hard for her to establish an award on the grounds of disappointment or some element of consumer surplus which had not satisfied her expectation interest. Contractual damages in the UK are not punitive. Following the decision of **Attorney General v Blake** it is possible for a claimant to recover profits made by the defendant by their breach of contract. In **Blake** the defendant had to account for all the profits he had made in the publication of his memoirs in breach of his contractual obligations to the government as his employer and his specific contractual obligation not to disclose certain information. Such an award will only be given in exceptional circumstances where the usual contractual remedies are inadequate and there is a legitimate interest in depriving the defendant of their profits. **Blake** appears to be unusual in that the defendant had to account for all the profits.[7] In **Experience Hendrix LLC v PPX Enterprises Inc.** [2003] 1 All ER (Comm) 830 the defendants had breached terms of a settlement which would allow them to avoid paying royalties to the claimants. The defendants were required to hand over a share of their profits. It would appear that the courts are more willing to make such an award where the subject matter concerns confidential information or property and the conduct of the party in breach attracts the disapproval of the court. Therefore, Sally would be potentially able to recover some of Peter's profit derived from his breach of contract. She would be unable to claim the difference between his profit and the £20,000 she would have got as her losses would be too remote (**Hadley v Baxendale** (1859) 9 Ex 341).[8]

[7] This has been summarised concisely and demonstrates an understanding of the development of the law following *Blake*.

[8] No need to discuss in depth, but alluding to this issue demonstrates a breadth of knowledge.

Sally would be able to recover nominal damages from Paul's Pots and Plants Ltd for a loss representing her interest in the exact performance of her contract, and potentially a share in the profit Peter made from the photographs.

✓ Make your answer stand out

- Consider if the UK courts might follow the lead of the Canadian case of *Whiten* v *Pilot Insurance Co.* 2002 SCC 18, where it was held that where there is an independent actionable wrong arising out of the same facts as a breach of contract then a punitive award would be possible.
- Support your analysis with the use of some academic authority, such as B. Coote's (1997) article Contract damages, *Ruxley* and the performance interest, *CLJ* 537, or perhaps A. Loke (1996) Cost of cure or difference in market value? Towards a sound choice in the basis for quantifying expectation damages, 10 *JCL* 189.
- Add depth to your answer by reading and possible reference to D. Pearce and R. Halson's (2008) article Damages for breach of contract: compensation, restitution, and vindication, 28 *OJLS* 73, which picks up on the themes of what the law is actually trying to compensate for.

! Don't be tempted to . . .

- Forget your application. The question raises issues which are the subject of much academic and judicial discussion. Adding depth to your analysis is good; forgetting the task in hand will lose marks.

📰 Question 3

Consider the limitation to a potential award of damages as a consequence of which the innocent party to a breach of contract can only be compensated for losses which flow from that breach, and only then if the contract itself has not restricted the amount which can be recovered in a liquidated damages clause.

Answer plan

→ Identify the purpose of an award of damages in contract.
→ Consider that the breach must have caused the loss claimed.
→ Give examples of the chain of causation being broken by the acts of third parties.
→ Articulate the tests for remoteness as laid down in *Hadley* v *Baxendale* and define the limitations this puts on the recovery of losses.
→ Illustrate the test with the case of *Victoria Laundry*.
→ Discuss the use of liquidated damages clauses and the limitations to their enforceability.

Diagram plan

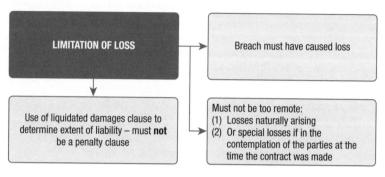

A printable version of this diagram plan is available from www.pearsoned.co.uk/lawexpressqa

Answer

Losses can only be recovered to the extent that the breach of contract caused the loss, and only if that loss is not too remote a consequence of the breach. The parties can of course agree between themselves what the remedy for a breach will be.

In order to claim for a breach of contract it must be the breach that is an effective cause of the loss.[1] In **C&P Haulage Co. Ltd v Middleton** [1983] 3 All ER 94 the claimants could not recover for outlay made in refurbishing fixtures and fittings when the tenancy was terminated early in breach of contract. A term of the contract provided that no money would be recoverable for improvements made to fixtures and fittings at the end of the agreement. These losses were therefore not incurred by the breach but by the forming of a bad bargain. The breach had merely accelerated the losses which would have been incurred eventually. The breach does not have to be the sole cause of loss but it does have to be an effective cause of the loss (**County Ltd v Girozentrale Securities** [1996] 1 BCLC 653).

The act of a third party may break the chain of causation (**Weld-Blundell v Stephens** [1920] AC 956).[2] However, in **Stansbie v Troman** [1948] 2 KB 48 it was reasonably foreseeable that in leaving the house unlocked in breach of contract the property might be burgled. It can also be that the claimant's acts may be so unreasonable that the chain of causation is broken. In **Lambert v Lewis**

[1] Stating the legal principle and then using case law by way of illustration is a good way to build a logical and clear structure.

[2] By discussing the general rule first, the analysis flows on naturally to the exceptions to that rule.

[1982] AC 225 a farmer continued to use a broken trailer coupling which caused further injury and loss. By continuing to use the faulty goods unreasonably, he broke the chain of causation between the defendants' breach of contract in supplying faulty goods and the ultimate liability of the farmer to injured persons.

In addition to the breach of contract having caused the loss claimed for, the loss must also be not too remote a consequence from the breach. The rule in **Hadley v Baxendale** (1854) 9 Exch 341 contains a two-limb test for determining the extent to which the consequences of a breach of contract can be claimed for.[3] First, a loss will not be too remote if it 'arises naturally' from the breach. This covers the type of loss that would be a normal consequence of the breach. The second limb of the test covers the type of losses which would have been in the contemplation of both the parties at the time the contract was made. This type of loss would cover special or unusual losses. The difference in these type of losses is demonstrated by the case of **Victoria Laundry (Windsor) Ltd v Newman Industries Ltd** [1949] 2 KB 528. In this case there was a delay in fitting new boilers which would give the business extra capacity. As such, the plaintiffs could recover an amount for the loss of the extra capacity and business during the delayed period for installation in breach of contract. The loss of the potential extra business capacity was a normal consequence of the delay in completion of the work. The plaintiffs had also secured an especially lucrative contract with the Ministry of Supply for the dying of army uniforms. No amount could be recovered for the losses as a result of being unable to fulfil this contract, as the defendants had no knowledge of this deal. It was not therefore in the contemplation of both parties at the time the contract was made.[4] Potentially the defendants would have been liable had the claimants made them aware of the 'special losses' which might be incurred. Lord Asquith in **Victoria Laundry (Windsor) Ltd v Newman Industries Ltd** suggested that losses would be recoverable if they were reasonably foreseeable. This would suggest that the test for remoteness would be the same for tort as in contract. However, in **Koufos v C. Czarnikow Ltd, The Heron II** [1969] 1 AC 350, Lord Reid stressed the difference between the test in tort and contract. The scope for liability had to be narrower in contract as the parties have it within their power at the time the contract is made to allocate risk between them.[5] It is possible to

[3] Any question on remoteness will require an explanation of this test, and most of the marks will be awarded for demonstrating clear understanding of the concepts involved.

[4] The facts of *Victoria Laundry* are an excellent illustration of the two-limb test.

[5] Depth of analysis will gain additional marks; this is achieved here by giving the rationale for a less wide test for foreseeability in contract than tort.

draw the attention of the other party to 'special losses' thus placing the loss within the contemplation of both parties. This line of argument has recently been followed in *Transfield Shipping Inc.* v *Mercator Shipping Inc.*, **The Achilleas** [2008] 3 WLR 345.

The parties can determine the extent of their liabilities using a liquidated damages clause. Provided that the liquidated damages clause is a genuine pre-estimate of loss, and not punitive, then it will be enforceable irrespective of the actual loss suffered by the breach. Therefore if the actual loss suffered was much less than the amount provided for in the contract, the full amount would be payable and recoverable, even if it would have been irrecoverable on the grounds of remoteness (*Robophone Facilities Ltd* v *Blank* [1966] 1 WLR 1428).[6] The distinction between a liquidated damages clause, which is enforceable, and a penalty clause, which is not, following the case of *Dunlop Pneumatic Tyre Company Ltd* v *New Garage & Motor Co. Ltd* [1915] AC 79, depends on whether the amount claimed is a genuine pre-estimate of the potential loss, or an extravagant and unconscionable amount in comparison with the greatest loss which could have arisen from the breach. The modern case of *Alfred McAlpine Capital Projects Ltd* v *Tilebox Ltd* [2005] EWHC 281 (TCC) has substituted the word 'reasonable' for 'genuine'. Therefore the pre-estimate of losses may be wrong, but where there is a substantial discrepancy between the amount in the clause and the actual loss then the pre-estimate will be unreasonable.[7] In drafting liquidated damages clauses, care must be taken to ensure that the clause is not presumed to be a penalty on the grounds that the breaches covered are broad and provide for the same amount for some serious as well as some trifling breaches.

The intention of the parties at the time of making the contract will to a large extent determine whether losses are not recoverable as being too remote, or whether their own clause will determine the remedy available. Whether the breach has caused the loss claimed may depend on the contract itself but the chain of causation can also be broken by the acts of others.[8]

[6] Directed to the question asked, which suggests that the amount recoverable could fall short of consequential losses; here there is depth to the analysis, suggesting that if the breach is covered then the amount is payable regardless of any question of remoteness.

[7] This demonstrates an up-to-date knowledge but also the ability to explain the development of a well accepted test to fit modern day requirements.

[8] A strong conclusion will potentially gain you that bit of extra credit between grade boundaries; this should directly focus on the question, but also pick up on the predominant theme in the analysis.

✓ Make your answer stand out

- Consider including some academic opinion in your analysis, particularly in the areas where there has been some recent developments: A. Robertson (2008) The basis of the remoteness rule in contract, 28 *LS* 172.

- S. Rowan's (2010) article Reflections on the introduction of punitive damages for breach of contract, *OJLS* 495, will help clarify why penalty clauses are not enforceable in UK law. H. Lal's (2009) article, Slaying some liquidated damages myths, 20(6) *CL* 17, will help explain the current tests used to distinguish a penalty clause from a liquidated damages clause.

! Don't be tempted to . . .

- Think that the question is deceptively simple; ensure you pick up the extra marks by giving depth to the analysis: for example, the criticism of Lord Asquith's judgment in the *Victorian Laundry* case in suggesting the test for remoteness in tort and contract should be the same.

- Drift away from the question set and include irrelevant material.

❓ Question 4

Cooledmagma Ltd has purchased a water jet cutting machine with live remote programming camera and dual cutting heads from Aquacuts Ltd. These machines are made to order and individual specification. The new machine replaces the traditional stone masonry equipment Cooledmagma Ltd had been using which had become obsolete. Cooledmagma Ltd instantly doubles their output at vastly reduced costs, which will mean they will be more competitive in the marble and granite worktop market. In March they are approached by Pashama Ltd to provide all the granite and marble fixtures and fittings for a new luxury spa and hotel to be opened in central London. The work has to be completed by the September opening and payment will be made on completion. The contract itself is worth £2,000,000. It would mean that all production would have to be focused on the one contract. This contract is worth double the projected profit forecast by Cooledmagma Ltd for their bank when securing finance for the investment in the new machinery.

In May, three months after the purchase of the machinery, one of the cutting heads has ceased functioning. Engineers from Aquacuts Ltd take the malfunctioning head away leaving Cooledmagma Ltd on half capacity. Through an administrative error the new cutting head delivered is incompatible and it is a full two months before the correct cutting head is fitted. Cooledmagma Ltd informs Pashama Ltd that they will be unable to make delivery on time. Pashama Ltd has found an alternative supplier and as the price of the Madagascan granite they wanted had fallen the contract will be cheaper for them, but they agree to take the completed work from Cooledmagma Ltd at a reduced price.

Advise Cooledmagma Ltd as to the likelihood of recovering for their loss of profits from Aquacuts Ltd.

Answer plan

→ Consider Cooledmagma Ltd's losses in terms of contract looking to satisfy expectation interest.

→ Evaluate whether Aquacuts Ltd's breach of contract caused the losses claimed for and whether any of the loss could be considered too remote.

→ Discuss if Cooledmagma Ltd has done enough to satisfy the duty to mitigate losses.

Diagram plan

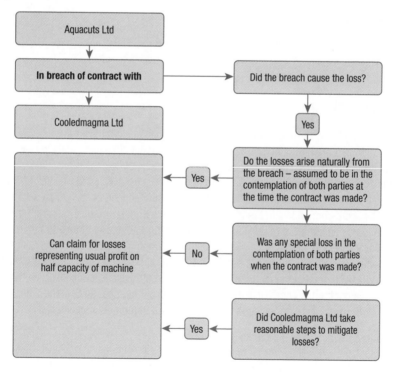

A printable version of this diagram plan is available from www.pearsoned.co.uk/lawexpressqa

Answer

Aquacuts Ltd is in breach of contract with Cooledmagma Ltd in supplying a faulty machine and then have caused further losses in delaying remedying the defect.[1] The measure of damages awarded for a breach of contract aims to satisfy the expectation interest of the innocent party to the breach, in other words to put them in the position they would have been in had the contract been performed properly. The extent of any such loss is limited by the rules on causation and remoteness.

The law of contract aims to put the innocent party to a breach of contract in the position they would have been in had the contract been performed without defect. This is called expectation interest (***Robinson v Harman*** (1848) 1 Ex Rep 850). Cooledmagma Ltd had an expectation that they would make £2,000,000 with their sole client in the period between March and September.[2]

The recovery of losses based on expectation interest is limited to the extent that the breach of contract must have caused the loss (***C & P Haulage Ltd v Middleton*** [1983] 3 All ER 94). The fault in the cutting head was a breach of contract which directly led to the losses incurred by Cooledmagma Ltd. These losses were further compounded by Aquacuts Ltd's failure to remedy the situation efficiently.[3] A promise to supply or repair goods must be undertaken in a timely fashion or liability will arise for the ordinary loss of profit suffered[4] (***Fletcher v Tayleur*** (1855) 17 CB 21).

The profit which would have been derived from the contract with Pashama Ltd was as a result of a particularly lucrative contract having been secured.[5] It must be established that those losses were caused by the breach and that they are also not too remote a consequence from the breach of contract. The test applied for determining the remoteness of damage is in the case of ***Hadley v Baxendale*** (1854) 9 Exch 341. In this case the plaintiffs' mill was reliant on a crankshaft to keep working. The defendants were contracted to deliver the old crankshaft to third parties to manufacture a replacement which the defendants would return to the plaintiffs. In breach of contract the defendants delayed delivery to the third party, causing an extra five days' complete loss of production. Anderson B formulated a two limb-test to determine whether this loss was too

[1] A good mark could be achieved in this question which is focused on the measure of damages even if the candidate is less sure of the law surrounding the breach itself (s. 14(2) Sales of Goods Act 1979).

[2] Succinctly put, leading neatly on to a discussion of any possible limitations to a claim for all the lost profits.

[3] In establishing in the problem that the breach caused the loss the marker knows that the candidate would be aware of the potential limitation to recovery if that were not the case.

[4] This raises the question as to the recovery of special losses.

[5] Starting with the application is unusual but does help signal where the analysis is heading.

remote a consequence of the breach or not. The first limb asks if the losses 'arise naturally' from the breach: in other words, losses which would be an inevitable consequence of the breach and could be assumed to be in the contemplation of the parties at the time the contract was made. The second limb of the test allows for the recovery of losses which could not be assumed to be in the contemplation of the parties at the time the contract was made, but would be recovered if at the time the contract was made both parties had actual knowledge of these 'special losses'.[6] In **Hadley v Baxendale** the loss of profits for the five-day delay was not recoverable as such a loss could not be regarded as being 'naturally arising' from the breach: it could be expected that a mill would carry a spare when so dependent on a particular part and as such the loss was not inevitable. Nor was it in the contemplation of both parties that the mill would have to cease production in the absence of the crankshaft. Following this test, it was in the contemplation of both Cooledmagma Ltd and Aquacuts Ltd that the machine would be working on half capacity. It would not have been in the contemplation of both parties at the time the contract was made that Cooledmagma Ltd was so dependent on one very lucrative contract.[7]

The case of **Victoria Laundry (Windsor) Ltd v Newman Industries Ltd** [1949] 2 KB 528 provides further illustration of this principle. In this case the installation of new laundry kettles was delayed by the defendants. As a result the increased capacity of the business was delayed. The amount of profits lost in this regard would be a natural consequence flowing from the breach of contract and was recoverable. An additional amount to compensate for the loss of a lucrative government contract could not be claimed for, as these special losses were not in the contemplation of both parties when the contract was made. **Victoria Laundry (Windsor) Ltd v Newman Industries Ltd** suggested that the test for remoteness was the same as for tort: that the losses must be reasonably foreseeable. However, subsequent decisions have raised the presumption that the standard is higher in contract, as the contracting party has the opportunity to disclose special losses (**Koufos v C. Czarnikow Ltd (The Heron II)** [1969] 1 AC 350). Following this line of argument it would have been in the contemplation of both parties that capacity would be halved, but not that no income would be made as only one contract for the whole of a six-month period was being worked on.

6 Good paraphrasing of the judgment and clear articulation of the test for remoteness.

7 Providing the application immediately following the analysis of the test demonstrates an ability to use and not just describe the law.

[8] The application is being emphasised again here in the context of the case law developed since *Hadley* v *Baxendale*.

Unless these special circumstances had been made known to Aquacuts Ltd they will not be liable for those special losses.[8]

Cooledmagma Ltd told Pashama Ltd that they would be unable to make delivery. In so doing they committed an anticipatory breach of contract which Pashama Ltd was free to accept or reject (**Hochester v De La Tour** (1853) 2 E & B 678). Pashama Ltd has accepted Cooledmagama's partial performance, for which Cooledmagma has been paid and as a consequence recovered some of their expenditure.[9] A claimant cannot recover losses which they could have taken reasonable steps to prevent or reduce once there has been an actual breach of contract.[10] Whether the steps taken are reasonable is a question of fact. The burden is on the defendant to prove that the steps are not reasonable. Providing that the action taken was reasonable at the time, the fact that with hindsight such action was inefficient is irrelevant (**Gebruder Metelmann GmbH & Co. KG v NBR (London) Ltd** [1984] 1 Lloyd's Rep 614). Even if the deal struck with Pashama Ltd was not as lucrative as the original deal, Cooledmagma Ltd acted quickly to stop losses running any further than necessary. As they were in breach of contract with Pashama Ltd their mitigation in the circumstances seems to be the best that could have been achieved.

[9] In moving into demonstrating that any recovery of losses would be limited if the innocent party did not attempt to mitigate those losses an opportunity has been taken to demonstrate a wider understanding of the topic.

[10] Which there has been with Aquacuts Ltd.

[11] Short conclusion focused on specific application to the problem.

The measure of damages available to Cooledmagma Ltd will satisfy expectation interest to the extent that Aquacuts Ltd's breach caused the loss claimed for, but will be limited to those losses which naturally arose from that breach and not the full amount of the contract with Pashama Ltd.[11]

 Make your answer stand out

- Follow the judicial reasoning in decisions such as *Borealis AB* v *Geogas Trading SA* [2010] EWHC 2789: this case includes a discussion of the cases and principles used in the solution to the above problem. It doesn't add anything new but demonstrates a breadth of reading and currency of research.

- Consider including some of the more recent case law, such as *Henderson* v *Merrett Syndicates Ltd* [1995] 2 AC 145 or *Transfield Shipping Inc.* v *Mercator Shipping Inc.* [2008] 3 WLR 345, that has discussed the narrower operation of the test for remoteness in contract than for tort.

! Don't be tempted to . . .

- Miss out the limitation on the recovery of losses which the claimant could have mitigated. The question openly directs you to the other losses. Higher marks will be gained by recognising this issue. Only the better answers would do this.

- Lose the opportunity to give depth to your analysis: in this question you really have the chance to have a good look at the decision in *Hadley* v *Baxendale*.

- Forget to do your application as you progress through your answer. It is tempting to cover all the complex issues surrounding remoteness and apply the test to both potential amounts claimed at the end. If you do this as you go along, it does also help illustrate the legal point you are making and so is doubly effective.

www.pearsoned.co.uk/lawexpressqa

 Go online to access more revision support including additional essay and problem questions with diagram plans, You be the marker questions, and download all diagrams from the book.

Bibliography

Andrews, N. (2001) Strangers to justice no longer – the reversal of the privity rule under the Contracts (Rights of Third Parties) Act 1999, *Cambridge Law Journal* 353.

Atiyah, P.S. (1986) Consideration: a re-statement, in *Essays on Contract*, Oxford: Oxford University Press, p. 179.

Baatz, Y. (2010) International sales: market price – illegitimate seller pressure, 16(2) *Journal of International Maritime Law* 88–9.

Beale, H. (2005) An unfairly complex law, 155 *New Law Journal* 318.

Birks, P. (2004) Undue influence as wrongful exploitation, 120 *Law Quarterley Review* 34.

Bojczuk, W. (1987) When is a condition not a condition?, *Journal of Business Law* 353.

Brown, I. and Chandler, A. (1993) Unreasonableness and the Unfair Contract Terms Act, 109 *Law Quarterly Review* 41.

Brownsword, R. (1992) Retrieving reasons, retrieving rationality? A new look at the right to withdraw for breach of contract, 5 *Journal of Contract Law* 83.

Capper, D. (2008) The extinctive effect of promissory estoppel, 37(2) *Common Law World Review* 105.

Chandler, A. and Devenney, J. (2004) Mistakes as to identify and the threads of objectivity, 1 *Journal of Obligations and Remedies* 7.

Cooper, D. (2008) The extinctive effect of promissory estoppel, 372 *Common Law World Review* 105.

Coote, B. (1997) Contract damages, *Ruxley* and the performance interest, *Cambridge Law Journal* 537.

Coote, B. (2004) Consideration and variations: a different solution, 120 *Law Quarterly Review* 19.

Dabbs, D. (2002) The risk of mistake in contract, 152 *New Law Journal* 1654.

Davis, P. (2007) Wynn or lose, 157 *New Law Journal* 535.

Dockray, M. (2001) *Cutter* v *Powell*: a trip outside the text, 117 *Law Quarterlp Review* 664.

Fisher, J. (1981) Contract – repudiation of substantially performed contract for delective workmanship, 84 *Law Society Gazette* 30.

Furmston, M.D. (2010) *Cheshire, Fifoot and Furmston's Law of Contract*, 16th edn, Oxford: OUP.

Gardner, S. (1992) Thrashing with Trollope: a deconstruction of the postal rule in contract, 12 *Oxford Journal of Legal Studies* 170.

Griffiths, M. (2010) Situation critical, 160 *New Law Journal* 1251.

Halson, R. (1990) Sailors, subcontractors and consideration, 106 *Law Quarterly Review* 183.

Hare, C. (2004) Identity mistakes: a lost opportunity, 67 *Modern Law Review* 993.

Hibbert, T. (2009) Sovereignty of the contract, 9 *Journal of International Banking and Finance Law* 524.

Hill, S. (2001) Flogging a dead horse: the postal aceptance rule and email, 17 *Journal of Contract Law* 151.

Hird, N.J. and Blair, A. (1996) Minding your own business – *Williams* v *Roffey* revisited: consideration reconsidered, *Journal of Business Law* 254.

Hooley, R. (1991) Damages and the Misrepresentation Act 1967, 107 *Law Quarterly Review* 547.

Kramer, A. (2004) Implication in fact as an instance of contractual interpretation, 63 *Cambridge Law Journal* 384.

Lal, H. (2009) Slaying some liquidated damages myths, 20(6) *Constitutional Law* 17.

Law Commission (2007) Insurance contract law: misrepresentation, non-disclosure and breach of warranty by the insured, Consultation Paper No. 182.

Loke, A. (1996) Cost of cure or difference in market value? Towards a sound choice in the basis for quantifying expectation damages, 10 *Journal of Contract Law* 189.

MacMillan, C. (2000) A birthday present for Lord Denning: the Contracts (Rights of Third Parties) Act, 1999, 63 *Modern Law Review* 887.

MacMillan, C. (2002) Evolution or revolution? Unfair terms in consumer contracts, *Cambridge Law Journal* 22.

MacMillan, C. (2004) Mistake as to identity clarified?, 120 *Law Quarterly Review* 369.

MacMillan, C. (2005) Rogues, swindlers and cheats: the development of mistake of identity in English contract law, *Cambridge Law Journal* 711.

Mayfield, A. (2010) Would I lie to you?, 160 *New Law Journal* 970.

Mitchell, P. and Phillips, J. (2002) The contractual nexus: is reliance essential?, 22 *Oxford Journal of Legal Studies* 115.

O'Sullivan, D.B. (2002) Developing O'Brien, 118 *Law Quarterly Review* 337.

O'Sullivan, J. (1996) In defence of *Foakes* v *Beer*, *Cambridge Law Journal* 319.

Pawlowski, M. (2002) Common mistake: *Law* v *Equity*, 152 *New Law Journal* 132.

Pearce, D. and Halson, R. (2008) Damages for breach of contract: compensation, restitution, and vindication, 28 *Oxford Journal of Legal Studies* 73.

Peden, E. (2001) Policy concerns behind the implication of terms in law, 117 *Law Quarterly Review* 384.

Peel, W.E. (2007) *Treitel on the Law of Contract*, 12th edn, London: Sweet & Maxwell, p. 18.
Peel, W.E. (2011) *Treitel on the Law of Contract*, 13th edn, London: Sweet & Maxwell.

Robertson, A. (2008) The basis of the remoteness rule in contract, 28 *Legal Studies* 172.
Roe, T. (2000) Contractual intention under section 1(1)(b) and section 1(2) of the Contracts (Rights of Third Parties) Act 1999, 63 *Modern Law Review* 887.
Ross, J. (2002) Seller beware, 152 *New Law Journal* 1884.
Rowan, S. (2010) Reflections on the introduction of punitive damages for breach of contract, *Oxford Journal of Legal Studies* 495.
Rutherford and Wilson (1998) Signature of a document, 148 *New Law Journal* 380.

Stevens, R. and McFarlane, B. (2002) In defence of *Sumpter* v *Hedges*, 118 *Law Quarterly Review* 569.
Steyn, Lord (1997) Contract law: fulfilling the reasonable expectations of honourable men, 113 *Law Quarterly Review* 433.

Treitel, G. (1974) Consideration: a critical analysis of Professor Atiyah's fundamental restatement, 50 *Australian Law Journal* 439.
Treitel, G. (1998) Affirmation after a repudiatory breach, 114 *Law Quarterly Review* 22.
Treitel, G. (2002) *Some Landmarks of Twentieth Century Contract Law*, Oxford: Oxford University Press.

Webb, C. (2006) Performance and compensation: an analysis of contract damages and contractual obligation, 26 *Oxford Journal of Legal Studies* 41.
Whincup, M. (1996) Reacting to repudiation, 146 *New Law Journal* 674 and 729.

Index

INDEX